The Breeze of Sahasrara

*Miracles of Shri Mataji Nirmala Devi
and Her Gift to the World*

Linda Williams

Blossomtime Publishing

Other books by the author:

Published by NITL:

Eternally Inspiring Recollections of our Holy Mother, Volume 1 – Stories from India

Eternally Inspiring Recollections of our Holy Mother, Volume 2 – Western Europe

Eternally Inspiring Recollections of our Holy Mother, Volume 3 – East Europe, Middle East and Extra Stories

Eternally Inspiring Recollections of our Holy Mother, Volume 4 – Australia, New Zealand and South East Asia

Eternally Inspiring Recollections of our Holy Mother, Volume 5 – The Americas

Eternally Inspiring Recollections of our Holy Mother, Volume 6 – The United Kingdom

Eternally Inspiring Recollections of our Holy Mother, Volume 7 – Stories that missed the printing deadlines of the previous volumes

Eternally Inspiring Recollections of our Holy Mother, Volume 8 – Stories, Diaries and Photos

Published by Checkpoint Press:

The Awakening of Navi Septa, Book One: The Keys of Wisdom

The Awakening of Navi Septa, Book Two: The Mountain Mouse

The Awakening of Navi Septa, Book Three: The Swarm of Bees

The Breeze of Sahasrara

*Miracles of Shri Mataji Nirmala Devi
and Her Gift to the World*

Linda Williams

Blossomtime Publishing

This edition is published 2012
by Blossomtime Publishing

Copyright © 2012 by Linda Williams
Cover design © by Linda Williams
Layout by Günter Woltron

The moral right of the author has been asserted.

Printed and bound by Lightning Source UK Ltd, Milton Keynes, in the United Kingdom and/or the USA/Australia.

All rights reserved. No part of this publication may be reproduced, stored in a retrieval system, or transmitted, in any form or by any means, electronic, mechanical, photocopying, recording, or otherwise, without the prior written permission of the publisher and/or the author, except in the case of reviewers who may quote brief passages in a review.

A CIP catalogue record for this book is available fom the British Library.

THE BREEZE OF SAHASRARA

ISBN-13: 978-0-9573769-0-8

Blossomtime Publishing
69 North End Road, London, NW11 7RL, UK
blossomtime.books@gmail.com

Acknowledgements:

Shri Mataji Nirmala Devi, Meta Modern Era, 1997
Shri Mataji Nirmala Devi, To My Flower Children, 1973
Dr Antonio Masella, video on the Vega machine, 2001, Italy
Nirmal Fragrance, NITL, India, 2005
Dr Ramesh Manocha, Australian Family Physician, vol. 29, Dec. 2000
Ross Francis, The Bedfordshire Journal, October 1982
Prof Umesh C. Rai, Medical Science Enlightened, L.E.T., 1993
Eternally Inspiring Recollections of our Holy Mother, NITL, 2002-11
The Mail, Wed July 30th, 2008, Australia

Every effort has been made to trace the copyright holders of work quoted in this book. Please contact the publisher if there any errors or ommissions and these will be put right in future editions.

When Shri Mataji saw the first draft of this book,

she said, 'There has never been a book like this;

it is too good, but it is too strong.'

That was in May 2002, at Cabella, Italy,

in the old castle which was her home there.

Nevertheless, again and again she asked me

to continue with it, so I did my best, although

it was very difficult to make it less strong.

I can only hope and pray that it does just a little

justice to her divinely altruistic and unique life.

Linda Williams

Content

Chapter 1	A Miracle Defined	9
Chapter 2	A Little about Shri Mataji	11
Chapter 3	Experiencing the Cool Breeze	16
Chapter 4	Despite Cultural Conditioning	19
Chapter 5	A Photo with Unique Properties	23
Chapter 6	Meta Physical Photos	28
Chapter 7	The Bandhan	36
Chapter 8	Help from a Distance	45
Chapter 9	The Wisdom of the Kundalini	53
Chapter 10	Traditional Practices, Untraditional Outcomes	64
Chapter 11	Time Becomes our Friend	69
Chapter 12	Fire as a Healer	74
Chapter 13	Lost and Found	77
Chapter 14	Transformation	81
Chapter 15	When the Five Senses are Enlightened	88
Chapter 16	Coming to Terms with the Weather	97
Chapter 17	Power over the Elements	112
Chapter 18	Animals, Fish and Vibrations	122
Chapter 19	Responsive Plants	129
Chapter 20	Chance Meetings	137
Chapter 21	A Perfect Sense of Direction	142
Chapter 22	Things Just Work Out	146
Chapter 23	Technology Enlightened	155
Chapter 24	Simultaneous Appearances	163
Chapter 25	Collective Awareness	173
Chapter 26	Traumatic Events	176
Chapter 27	Incidents and Accidents with Cars	190
Chapter 28	Grave and Chronic Health Problems	197
Chapter 29	Dreams and Visions	206
Chapter 30	The World Stage	213
Chapter 31	A Little More about Shri Mataji	220
Chapter 32	The Mother who 'Just Knows'	227
Chapter 33	The Last Word	234
Appendix 1	Instructions for Awakening the Kundalini	238
Appendix 2	Contributors	247

This book is dedicated to

Her Holiness Shri Mataji Nirmala Devi

and all seekers of truth

Chapter 1

A Miracle Defined

Today, science, despite the triumph of technology, is unable to tell us the absolute truth about who we are and why we are here. Scientists are unable to cope with the ecological problems that we have created for ourselves, and we know little about our inner selves. It seems too much to propose that a simple solution could be at hand which could help resolve our dilemmas, heal our afflictions and reveal the truth we have been searching for. We would like to tell you of our experiences, which suggest that a solution is not only possible but accessible to all of us.

This book is made up of first-hand accounts of close coincidences, unusual occurrences and miraculous events that could happen to anyone who reads it with an open mind. Some readers will put a number of these stories down to luck or coincidence, but other reports are almost impossible to explain rationally. Read on, and make up your own mind.

If one considers a miracle to be an event which does not follow the normally accepted laws of nature, then Sahaja Yoga is a miracle. In the recent past humanity has made enormous strides in the worlds of science and technology, in other words many 'miracles' have ceased to be miracles in the material world. Imagine trying to explain to someone in 1900 the technology behind satellite TV, the internet or mobile phones – all conveniences of life we take for granted.

Most of us know little about the subtler side of our being. However, in many scriptures spiritual experiences are reported as being accompanied by a wind, or coolness, for example the 'mighty rushing wind' of the Holy Spirit in the Christian Bible.

In the Hindu tradition it is the 'sali lam' or 'cool wind' which accompanies the awakening of the Kundalini, the inner subtle system, dormant at the base of the spine before awakening, at which time it rises to the top of the head through the main chakras, or subtle centres within us. This is necessary to attain moksha, or realisation of the self as spirit, and is considered by millions to be the ultimate goal of life. One great saint, Gyaneshwara, who lived in Maharashtra in the thirteenth century, described it like this:

'The Kundalini uncoils herself ... she then reaches the palms of the hands ... creating a draft, the life wind emerges ... and creates a cooling sensation internally as well as externally.'

This experience is not common to humanity, and does not follow the accepted laws of science, so could at present be defined as a miracle.

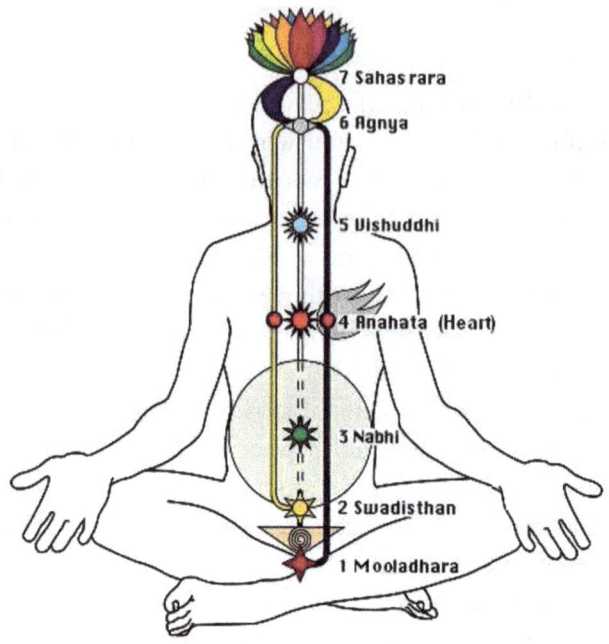

The Kundalini and the seven main chakras

It is interesting that in many languages, the word for the Holy Spirit, or 'Adi Shakti' as it is in Sanskrit, is a feminine noun. Christ used an Aramaic word which was feminine, and in Islam, the word is also feminine: 'ruh'. In at least two African languages, Zulu and Xhosa, the word for Holy Spirit and wind are the same: 'imoyo'.

In the course of this book we will show that this cool breeze, and many other interesting phenomena can be easily experienced, and it is likely that the reader will also do so by the time he or she has finished reading it. This is the result of a simple method of en masse Kundalini awakening, developed and given to the world by a very remarkable lady, Shri Mataji Nirmala Devi. Firstly, here is a short account of her life.

Chapter 2

A Little about Shri Mataji

Many people whose stories make up this book met Shri Mataji personally. She was majestic, awe inspiring, kind, gentle, wise, wonderful company, loving and caring and radiated many other beautiful qualities.

Shri Mataji Nirmala Devi was born at midday on the 21st of March 1923, in Chindwara, India. Her family, the Salves, were Christians and were descended from the Shalivahana dynasty, which ruled over large parts of India many centuries ago. Her father, Shri Prasad Rao Salve, was a distinguished lawyer and a member of India's Constituent Assembly. He knew Mahatma Gandhi well, as did all the family. He was a great scholar and translated the Koran into Marathi in an effort to bridge the gap between Hindus and Moslems. Shri Mataji's mother was one of the first ladies in the country to graduate in mathematics.

Nirmala Salve was often sent to Mahatma Gandhi's ashram during her school holidays, because her family were actively involved in the freedom struggle. He saw something special in her, and would talk with her about spiritual matters. She later studied medicine at a medical college in Lahore and spent two brilliant years there. She was also involved in the independence movement, as India strove to shake off the colonial imperialism of England. She spent some months in hiding from the police, before being imprisoned – like her father, who sacrificed all the family possessed for the cause of freedom.

In 1947 Nirmala Salve married Mr, later Sir, CP Srivastava, who soon became private secretary to the then Prime Minister, Lal Bahadur Shastri. After his death Mr Srivastava and his family moved to Mumbai, where he became the first chief executive of the Shipping Corporation of India. Mrs Nirmala Srivastava devoted her life to the care of her husband and two daughters. Shri Mataji, as many of us called her, later became a grandmother and great grandmother.

In Mumbai, Shri Mataji attended meetings where people were seeking something 'beyond', an inner transformation. She always had the power to cure and was able to help many people, but as yet had not given anyone self realisation, the experience by which we become our real self, the spirit. Shri Mataji's father was aware of her mission and told her that a way had to be found for many people to receive this, otherwise nothing could be done with the human race. Shri Mataji saw how many sincere seekers of truth were being damaged by false prophets or 'gurus'. They were deceiving the very people she wanted to help.

On the 5th of May 1970, after solitary meditation at Nargol, on the west coast of India, Shri Mataji found the answer. She experienced the cosmic opening of the uppermost subtle centre, the Sahasrara chakra. In her own words:

'As soon as the Sahasrara was opened, the whole atmosphere was filled with tremendous chaitanya, (vibrations) and there was tremendous light in the sky, and the whole thing came on this earth as if a torrential rain or a waterfall with such tremendous force as if I was unaware and got stupefied. The happening was so tremendous and so unexpected that I was stunned and got totally silent at the grandeur.

I saw the primordial Kundalini rising like a big furnace, and the furnace was very silent but (a) burning appearance it had, as if you heat up a metal and it has many colours. In the same way, the Kundalini showed up as a furnace like a tunnel, as you see (in) these plants you have for coal burning, that create electricity, and it stretched like a telescope and came out one after another: Shoot! Shoot! Shoot! Just like that.

And the deities came and sat on their seats, golden seats, and then lifted the whole of the head like a big dome and opened it, and then this torrential rain completely drenched me. I started seeing all that and got lost in the joy. It was like an artist seeing his own creation, and I felt the joy of the great fulfillment. After coming out of this beautiful experience, I looked around and saw human beings so blind. I became absolutely silent and desired that I should get the cups to fill the nectar, not all stones.'

The Kundalini energy has long been known in India, but only to a few individuals who devoted years to their spiritual ascent. This energy exists in every human in a dormant form at the base of the spine, but now the primordial Sahasrara was open, it could be awakened in everybody. Once the Kundalini has risen to the Sahasrara chakra on the top of the head, it becomes the source of wisdom, peace and bliss, and can transform humanity both individually and collectively.

Shri Mataji's role was to give en masse awakening to the world, and she worked tirelessly, selflessly and endlessly to achieve it. In 1970 Shri Mataji gave a few seekers from Mumbai their Kundalini awakening and self realisation.

Here is a first-hand account by Suresh Thacker of Nargol.

'After opening the Sahasrara at Nargol, Shri Mataji raised the Kundalini Shakti of seekers who came to her, and they all felt the cool breeze, on their fingertips, hands and at the Sahasrara chakra. In 1971 the first public programme was organised in Mumbai and Shri Mataji gave a lecture and self realisation to a few seekers.

They attended a seminar at Bordi beach, near Nargol, in January 1972 and Shri Mataji helped them to further establish the power within that they felt. Sahaja Yoga spread like a fire. Shri Mataji established the first weekly meditation meeting in 1971 at Bharatiya Vidya Bhavan, Mumbai, every Tuesday evening.'

In 1972, Shri Mataji visited the United States, where she publicly denounced the many false gurus who were peddling pseudo-spiritual techniques to the credulous public, and firmly stated that one cannot pay for one's self realisation. In 1973 her husband was elected Secretary General of the International Maritime Organization of the United Nations, based in London, and Shri Mataji moved with him to England.

Here is an account by Toni Panáayiotou of her first public programme there.

Shri Mataji during a public self realisation programme in the 70s

'It was my good fortune to meet Shri Mataji in 1973, at 17, New Oxford Street, London. A reception was organised by the London Bharatiya Vidya Bhavan to welcome the newly elected United Nations diplomat, Mr (now Sir) CP Srivastava and his wife Shri Mataji Nirmala Devi. The reception was well attended, with about two hundred Indian people, and musicians.

After the thank you's and welcomes, Shri Mataji was asked to grace us with her spiritual knowledge and her new Sahaja Yoga. She had a commanding presence which was nevertheless flexible, always just enough, but never too much so as to intimidate anyone.

Here was no ordinary saint, but someone surpassing all the norms of holy persons. Shri Mataji was able to empower ordinary people and give them access to their inner being by raising the Kundalini. She could enable individuals to experience thoughtless awareness and vibratory awareness, tangible tools for the verification of truth and one's state of being.'

For the next seventeen years Shri Mataji lived in London and spread Sahaja Yoga around the world. With more and more people getting self realisation the process of awakening the Kundalini became easier. She travelled endlessly, often at her own expense, giving thousands of lectures and self realisation to

Shri Mataji speaking at the United Nations Women's Conference in 1995

any who asked for it. She also taught those who received it how to hand it on to others, and how to use the new level of awareness to help and heal.

Sahaja Yoga is now established in over a hundred countries with more being added every year. Shri Mataji first visited Russia for Sahaja Yoga in 1989, where some senior members of the Ministry of Health were interested in yoga as it pertained to medical treatment. She demonstrated its power to help combat many diseases and Sahaja Yoga was officially recognised.

In 1995 she was a keynote speaker at the UN Conference on Women in Beijing, China. This is a short report by Alex Henshaw, who accompanied her.

'When Shri Mataji came to Beijing in 1995 for the UN Conference, we received her at the airport and she was very happy to be in China. She spoke about the Chinese, and what gracious hosts they were. Shri Mataji gave a very beautiful and moving address and in her speech was the only speaker who actually thanked the Chinese government, who were the hosts of the conference.'

Shri Mataji received awards and official recognition in many countries, such as Italy, Russia, India, Canada, the U.S.A, Romania and Brazil.

The words Shri Mataji mean respected, blessed mother, and a mother always wants the best for her children. She enabled the experience of Kundalini awakening to become accessible to all, so we can begin to take responsibility for our own evolution. She passed away peacefully in 2011, having spent the last forty years of her life giving her great gift of en masse Kundalini awakening to the world.

Chapter 3

Experiencing the Cool Breeze

Let us begin our story proper in Greece, the seat of Western civilization, where Shri Mataji was conducting an introductory programme of Sahaja Yoga. She gave programmes like this in many countries and numerous other people who have themselves had their self realisation regularly give them with the same results.

This report is from Meera Szegvary, a Swiss accountant.

'We were in Athens in October 2001. It was a warm evening and Shri Mataji was giving a public programme, an introduction to Sahaja Yoga, in a hotel there. At the end of the programme, Shri Mataji gave the experience of self realisation or Kundalini awakening. In many traditions, one of the signs of self realisation, or as the Christians say, the awakening of the Holy Spirit, is a cool wind. Nearly all the people who came for the first time said they had indeed felt a cool breeze, on their hands and above their heads, but some insisted it was the air conditioning. Someone went to find the hotel staff to ask them to please turn it off, and the staff, when found, said it was not on in the first place.'

Heidi Zogorski, from America, tells of her experience of feeling this cool breeze.

'I was staying in an apartment in Florida where Shri Mataji was visiting, and the owners asked me to sit outside her room while she was resting, in case she asked for something. I felt the cool air, so intensely cool, coming from the crack under the door. It was so enjoyable, different from air conditioning which is just cool on the surface, and more penetrating. Later I went near the open door when Shri Mataji had gone out. I was surprised at the feeling coming from the room; a deep coolness, deeper somehow than air in a refrigerator or freezer, but not at all cold - cool, but not cold - a very pleasant feeling. I usually feel it strongest on my hands.

I loved greeting Shri Mataji as she arrived in a city. I remember many times waiting for quite a long time for her to arrive at an airport, then all of a sudden, we'd feel cool on our hands and we'd look at each other.

"She's here," we'd say.

Then we would hear the announcement, "The plane has just landed," but we all knew, just at the same moment, before we were told.'

Bala Kanayson, an aerospace engineer from Singapore, now lives in America.

'I was at a public meeting in 1978, in London. I had been coming to Sahaja Yoga for a few months and a Sahaja Yogi (someone who practices Sahaja Yoga) gave me healing treatment, particularly in the area of my head. All of a sudden, I began to feel a tremendous cool breeze flowing. In those days, if Shri Mataji was taking the meeting, she used to come by and talk to each one of us.

"Are you feeling the cool breeze?" she asked.

"Yes," I replied.

Then she told me to put one hand towards her and one hand towards a long-haired person who was next to me. The hand towards Shri Mataji felt this fantastic cool breeze, whereas the one towards this guy felt tremendous heat. As I was doing that, this man, a complete stranger, turned around and for no apparent reason said he didn't like me at all. It was the first time I had felt the difference between the cool and the heat.'

Editor's note: In any system heat can indicate friction and a problem. Once a person has self realisation he or she can become aware of this subtle heat or beneficial coolness, which is actually a form of vibrations, and can also learn how to direct the cool vibrations to help heal people of diseases and other problems.

Chris Kyriacou, from Sydney, Australia, writes about an incident which occurred in the 1980"s.

'I was never what is termed a seeker. My brother was always looking for something, and said he would tell us once he found it. One memorable day, I was seated in front of the television watching a football game, when my brother came home and said the most incredible thing had happened. He had just met an Indian lady called Shri Mataji Nirmala Devi and had received his self realisation. He told me he had spent the day with her and a group of people and he had felt an incredible cool wind coming from her, when he put his hands in her direction.'

This is by Mrs K.T. Tan from Malaysia.

'My mum was 86 when she received self realisation in 1990. I didn't ask her to feel the cool breeze above her head. Instead I felt it and after that I taught my mum to meditate in the simplest way. We never explained to her about the cool breeze and when I asked her if she felt it on her palms while she was meditating her reply was no, she wasn't putting attention on that.

"Now that you mention it," she said after a while, "there were a few times while meditating I felt some wind blowing towards me but when I opened my eyes, the leaves were not moving." How simply put!

When new seekers ask if this cool breeze they feel is some auto-suggestion or self-hypnotism, I tell them about my mum who didn't know she was supposed to feel it during meditation but still did, therefore definitely ruling out any imagination.

She passed on in 2005, aged 100.'

Chapter 4

Despite Cultural Conditioning

The cool breeze we feel, a subtle form of vibrations, is the experience of everyone who has had the experience of self realisation. To quote Shri Mataji, 'The temperature of the spirit is absolute zero,' and at absolute zero all is still and orderly. This is why in Sahaja Yoga meditation, the ideal state is one of nirvichar, a Sanskrit word meaning thoughtless awareness – absolute stillness, absolute order.

The religions of the world fall into two main categories. The first group believes that to worship, or pay respects to an image is wrong, (the exact instruction is not to worship a graven image) while the second uses images in their doctrine. If the image is created by someone who is themselves awakened spiritually, and emits cool vibrations, or if it has spontaneously emerged from the earth, then these can be beneficial. But if we worship an image which is made by someone who is not awakened spiritually, it could give problems.

The solution is to have a heightened awareness so as to be able to distinguish between what is 'holy' or cool, and what is not. Once a person has settled into Sahaja Yoga he or she can generally do this. A photograph is not a graven image, ie a sculpture or painting made by someone's hand, as it merely records light waves, but the principle is generally the same; if the original subject emits cool vibrations, so will the photograph.

Here is a story of a visit to a famous artwork, by Auriol Purdie.

'My mother is somewhat intellectual in her approach to life, and I am a research scientist. We have visited many art galleries together, but one stands out, in Milan, Italy in 1998. It was a warm day and we went to the Castello Sforzesco. We walked around for about an hour until we reached the room which has a statue called the Rondanini Pietà by Michelangelo in it. There were some benches, and being hot and tired, we sat down to look at it. Suddenly, we both felt a blast of cool wind, like air conditioning on full. It seemed to be coming from the direction of the statue.

"You've got strong air conditioning on in here," my mother said to the attendant.

"No, signora, there isn't any in this room," he said, looking rather puzzled.

"That was a bit slow of us," laughed my mother, "after all, Michelangelo was a great realised soul."'

Djamel Metouri, originally from Algeria and these days a bank executive living near Paris, discovered a verse in the Koran which says, 'On the day of resurrection your hands will speak and bear witness to all that you have done ...' Could this refer to the time when the second birth of the Kundalini awakening, or self realisation takes place? Because, as will be seen in later chapters, after self realisation our hands can tell us a great deal of our, or another person's inner state, based on our present and past experiences. Other Sahaja Yogis who come from a Moslem background, have discovered that the Kaaba, the sacred stone which all Moslems are asked to visit at Mecca, also emits cool vibrations. This is Djamel's story.

'Shri Mataji arranged a weekend at her house at Hurst Green in Sussex, England, in 1976. There was a big drawing room downstairs with statues of Indian deities, and one was a beautiful wooden Shri Ganesha. One of the Sahaja Yogis who had been there before showed it to me.

The statue referred to is in the background of this photo

"This statue has such vibrations," he said.

"Hang on," I replied. "What is he talking about?" I thought. Although I had received my self realisation and could feel the cool vibrations, because of my cultural conditioning I was sceptical that this statue would emit them. So I tried feeling the cool vibrations and it did have them.

One of the things that struck me in Shri Mataji's house was that it felt as if every statue was vibrating with power. Everywhere you went you felt a kind of silent, peaceful, but extremely powerful environment, which is difficult to describe, except that you knew something very powerful was working deep inside you and working it out. You felt you were in a different universe altogether.'

This next account shows the similarity of all the religions, and how, once we have self realisation, we can experience them as being different flowers of the same tree of universal wisdom. This report is from Ray Harris, a businessman.

'My parents were very religious Jews. The first weekend after I got my self realisation, I went to see them at our home in Sheffield, England. I was still working the whole thing out myself, but I gave my mother self realisation and she felt the vibrations as a cool breeze.

Shri Mataji and the Harris family in their garden, 1981

She went to the synagogue the next Saturday, as she always did. At a certain point in the service the scrolls of the law would be taken out. They are kept in a beautifully decorated altar, which we call the Ark, a replica of the place where the Ten Commandments were kept after they were given to Moses on Mount Sinai. The scrolls are all parchment and beautifully written and decorated, by hand. As soon as they opened the Ark, my mother couldn't believe it. She felt a cool breeze pouring out of it. The rest of the people in the synagogue had no idea of this. As soon as the Sabbath was finished and she could use the phone, she phoned me.

"Ray, the most extraordinary thing happened," she said. "When they opened the Ark, I felt the same cool breeze pouring out of it as I felt from Shri Mataji. Now I know this is right."

Sadly my mother died in 1987, but before that, although she was always a firm follower of Judaism, she understood about Shri Mataji. Shri Mataji came to stay in our house and my father, a deeply learned and religious Jew, also understood her and respected her profoundly.'

In many cultures places where saintly people have lived are considered to be intrinsically special. This Sahaja Yogi, who prefers to remain anonymous, had an experience which explains why.

'I am from Austria. In January 1987 I got married, and my wife is from India. I wanted to visit my in-laws in Nagpur, India, so I went there, where I met Shri Mataji's brother, the late Baba Mama. He asked me if I would like to visit the house at Chindwara where Shri Mataji was born, then used as a hospital. Two days later, my new family and I visited it.

"I'm not telling you in which room she was born. You'd better find out for yourselves using vibrations," Baba Mama said.

When we gave the letter of introduction Baba Mama had given us to the hospital director, he asked one of the doctors to show us around. We were all very eager to find the right room. So round we went, our hands stretched forward with palms turned upwards, ready to register every slightest cool breeze or vibration on our hands. We felt coolness and peace all over the hospital, and in one laboratory both my brother-in-law and I could feel more vibrations. Standing in this small room, about two metres by five, and holding my hands like a radar scanner, I directed them to each part of the room. I never doubted that we would find the spot, but as we did, we became excited like children.

"You felt it too?" I said.

"Yes, it's there in this corner," said my brother-in-law. We went round the whole corner, from the left side to the right side, then raising our hands from the bottom to a height of about two metres to check how high this breeze was reaching. After a little while we remembered our guide, the doctor, who was standing there patiently. We asked him whether he had any idea what we were doing.

"No," he said, "but two years ago, a doctor from Saudi Arabia was here in the same room doing the same thing." He was a Sahaja Yogi and had found the same corner as us. We were later told that this was indeed the right place.'

Chapter 5

A Photo with Unique Properties

Previously it was explained that many people have felt a cool breeze coming from the photo of Shri Mataji. This chapter takes it a step further.

Experiment with the Vega Machine

This is a summary of a video made in Italy, of an experiment conducted by an Italian surgeon who specializes in integrated medicines. The patient is a young woman and the doctor is using Voll's electropuncture diagnostics.

The doctor starts using a pen-like device to measure the patient's meridian energy levels on her right hand. The scale ranges from 0 to 100 and 50 represents normality. If higher than 50 they indicate an inflammatory reaction and if lower than 50 they indicate a degenerative phenomena. If a white line appears on the computer screen it means there is something wrong.

He runs through all the meridian points on the right hand and then on the left hand, then starts probing various positions on the patient's feet. A chart appears on the computer screen. He points out that there are problems in the liver, the endocrine system, there are some allergies and the gall-bladder is not totally all right. The patient says that she suffers from horrendous conjunctivitis, and the doctor says it is a virus which is causing pain in her joints, and which is also present in her eyes.

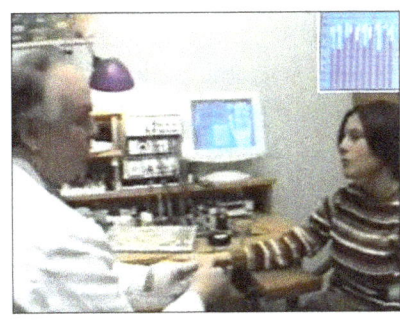

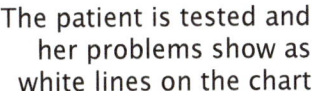
The patient is tested and her problems show as white lines on the chart

The Doctor repeats the tests while the patient holds Shri Mataji's photograph in her left hand. He is very surprised at the results. The Doctor asks the patient to switch the photograph to her right hand while he tests the left hand again.

Doctor: 'Yes it really is incredible. I don't know what is happening but it would take six months of treatment to get to this stage. I don't know who this person (in the photo) is but it is incredible. Look at the differences – first the test carried out without the photo, this is the difference between the two tests.'

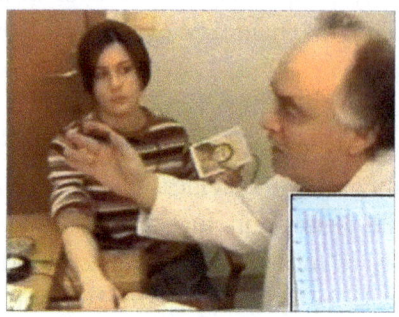

The patient holds Shri Mataji's photo and the symptoms have almost disappeared

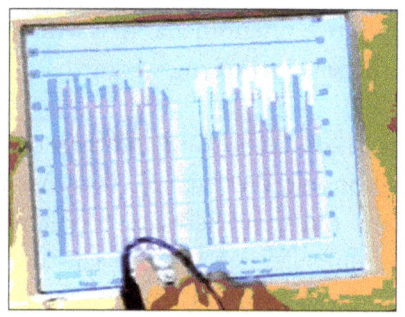

A comparison of the two charts

The interviewer then asks if it could be due to some placebo effect or whether some sort of suggestion was being used. The doctor replies that it is impossible. He says the machine is like a lie detector. He then repeats all the tests again with the patient holding a plain piece of paper in her hand. The patient reverts back to her former results.

Doctor: 'It's really incredible, I mean in theory by carrying this photo on her person, her regulating systems are regularized automatically without medication. That's incredible. Look at the effect – it's really clear cut. We can take anything else, but nothing else changes. I don't know what this photo (of Shri Mataji) has got but the patient touches (any other) piece of paper, of any kind, of any thickness, size or colour - nothing happens. She just goes back to being as ill as she was before. We can try some other things. This is no placebo effect.'

Two Sahaja Yogis then raise the patient's Kundalini and give her vibrations. The Doctor then repeats the tests after the patient's Kundalini has been raised.

He again compares the results with the results from the original diagnostics. He cannot find any trace of the original bacteria.

Doctor: 'Nothing. I could not even prescribe a treatment at the moment because to all intents and purposes – she's cured. The only thing is that we would have to see if this phenomena lasts, that is I ask myself is this just a transfer of energy, once the transfer has passed, will the normal energy levels come back and will the bacteria reappear? Certainly if by meditating every day, a person always has optimum levels of energy, it is possible - but how can this be brought to the masses?'

Rama Iurili is from Italy.

'My mother went to an introductory programme of Sahaja Yoga and received her self realisation. This was in Italy, and Shri Mataji was not present. It was conducted by the local Italian Sahaja Yogis. She brought home a photo she had been given of Shri Mataji. She showed it to me and two extraordinary things happened. Firstly, I smelled a very strong and beautiful aroma of roses, and then I felt a cool breeze coming from the photograph.'

Guillemette Metouri is French.

'I got my self realisation in November 1980 in London. I had spent the three previous years in Sicily, in the south of Italy, and was eager to go back there and tell my friends about my magic encounter with Shri Mataji. I got the opportunity to do so in August 1981.

I was quite excited to visit again a land whose people I loved very much. As expected, the hypothesis of vibrations was accepted very well. Italians are always open to magic and the irrational; they are ready for dreams to come true. My friend Mariella remained opened-mouthed when discovering Shri Mataji's photograph, unable to speak for a short while.

"This is incredible," she said a few seconds later. "I've seen this lady in a dream a couple of nights ago. Yes, it's exactly her. I'm sure." Mariella felt the cool wind of the spirit on her hands, on top of her head, on her face and all around her, filling the room with ecstasy and bliss.'

Rekha Das is from India.

'In September 1999 I became very ill and went to the Apollo Hospital in New Delhi. After a thorough check up I was diagnosed with a cyst in my left breast, which the doctors suspected to be breast cancer. I went to our local Sahaja Yoga centre, sat in front of Shri Mataji's photograph, and the lady running the centre gave me vibrations, and I felt a cool breeze on my head, hands and heart. I meditated in this way daily in the morning and evening.

After one and a half months, I went to the hospital for the biopsy. The doctors could not find any cyst and I had again to go for another round of monograms etc. as a checkup. The doctors were very surprised that the cyst had vanished and they could not find any reason. They were nervous and perplexed and paid me back the large amount of money which I had spent.'

Françoise Kazakov lives in France.

'Two years ago, I suddenly had spasms in my diaphragm as soon as I got up in the morning and unbearable pains in my belly. Medical check-ups and radiology were unsuccessful. They found nothing wrong, yet I was suffering like a martyr for hours together.

One day when the pain reached its peak, and unable to bear it any longer I phoned a Sahaja Yogi and she suggested that I should take Shri Mataji's photograph and place it on my belly. I kept it there for at least two hours. Three hours later, the pain which had been there for a week vanished. Since that day, I've never had the pain again.'

It is important to understand from the outset that Sahaja Yoga does not in any way replace or conflict with conventional medical practice, and in fact there are, in many countries, a number of regular doctors, surgeons, psychiatrists, consultants, medical researchers and others in similar fields who practice Sahaja Yoga and recommend it alongside but not instead of regular medical treatment.

There is a fair amount of confusion in the Western world about the meaning of the word meditation. From a quick search around the internet, contemporary definitions of meditation include concentration, contemplation, speculation, sitting in a certain way, endlessly repeating a meaningless word, reflection on a sacred text, continued thought, experiencing some inner conflict, exploring the nature of one's experiences, breathing in a special way and even dancing ecstatically - one can go on forever, through thousands of websites.

Dr Ramesh Manocha, a medical doctor and a Sahaja Yogi from Sydney has discovered the following:

'Meditation (in the Western world) is popularly perceived to be any activity in which the individual attention is primarily focused on a repetitive cognitive activity…If one closely examines the authentic (ancient) tradition of meditation it is apparent that meditation is a discrete and well defined experience of a state called 'thoughtless awareness'. Authentic meditation

enables one to focus on the 'present moment'.... is said to be therapeutic both psychologically and physiologically and which fundamentally distinguishes meditation from simple relaxation, physical rest or sleep.'
Ramesh Manocha, Australian Family Physician, Vol. 29, no 12. Dec. 2000

Sahaja meditation is different from the Western understanding of the word and is similar to the ancient traditions. All the types of meditation which involve thinking and physical activity put the cart before the horse. By allowing the Kundalini to rise, the result is a different state of awareness, and when this has happened and we then allow our attention to either be on the top of our head or on a photo of Shri Mataji, a state of thoughtless awareness and inner peace often occurs. This is the result of, not the cause of, an altered state of awareness.

It is well known that thinking uses up a lot of brain energy, so when this is reduced, the life energy can go elsewhere. The autonomous nervous system can take over and the body and mind can often be healed. These are the outer expressions of the Kundalini, and may account for some of the many stories of cures in this book that defy conventional medical explanation.

What about all the other amazing, extraordinary and downright bizarre stories in this book? As a scientist once said, 'The universe is not only stranger than we imagine, it is stranger than we can imagine.' And therein is the crux of the matter. Until the Kundalini takes our consciousness beyond rational thought and our emotions or feelings, we are bound by them. Or, to put it another way, in traditional Sanskrit philosophy, one of the qualities of the Adi Shakti or in Christian terms, the Holy Spirit, is Shri Achintya Rupa, meaning, 'She is inaccessible to thought since mind, the instrument of thought, is her creation'. In other words, you can only experience that which is beyond normal human intelligence if you stop thinking and analyzing and humbly allow this higher level to spontaneously filter into your consciousness.

Quantum mechanics recognizes that we influence our environment so that the act of observation itself influences the outcome. Similarly, Sahaja Yoga teaches us that the state of consciousness when the Kundalini is awakened allows us to perceive and observe what would otherwise not have been possible. This may be why Sahaja Yogis experience so many unusual occurrences, because when the Kundalini is awakened one is a channel or instrument for a different order of reality. |

Perhaps you, the reader, would now like to do an experiment to enable you to also feel the cool breeze and inner peace. If so turn to the Appendix at the end of the book.

Chapter 6

Meta Physical Photos

In the early 1980's, more and more people started taking photographs of Shri Mataji and the people who did her Sahaja Yoga. Sometimes it seemed that light was getting into the cameras, and all sorts of other phenomena started appearing. On the cover is a photo of Shri Mataji blowing on her hand, and one can see a white light where she is blowing. This photo, like many in this chapter, was taken nearly thirty years ago, before the advent of computer graphics programs. Literally thousands of photos like this have been taken, and more are taken daily by Sahaja Yogis, but these few will serve as examples. Below are some of the earliest ones, taken in 1979.

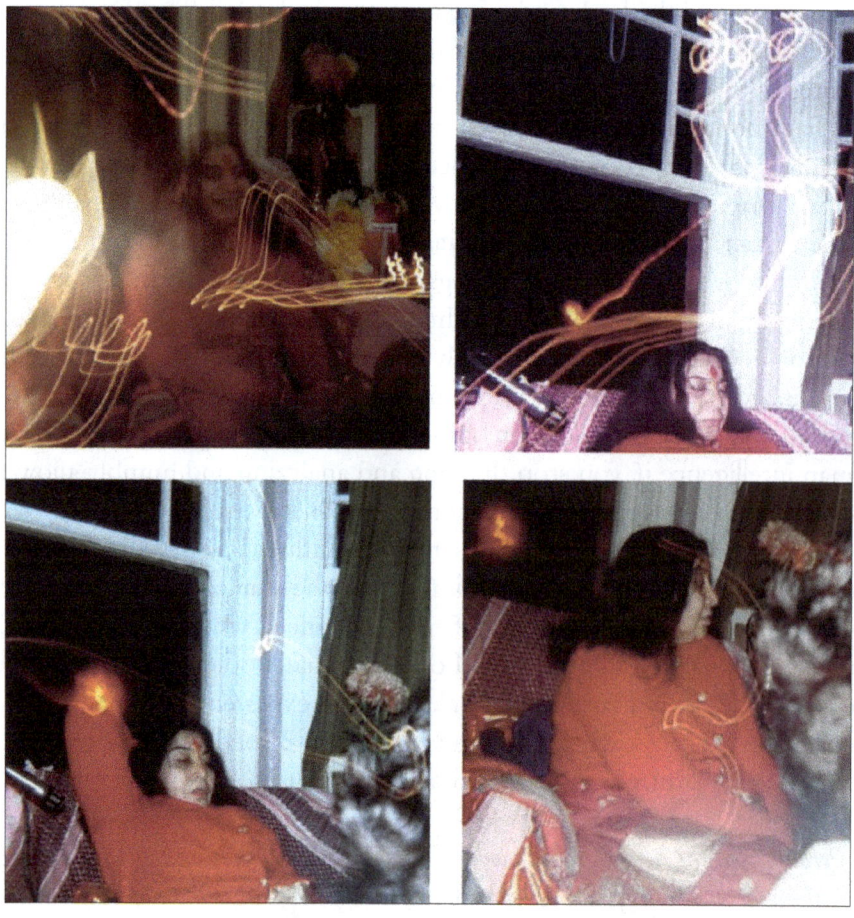

We began to realise that although we did not, and should not see the vibrations as light, the camera often picked up what was going on at wavelengths beyond what our eyes could see. Here are a few more examples. These photographs cannot be taken to order – they just happen spontaneously.

In these days of digital cameras the situation is even stranger – one can be in front of a perfectly normal scene, and if one looks through the viewer on the camera the scene may be bathed in light. Or – one person's photo will show light, while someone sitting next to them will take the same scene and it will be normal.

Kay McHugh is a businesswoman from Australia and was present when Shri Mataji was giving a programme in Maharashtra, India, in the early 1980's. The photos below are three of a series of seven from that occasion.

'There was a village we went to on that trip, where the pictures were taken, and the light is coming down. I was sitting next to my friend who took the pictures, so I can vouch for the fact that it was completely open, no cover. It was an overcast day and there was no sunlight.

Later, I took the pictures to London, to Shri Mataji at her flat.

"These amazing pictures have come out, Shri Mataji," I said, and took three or four of them and showed them to her.

'There's another picture in the series. It's the last one and you have your hand up over your head like you're saying, "It's enough now,"' and she laughed.

Shri Mataji said the reason for the light was because there was a saint buried there.'

These next photos, three of a series of twelve, were taken on a boat trip to Capri, an island off the coast of Italy. In Sorrento, Italy, in 1989, the assembled Sahaja Yogis had the privilege of a boat ride to Capri with Shri Mataji. During the trip a series of extraordinary photographs were taken. None of the many people on the boat with Shri Mataji had any idea that anything unusual was going on, until the photos were developed. This is always the case with these photos.

In the first, one can see the people sitting in front of Shri Mataji; she is on a bench and more people are sitting around and to the side of her. The picture is normal, although a little blurred.

In this later picture a few individuals can be made out around Shri Mataji, but the whole photograph is dissolving into light.

The last photograph is practically nothing but sheets of light pouring from Shri Mataji. No more Sahaja Yogis are to be seen. Shri Mataji said this photo showed the fully open Sahasrara.

Edith Petermann, together with Madhavi Dejust and Günter Woltron were with the professional photographer from Austria, who Shri Mataji had asked earlier to take some pictures.

'After coming back from the boat trip we had just enough time available to order a one-hour express service from a local film shop. When the prints returned about ten of us circled around him curiously watching the sealed envelope being opened. We were all wonderstruck when we saw the vibrations emenating from Mother's Sahasrara.'

Mara-Madhuri Corazzari was on the boat trip when Shri Mataji was with us near Capri.

'We were so very surprised when we saw them with the light coming in every photo on the boat. In every successive photo there were more and more vibrations (light) coming. We didn't understand about them at all. When we were on the boat we didn't see any light coming. It was a wonderful trip with Shri Mataji but there was nothing unusual happening. Also there was no light in the other photos on the same reel of film.'

The vibrations can often be seen in photos of Sahaja Yogis. Next is a photo of a group of Sahaja Yogis giving vibrations (healing) to a lady sitting in front of them. This took place in the house of Mr Saundankar, a musician and composer from Nasik, Maharashtra, India, in the late 1980's.

Dr Ambar Chatterjee is a leading nuclear physicist and lives in Mumbai, India. The unexplained light in his photo is not nearly so dramatic as many others, but it served to convince him.

'After I started Sahaja Yoga I was happy with the way my concentration improved and I was able to do better in my scientific work. There were people who used to ask me how I could reconcile my scientific beliefs with Sahaja Yoga. I told them I found no contradictions. The world is constructed by the Adi Shakti and she allows us to investigate its laws and properties for the benefit of mankind. Each new scientific discovery is a revelation about the beauty of the world we live in.

There was however one part of Sahaja Yoga which I could not accept. I examined some photographs with vibrations and concluded that the observed effects were caused by artifacts ranging from a finger in front of the lens to diffraction and reflections, and the subject was put out of my mind.

Then, one day, I was taking some random pictures to finish a film. One of them was of my wife's study table where she had several pictures of Shri Mataji. When the prints came back from the shop, I was amazed to see the result.

There was an orange glow emanating from the lower left of the picture. In those days I was still using a film and I had seen effects in sunset pictures or on the beach where the angle of the sun is low and in night time pictures where flash or backlighting creates strange looking streaks. But this photo was taken in broad daylight, the flash was not attached to the camera and there was no electric bulb switched on in the room.'

Hermann Haage is an architect living in Vienna.

'In the autumn of 1985 I went with some Sahaja Yogis to the Frankfurt Book Fair, in Germany, where we had a stand for a book on Sahaja Yoga. We also placed some information about Sahaja Yoga where a lot of people passed. We put up a big poster showing Shri Mataji dressed in a white sari, standing on the shore of the Indian Ocean. When I saw this picture, in the middle of the crowd, I felt very touched. Spontaneously I took a picture of the picture. Back in Vienna we developed it and I was amazed when we could see a white light on Shri Mataji's heart, and we all said what a coincidence it was that the reflection of the flash light was exactly on her heart.

Some weeks later, the Diwali Puja, the festival of light, was celebrated in Rome with Shri Mataji. We asked her about this light and it was shown to her.

She said it was the paramatma (the supreme spirit) and not the reflection of the flash light.'

Editor's note: in Sahaja Yoga we accept that the seat of the spirit is in the heart.

The photo of the photo, taken at the Frankfurt Book Fair

'A photograph of mine was taken there ... and in some photographs, in my heart there's a light coming out, and some told me that some photographs ... did not have the light, but when they re-took, and again they took a photograph with that, then the light came in there.'
Shri Mataji Nirmala Devi, May 1986

Chapter 7

The Bandhan

When we receive our self realisation we learn how to make a bandhan to protect our awakened Kundalini. With our right hand we trace an arch around our body seven times each way to protect our subtle system. The details are in the Appendix. There is also another sort of bandhan, which can help whoever or whatever we have our attention on when we do it, and again, for instructions please consult the Appendix. Before the contributor went to Shri Mataji's birthplace, in the story related in Chapter 4, he did this.

'In January 1987 I got married. Soon after the wedding I had to return to Europe. However, since I wanted to visit my in-laws in India, I tried to extend my ticket to return a few days later. I was told by the airline I would have to buy a new ticket, but I had no money for this. I asked my Sahaja Yogi friends what to do.

"You are a Sahaja Yogi," they told me, "ask the vibrations."

"Shall I stay in India?" I wrote in my palm, making a bandhan on my hand, and a cool breeze was coming. Then I wrote, "Shall I go to Nagpur?" and made another bandhan. The breeze was flowing again. I asked again, "Shall I go straight back home to Austria?" Very clearly the answer came, no cool breeze, no vibrations at all.

"You have felt the answers yourself. We cannot decide for you," my friends said, so I stayed in India. They promised to try to extend my ticket home, so I left Mumbai and went to Nagpur.

After my visit to Nagpur, my flight home to Austria was scheduled to leave Mumbai at 3:45 am. I finally reached Mumbai at 2.45 am, where a Sahaja Yogi was waiting for me at the National Terminal. I was incredibly late, because my plane from Nagpur had been very delayed. Then we had to go to his flat to pick up my luggage. I checked in at the International Terminal at 3:20 am to find my Indian friends waiting for me. They thrust a boarding card into my hand and a few minutes later I was sitting comfortably in a First Class seat – the other compartments by now being full. In the plane I found some other Sahaja Yogis, who told me that they had somehow been able to exchange my ticket with somebody else, usually quite impossible. They also told me that boarding a plane in India normally takes at least two hours, not twenty minutes, and the check in time was usually even longer during the night, the peak period.'

Three Italians helped renovate Shri Mataji's house in London. Alessandra, seen in the photo, is a farmer, Giovanni has a guest house and Duilio is an architect.

Alessandra: When we were in Brompton Square in July 1983, Shri Mataji was still doing some work in the house. There were about ten of us, mostly Italians, staying there. The Italian boys were doing the pavement with blocks of Carrara marble.

Giovanni: Shri Mataji asked me and another boy to put some marble tiles on the floor. I had never done this before, but she told me to try.

Duilio: As an architect, I was familiar with this kind of job, but only from a theoretical standpoint and none of us had any practical experience in this domain. We started, and some time later, Shri Mataji came to see how the work was going and we told her that we were running out of cement. We had only done one small corner of the room and had used half our last bag. We asked an English person to go to the shops and buy more, but he soon returned saying the shops were closed, because it was Saturday afternoon. Shri Mataji very gently pointed out the urgency of finishing that day.

"Just give a bandhan," she said, smiling.

Giovanni: She said we should give a bandhan. I thought maybe this meant that we would find a shop open.

Alessandra: "Don't worry, just keep going on with your work," said Shri Mataji.

Duilio: It was my job to mix the cement with the water and the more I took out from the sack, the more I found inside. When we finished the marble floor, we found we still had cement left over, which turned out to be precisely sufficient to tile the corridor leading to the kitchen. The bucket emptied just as we finished.

Alessandra: They went on and the bucket with the cement never ended; it was still full. They could finish the whole room by the time we all left for the Sahaja Yoga programme we were all going to in the countryside.

Duilio: While we were working, a little child walked up to the freshly laid tiles and disturbed them. When the child had left we spent a few minutes putting the tiles back into place.

Alessandra: Giovanni had just finished the tiling and he put two pieces of wood on the entrance of the dining room because he didn't want people to step on the tiles just yet. Then Shri Mataji came down the stairs and into the corridor, which was also just done and he had put some wooden pieces there too. She walked on the corridor and went to the dining room, looked inside and went in. Giovanni was thinking: "Oh, now I'll have to do it all again." I was also sure it must be all out of place and would have to be redone.

Duilio: "Well," we thought to ourselves, "that's fine. We can reset the tiles afterwards, no problem." But when she left, we looked closely and discovered that the only tiles that had moved were those which we ourselves had slightly mis-set. Now even they were in exactly the right position.

Alessandra Pallini, Giovanni Albanesi and Duilio Cartocci

The front door and hallway of 48, Brompton Square, London

Ruth Eleanore is a diplomat.

'The first time Shri Mataji came to Rome was in November 1981. We were at the airport. I had met her for the first time only about five or six days before, when she had arrived in Rome, and I was travelling back to London with her. She had done some shopping and there was a lot of hand luggage. I had taken an Economy Class ticket, and Shri Mataji had her Business Class one.

We arrived at the gate and the flight attendants started shouting at Shri Mataji because of her hand luggage. I was a bit panicky, but she said she was thirsty, so I went to fetch her a cup of tea. On the way I gave a bandhan for this situation to resolve itself because I was worried about all this hand luggage. When I came back, I could not believe it. Before this, the airline attendants were being so aggressive with Shri Mataji. Now they were so kind and even said they would accompany us right to the plane. They carried our hand luggage, and even upgraded me to Business Class so I could sit next to her. I was absolutely stunned, and Shri Mataji laughed.

"Did you give a bandhan for the situation to change?" she said.

"Yes," I replied. It was just so amazing to see these people change their attitudes so much.'

Christine Haage gives an explanation.

'Another lady and I from Switzerland were in Poland in the early 1980's, doing an introductory programme. We were giving vibrations to people and there were only the two of us, and five hundred new people queuing, so we couldn't give much attention to every single person. We just gave a bandhan before and the Kundalini did the work. Many felt the cool breeze.

Later when Shri Mataji came to Warsaw, we told her about this. We said it was like phoning to the divine power.

"Do you know what it means when you do the bandhan?" Shri Mataji asked. "It is like when you make a circle in the water and it goes deep, like a turbulence. When you do this on your hand, you do the same in the param chaitanya (the all-pervading, divine power). It's acting immediately."'

Chris Kyriacou has a story which shows how a bandhan might help save lives. Many people have similar tales to tell.

'One night I was driving along the coast to visit a friend, near Sydney, Australia. This particular night a very fierce storm was raging, with driving rain, gale force winds and freezing temperatures. As I drove, I kept thinking to myself what a terrible night to be outside, and listened to the radio. A news reader announced that there was an emergency; a yacht had been battling the winds and was trying to make it to a safe haven, however it was still a few miles from the coast. Mountainous seas had closed the port so that no rescue ship could go out to help.

'I hoped the crew would be rescued, but the weather got even worse. About fifteen minutes later the news reader gave us an update, and said the rescue helicopter could see the two crew members on the deck, but because of the winds and the huge seas it could not get close enough to winch them to safety. The helicopter returned to the shore, taking with it the men's last hope of rescue, as the yacht was sinking. Suddenly, I realised that there was something I could do. I pulled the car over to the curb and started to place the men in a bandhan, then resumed my journey. Nothing more was mentioned about them on the radio.

'The following morning I was having breakfast and one of the people I lived with read a miracle story on the front page of the newspaper. As the helicopter was leaving the men on the yacht to their fate, they reported that a huge wave, bigger than any they had seen, had swamped the vessel. They felt sure the men were finished, but to their amazement the wave picked up the two men and carried them for over a kilometre to the beach, where both men had woken up safe and sound.

'I then related the story of the previous night to everyone and how at about the moment of the sinking I had put the men into bandhan.'

Bhakti Iro now lives in Slovakia.

'I was a nurse in the UK, assisting at a very serious operation – an aneurism in an artery near the heart. It was not going well, and the surgeon had to manually massage the patient's heart to keep it going, after the operation had been in progress for three or four hours. He was not optimistic and the patient's blood pressure was going down and down. I was standing at the base of the table, and as a last resort gave a bandhan on my hand. After a minute or two the anesthetist said to the surgeon, "What did you do? The patient's blood pressure and vital functions have suddenly returned to almost normal."'

This story is by Major Naveen Navlani, an officer in the Indian Army.
'I was posted to Kargil, North India in 1999. One day I, along with some fifteen to twenty other soldiers, was sitting inside a bunker when suddenly shells started falling on our camp. Shells were soon falling all around our bunker and it was shaking badly. I gave a bandhan and prayed: "Please save all the people of our camp."

The shelling continued for about five hours, but not one person of our camp (approximately 150 people) was hurt. Later, when the shelling stopped, we saw that shells had fallen all around our bunkers but not even one shell out of about 2500 that were fired on us had fallen on any of the bunkers where people were hiding. Shells had fallen on our rooms, our office complex, our store houses but it was as if the divine power had put some protective shield on us and we all came out unscathed.'

From an anonymous Sahaja Yogi
'In the 1980's, I woke up in the middle of the night, in Pune, India with an awful fear and foreboding for my brother, who lived several miles away in a

village. Somehow I knew he was in grave danger. I immediately placed him in bandhan. It was all I could do. The vibrations felt cool and so, reassured, I lay down again and went off to sleep.

The next day, news reached me from my brother's village of a sensational story which was the talk of the area. At the precise moment I had woken up with such fear in my heart, my brother had fallen down a well, having missed his footing in the darkness, but as he fell, believing himself to be lost, a hand came down, grabbed his outstretched arm and heaved him out onto the ground by the side of the well. With the shock of the moment he could remember little of what had happened, but one amazing detail stuck in his mind. "It must have been a lady," he said; "I can just remember seeing glass bangles, which sparkled in the dim light, and hearing them jingle as I was pulled out.'

This was one of our group emails, on September 13th, 2006, posted by Edward Saugstad of Vienna.

Many of us have heard of this incredible kidnapping case in Vienna, Austria. Eight years ago, in 1998, at the tender age of ten, Natascha was taken prisoner by a psychopath and locked in his basement, just a few minutes away from her home. He threatened to kill himself and to murder her and anyone who assisted her if she ever tried to escape. Despite the apparent hopelessness of the situation, she never gave up hope, all these years, that she would somehow be freed.

Early this year an article appeared in a Vienna newspaper stating that Natascha's mother recently consulted a psychic who told her that her daughter was still alive and was underground, somewhere north of the Danube River.

A Sahaja Yogi read this article and gave a heartfelt bandhan that this unfortunate, suffering girl should be found.

A few days ago, just after Natascha's escape, the police phoned the office of this yogi, saying that a call had gone out from there to the house of the kidnapper. As it turned out, a colleague of the yogi who made the bandhan had phoned the kidnapper about an advertised apartment (the man worked as a real-estate agent), and had, by a wonderful twist of fate, unknowingly kept the kidnapper talking long enough for the girl to get out of the house and call the police from a neighbour's home. After eight years, she had suddenly felt that her chance had come.

Very often it is difficult for doctors to explain what happens to Sahaja Yogis.

'My daughter was four months old and had been in hospital since her birth,' explained Gaelle Sattarshetty. 'We knew that the child had a genetic illness and on top of that had caught two bad bacteria. She had permission to be out of the hospital for one week so we took her to Cabella, Italy where Shri Mataji then was. Upon our arrival, we were asked to work on (give vibrations to) the child ourselves.

So we did so. While giving vibrations I was thinking that Shri Mataji was showing us how we could save our own child. Then my husband and I were introduced to a yogini who was also at the castle (Shri Mataji's home) at that moment. Her own child had got the same rare disease as our daughter and there she was that same day, also in the castle at Cabella. We had never seen this lady before and as yet have never met her again. She told us all Shri Mataji had said to her ten years before, when she came to see her, just like us.

The next day we got the message that Shri Mataji had given a bandhan in the night.

"She'll be alright," she said, regarding our child. We were advised to take some vibrated water from the castle. These four little words of Shri Mataji dissolved all fear and sadness in my heart and I left the castle very serene. When we returned home and brought the child back to hospital, the doctor told us that the tests showed no more bacteria.

"How do you explain that?" I said, because as yet no antibiotics had been given to the child.

"Tests are not 100% reliable," the doctor replied.'

This story, by Catherine Hallé, speaks for itself.

'I live in France, and in 1992, our baby Daya was a few months old. I decided to prepare a little vegetable soup for her. We decided to go out for a drive and a walk, and I completely forgot about the cooking. It was only on the way back, two hours later, that I realised I had forgotten to turn off the gas under the pan.

I got scared of the consequences, then decided to give it a bandhan anyway, even if it was too late. We arrived home, saw no firemen around, opened the door and went into the kitchen. Everything was safe and the vegetables were boiling nicely in the little pan as if I had just put them into the water a few minutes before.'

Calin Costian was living in Indiana, USA, at the time of this story.

'Once, as I was giving a Sahaja Yoga public programme at Purdue University, Indiana, the tornado warning siren got activated. I had never heard one before and since I didn't know what it was, I ignored it and went on. In the meantime, the people in the room started to get restless and some even got up and started to make for the door, trying to find shelter. As I came to understand what this was about, I said, "Why should we let the tornado interrupt our class, when we have spiritual powers to stop it?" I was not going anywhere, so I invited everyone to sit back down. It was an advanced class, so we all used a Sahaja Yoga technique called bandhan through which we directed our attention and the energy of the vibrations to the problem at hand.

Less than thirty seconds later, the siren stopped and we continued our class undisturbed. The next day I found out what had happened from a friend, corroborating the sequence of events based on when the siren went off and subsequently stopped. Apparently, two tornadoes had been sighted close to the campus that afternoon. One had touched down two miles away and another was forming right above us and was preparing to touch down. Then, all of a sudden, at the time we used the power of the bandhan, the first tornado lifted off the ground and went away, while the second one dissolved in the sky before touching down.

The next day I received an email from a Sahaja Yogi friend in New Jersey. Among other things he asked, "What about those tornadoes?" I feigned ignorance in my reply, "Which tornadoes?" He then emailed me back saying that the day we had the public programme there had been very intense tornado activity throughout the state of Indiana. What had also made news was the fact that on that particular night the number of emergency calls associated with tornadoes was 33% less than the average, and none of the experts could find any logical explanation for this.

One may think that such occurrences are pure coincidences – when they happen the first time, the second time, maybe even the tenth time. But as they keep on happening, as if because the divine power wants to convince us that we are indeed connected to it, after a while we get used to such happenings that become part of our daily life. Also, it is important to know is that such powers can never be misused, because in reality it is the all-pervading power that does everything, we only submit to its all-pervading attention the problems we would like solved. Interestingly enough, sometimes things get resolved in a different way from what we had envisioned, but they always get solved in the best possible way. For example, we may desire and put our attention on moving to a different place, but it may not work out. Later we can realize that it was better to stay where we were, and thank the divine power for creating 'obstacles' to our move.'

Christophe Sous from France was doing some home improvement.

'I recently went to IKEA, the large furniture and household appliance store, for a product return. It was a bathroom lamp, purchased in two pieces, one of which we broke when trying to fix it on the wall. When I asked for a replacement, they told me they didn't have the spare part. We placed the order and waited for them to call us after they received it from their supplier.

After three months, we visited the shop and asked for the lamp. The saleslady was embarrassed but said there were none in stock because the model had been discontinued.

I made a bandhan, which I normally never do for such small things. At this very moment, I saw, among the piles of documents, fax machines, phones and returned products, in one of the hundreds of small compartments containing spare parts, exactly the same lamp as ours, which among the hundreds of thousands of articles available at IKEA was rather unexpected. We pointed it out to the saleslady and she tried to find out about it. No one knew anything about it and it was not registered anywhere. She was a bit puzzled but realized she could get rid of a customer claim issue!

"Don't say anything to my manager, but I'll hand it over to you, free of charge," she said quietly.'

Chapter 8

Help from a Distance

When we get our self realisation, we are in touch with the underlying power of divine love, which permeates all creation, and each and every one of us. Shri Mataji expressed this in its most powerful and effective way, but we can all tap into it. Because she was so totally at one with this power, when our attention is on her, we are automatically helped by it.

When music from a symphony orchestra, or a sitar player, strikes the listeners with sound vibrations, they can be felt by everyone present in the hall, so in a similar way, once our Kundalini is awakened, we become able to detect even subtle vibrations from many sources of life. Most especially, the awareness of the vibrations of collective consciousness becomes heightened. Shri Mataji expressed this completely and gave us the knowledge of how to tap into that consciousness, even from great distances. The following stories illustrate the point.

This first story, by Anna Chicos of Australia, shows how Shri Mataji was often aware of us when our attention was on her via her photograph.

'We were having a simple programme to celebrate the fifth birthday of the Sahaja Yoga Treatment Centre at Belapur, Vashi, India and were all sitting in the meditation room with our attention on the photograph of Shri Mataji. Then the phone rang and the man who kept watch at the front gate answered it, came in and spoke to the director. It seemed odd to disturb a meditation programme and he would never normally do it, but it turned out Shri Mataji had told someone to ring up from her home some distance away in Pune and give this message: "I felt such good vibrations coming from Vashi."'

Here is a story from Grazyna Anslow, who was visiting Poland at the time, which shows how we can all share in this collective awareness.

'I stayed on in Poland after Shri Mataji visited Warsaw in 1992 to help with public programmes and to be with the newly formed and vibrant Polish collective. One day I went to see my friend, a Polish Sahaja Yogini called Marta. She kindly offered to make a dress for me from some material I bought in a local shop. We stayed up half the night and got up quite late the next morning - it was about 11 am when we finally started to meditate. Marta was hoping that her dog would behave as he was a very lively creature.

We put our hands out and if the cool breeze could be measured by any instruments or the movements of objects in the room everything would be blowing in this wind, which was on our hands, on our faces, in our hair. It was all around us as though it wanted to lift us up high, out of this world into another dimension and penetrated to the core of our beings. It felt as though it enlightened every cell in our bodies. The extraordinary thing was that we were in it together as one, including the dog, which during the whole time did not move and enjoyed the vibrations equally, just lying there totally relaxed. We looked at the clock at one point and to our astonishment almost three hours had passed. Even the next day we were still experiencing the effects of our amazing meditation and it felt like we were walking on air.

I found out couple of days later that Shri Mataji was waiting for the plane at the Heathrow airport on her way to Italy on that day and at the same time as our experience. Shri Mataji was talking to some Yogis and she commented the vibrations were so strong, as though the puja was happening there and then. Warsaw is on the same latitude as London.'

Chris Coles lives in America

'In September 1995 I was visiting Darwin, Australia. I was bitten by a cattle tick which was carrying a very toxic virus and after several days I ended up with a boil under my arm. For the next six months I was plagued with huge seeping boils under my left arm. Homeopathy did not work, and even the most powerful courses of antibiotics only kept them at bay for a few days. Still the boils kept coming back, getting worse each time.

In April 1996 I was on my way back to England and stopped over in India to visit friends. I took another course of antibiotics to enable me to travel, and the boils were temporarily under control. I was in New Delhi and stayed for a couple of weeks and inevitably the boils returned. My friend asked a doctor she knew to meet me – he was a General Practitioner who also used homeopathy and ayurvedic medicine. He arranged to meet me at a medical seminar he was attending the following day.

The next day we went to the seminar to meet him. We sat at the back of the auditorium and waited for the conference to finish. Suddenly the boils under my arm started to throb quite violently and a few seconds later Shri

Mataji herself walked out onto the stage. I was not even aware that she was in India at the time! She sat down and although there were a lot of people in the room, she immediately stared very intensely in our direction. The thumping pain under my arm got faster and faster and Shri Mataji continued to stare in our direction for about thirty seconds. All of a sudden the pain stopped and Shri Mataji smiled, looked around the room and the conference continued very successfully.

Afterwards we met the doctor and I explained what had happened during the seminar. He laughed and asked me to move my arm – something that was normally too painful for me to even attempt. I moved my arm and found there was no pain. He said I needed no further treatment. Two hours later the boils had shrunk from about the size of half a hen's egg to one quarter of their original size and the following morning they had disappeared completely. The scars of all the boils, at least twenty, had also disappeared and since that day I've not had another boil.'

Sergei Utenkov from Russia tells a simple story with an interesting twist.

'In 1996 Shri Mataji came to Moscow for some programmes. Through the leaders, she distributed presents. Afterwards there was an opportunity to come nearer to the stage. My aunt was seriously ill at that time and the leader gave her a chain as a present from Shri Mataji. She approached the stage.

"Have you got a present?" Shri Mataji asked and in answer my aunt showed the chain.

"It won't suit you," Shri Mataji replied and asked for a box with presents and chose another chain, thicker. Someone gave that chain to my aunt from Shri Mataji and the first chain was taken back from her.

"Do you like it?" Shri Mataji asked.

"Yes, I do," my aunt answered.

"Then wear it," Shri Mataji replied.

At that point my aunt realised the conversation with Shri Mataji was taking place at a distance. She was sitting about thirty metres from the stage and communicating with her on the level of thought. She did not know the English language and had not opened her mouth.

At that time the doctors told her that she would live for only three months but she was still alive in 2007, when this story was written.'

Editor's note: When Shri Mataji touched something she gave it vibrations, which can be very healing to whoever else touches the same thing.

Sometimes these cures have happened even if the subject was not a Sahaja Yogi, as related by the Editor

'Here is a story which concerned my mother. Although she was not a Sahaja Yogi, Shri Mataji, from a distance of a hundred miles or so, did something extraordinarily compassionate for her.

I returned to the UK in June 1986 after four years absence to find my mother looking grey in the face and very aged. She told me that both her GP and the specialist from the local hospital were virtually certain she had lung cancer. She told me there was little hope and that she would go for a biopsy the following week, but doctors don't tell patients they probably have lung cancer until they are pretty sure.

I went back to my house in London from the countryside, where my mother lived. Shri Mataji was in London at the time, but I didn't see her.

My mother went for the biopsy but there was no trace of cancer. The specialist was amazed. He said the lungs were very inflamed, but there was nothing malignant at all. He'd never seen anything like it. Three days later I saw Shri Mataji.

"How is your mother?" she asked me.

"Strangely enough, she's all right. The doctors thought she had cancer," I replied.

"Yes, the Sahaja Yogis told me. I thought I had better cure her," said Shri Mataji.

She lived another twenty-four years and passed away in 2010, aged 91.'

Shri Mataji has talked about the following incident in one of her lectures.

"There are a lot of miracles which have taken place about Sahaja Yoga, I must say; and in that you should see that the wisdom helps you. Of course, my attention is there always, no doubt, but still you should not take it for granted. You have to ask. One day you see, I was just sitting. I just thought that I should telephone somebody in the ashram of New York. I never telephone there. So I found out the number. We telephoned and asked if, I said, 'Is the child all right?" So the leader there was surprised because that boy had fallen in the water and was in the water for quite some time, and he was all filled with water, even his brain was filled with water.

As usual, there were some doctors who said that he cannot survive, and even if he survives his brain has so much water that he cannot be normal. So, I just said that, "Don't worry," – I didn't know, nobody told me – "Don't worry. The boy will be all right, completely." So, they were surprised how I said so. Firstly, how I knew that the boy had fallen, that there was some boy like that, and then they didn't know how I said that he'll be all right, and he was all right – perfectly all right. So they were surprised at my knowing about it, that how is it that Mother knows that there is a boy who is so sick?

Here I will say that it is pure knowledge. You see, my attention is always around you people, always dealing with you people, and how I know is this: that this attention of mine is global.

So, anything happens to you, any upsetting takes place, any, I should say, deviation takes place, my attention is there and immediately I know that there is something wrong somewhere. And I don't know how my attention goes to particular places, which makes life better – it helps people in need."

Shri Mataji Nirmala Devi, Navaratri Puja Talk 1998, Cabella Ligure, Italy

Maryanne Berman was there.

'It was a Sunday visit to the ashram in New Jersey, U.S.A., in about July/August 1998. My two sons David, then thirteen, and Phillip, then eleven, were playing outside with Jay, who was sixteen. They wanted to go swimming and I said it was OK. Jay asked his father who also agreed. My children were well adapted to water. The kids were in the pool about thirty to forty-five minutes, when I saw an Indian woman race through the room and out of the door, and then we all followed her.

Jay was at the bottom of the pool motionless and my sons were still swimming, because they thought Jay was playing and holding his breath under the water after jumping off the diving board. I yelled for David to go down to the bottom of the pool and pull Jay up, which he did. When he got him to the edge of the pool more people realised something was wrong, and came out to help. Two people jumped in the water to pull Jay out. 911 (the emergency number) was called. I went into the meditation room and started to give bandhans.

'I know we get boons for doing good deeds but right now I don't need any boons because I am alive so please, give Jay all my boons,' I said strongly. About two minutes went by and the phone rang. I already knew who it was. It was Shri Mataji who, quite spontaneously, called from Cabella, Italy, to say that the boy will be alright.

The ambulance came, and he was in the hospital for about two weeks. Two Sundays after the accident Jay and his parents came back to the ashram for meditation. Jay looked better after then before. His face was gleaming.'

Heidi Stornier was the lady who pulled Jay out of the pool.
'I dreamt of Shri Mataji one night.

She is seated, at the far end of a swimming pool on a throne bedecked in jewels. It is night but light emanates from her face as she gazes into the water. She sits as still as a gilded statue. I stand at the other end of the pool, gazing at her face and waiting. There is no one else around. It is silent save for the lapping of the water, silent and still, like the night and the stars with the blue light of the pool dancing around Shri Mataji's face. Slowly, deliberately she lifts her face to mine.

"Jump in," she says and I wake with these words echoing in my brain.

In the days that follow I try to interpret this dream and understand the words that Shri Mataji said to me. I know that her words, even in dream always have tremendous meaning. For two weeks her words beside the pool inspire me as I 'jump in' to my Yoga, 'jump in' to my day, my work and my relationships. These words become very freeing and I am grateful for the metaphor given so lovingly to me by Shri Mataji. Little do I suspect that these words are not just a metaphor but a tangible command to be carried out in the real world.

Two weeks after the dream I sit in the living room of the New Jersey ashram, a large spacious suburban American home chosen by Shri Mataji complete with outdoor patio and swimming pool. We have just finished a collective meditation, Elizabeth, my baby, is on my lap and I feel very quiet and at peace. The house is full of people, some like me still seated, some milling about on the patio, some outside by the swimming pool. Suddenly there is a commotion outside by the pool. Without thinking I hand Elizabeth to someone and stand up. I pass through the open doors of the living room onto the patio and out into the pool area. There are people standing by the pool pointing in the water and shouting. I cross the grass and jump fully clothed into the pool.

And from one moment to the next I am in another world, a world of blue water and muffled sound with everything passing as if in slow motion. There, before me in the water at the bottom of the pool, floats a young boy. He is beautiful, his black hair floating about his face like seaweed; his eyes closed as if asleep. He is an Indian boy, smooth skinned, long and lean, about sixteen years old. I am aware of other people in the water, diving in and out, perhaps they too are trying to reach him, but I only see him, floating alone in the blue water as if in a dream. I rouse myself and swim to him, put my arm across his chest and under his chin the way I was once shown by a lifeguard friend of mine. We are both weightless under the water and for a moment I am unsure how to propel us to the surface. Then my free arm and feet begin to move reflexively and we glide to the surface and over to the side ladder. Hands are there to lift him out.

The many hands lay him on the concrete. I climb out of the pool. An Indian woman I have never seen before kneels beside him and takes his pulse.

"I am a physician!" she calls out. "He has no pulse, call an ambulance, someone help me!" Someone leaves immediately for the house to call; I kneel down opposite her on the other side of the boy. She orders me to give him breaths while she pumps his heart. I follow her instructions but my breath does not seem to go anywhere. The boy does not respond. We take a break and turn his head to the side; water and bile flow from his mouth. Someone relieves me to resume giving breaths. I move aside with a gripping fear that we will lose the boy, a sickly awareness of the time passing, the minutes slipping by.

Finally we hear a siren. An ambulance arrives after what seems like an eternity and the emergency medical team sweeps up the stairs to the pool. They swarm the boy working quickly, fighting the time.

"He's not responding, we're going to lose him, what's his name, call his name!" one of the team calls out,

"Jay," someone yells. We all begin to call to him. I am close enough to lay my hands on his ice cold feet…

"Jay, Jay …"

"OK, we got something, get him out of here!" the medical technician shouts finally. Within seconds he is gone, whisked into the ambulance with his parents, the whirring siren receding into the distance.

Slowly the silent crowd by the pool begins to break up. I go upstairs to change into some dry clothes. In the hallway I run into the physician. We stop to talk. She is the sister of one of the Yogis, living in the ashram, she just happened to be visiting, a remarkable coincidence considering what just transpired. Suddenly she bursts into tears, I put my arms around her:

"He'll be alright," I assure her. She shakes her head.

"He was without oxygen for too long," she replies, "even if he lives, he will be a vegetable."

When I come downstairs after speaking with the physician, there is tremendous excitement in the house. Apparently Shri Mataji had just telephoned directly from Cabella, Italy, something she never did. In her call she asked after the boy and reassured everyone that he would be all right! Later when I am home I sit with my three children and discuss the day's events. I tell them that I know this boy is being looked after.

The next day I call for news. Jay is in a coma. I call for seven days and still there is no change. I toss and turn each night remembering the physician's words; technically the boy was dead when she declared he had no pulse. I try to calculate just how long the boy was without oxygen, I know it was long, too long; the time in the pool, time by the edge, the time with the paramedics; it had to be at least eight to ten minutes, perhaps the physician was right, perhaps there is no hope.

A week later I return to the house where Jay had floated between life and death. As I climb the stairs of the ashram and pass the pool, I shudder. I take off my shoes and enter the living room. The sun is streaming through the window and a light breeze lifts the curtains. There is stillness and a strange quality in the room.

I look around and stop as I see seated on the carpet in a patch of sunlight, the boy, Jay. He seems in perfect health. I go to him and tentatively call his name. He turns his face to mine and smiles. I ask him how he is and though his voice is hoarse from all the tubes that have gone down his throat; he lets me know that he is fine. I feel like jumping for joy but sit instead beside Jay to meditate wondering if now that I am in Sahaja Yoga, miracles are just another part of everyday life.'

Chapter 9

The Wisdom of the Kundalini

These days nearly all of us have a computer, but many of us do not really know how it works. What we do know is it is a box with what is called hardware, which we can see, and software, which we can't, but if the software is not alright the whole system is in deep trouble. If the software and hardware are both working well the computer will most probably be fine. In a way the Kundalini is our vital software. We can't see it, but it is incredibly important and an essential component of the whole system that we call a human being.

Before self realisation the Kundalini is a coiled, dormant force in the triangular sacrum bone at the base of the spine. When we receive our realisation, this rises through the chakras, or energy centres, pictured in the diagram below, and enlightens them. Finally it reaches the top chakra, the Sahasrara, at the top of the head. Here the individual awareness becomes united with the all-pervading power of the divine and self realisation takes place.

All diseases and many other problems can be traced back to an imbalance or imperfection in one or more of the chakras, so by giving vibrations to the chakras, one can often help cure diseases. There are also three energy channels within each of us. The left side channel governs our past, our conditioning, our emotions and is our more feminine side. The right side channel governs our ego, our intellect, our physical side and is our more masculine side. If there are imbalances health problems can also occur.

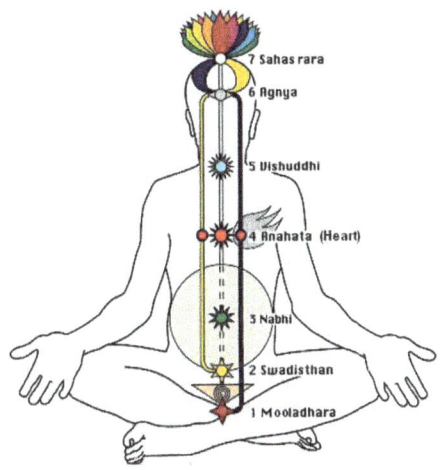

The Kundalini and seven main chakras

Left side channel – blue
Right side channel – yellow
Central channel – no colour

Below are some stories of people who have been helped and cured by using this subtle energy. These stories show the relationship between problems in certain chakras, and diseases. When the problems in the chakras are eased with vibrations and other Sahaja Yoga treatments, the health improves. In some of these stories Shri Mataji was there in person, but in others, and many more which could be told, vibrations and healing were given through the Sahaja Yogis themselves.

A major cause of death in the West is cancer. It can occur if the left side channel is adversely affected. Kay O'Connell, from Canterbury, England, tells of her experience.

'I received self realisation in 1979 when I was twenty. Some months later I became pregnant, but had a miscarriage, which unfortunately led to serious complications. It was eventually discovered that there was a tumour in my womb. The news didn't come as any great shock, as I'd felt for some time that there was something wrong with me. It had been impossible to stop thinking and my thoughts were morbid and depressing, often about death.

Shri Mataji at this time was in India and, although I knew she could cure me, it didn't seem right to expect to be cured just when she returned to England. I went to Charing Cross Hospital in London, where they specialize in the type of cancer I had. It was a depressing place to be in, and they started me on a chemotherapy treatment. The first week wasn't too bad, but by the third week the pain was unbearable. So, to the horror of the doctors, I discharged myself. They told me that, without the full course of treatment I'd have at most eighteen months left to live.

By this time, Shri Mataji was back in England, so I wrote a letter to her about the illness. Shortly afterwards I was invited to spend some time at her house at Brompton Square in London. On arrival, Shri Mataji asked me to sit down in front of her and gave me vibrations. After a few minutes she told me that the main causes for the cancer were drugs and getting involved with, and practically hypnotized by, a very negative person.

Immediately, I started to feel guilty. How foolish of me! So Shri Mataji very sweetly told me not to feel guilty because the vultures swoop down to attack the baby chicks when they're born and she is like the Mother hen who has to keep the chicks under her wing. Shri Mataji then asked me to go upstairs and rest. I fell asleep and dreamt of being on a bus full of Sahaja Yogis, driving along a road. Suddenly, we came across the negative person and he was destroyed. I woke up feeling much better. Shri Mataji worked on me every day for a few days. After two days, the colour came back into my cheeks and the darkness around the eyes disappeared. After another two days, Shri Mataji told me I was cured. I felt transformed.

I returned to the hospital for a checkup and to show them the results. Only one doctor was interested in how it had happened. The others, reluctant to recognize that the spirit is stronger than their treatments, put the cure down to luck! There are no words to express my gratitude and love for Shri Mataji. The feelings run much too deep for that.

Some time later I went for a check-up which included a chest x-ray. On the x-ray my lungs appeared perfectly clear of all contamination by nicotine. Normally when a person smokes twenty cigarettes a day, as I did for several years, the lungs continue to bear the traces of the habit long afterwards, but the doctors looking at my x-rays refused to believe that I had ever smoked.'

Editor's note: Over thirty years later Kay is still in excellent health. Generally, Sahaja Yogis are advised to accept the advice of doctors, but to do Sahaja treatments as well.

Heart disease, often caused by an imbalance on the right side channel, has also been helped through the power of the vibrations. Lyn Roles of Australia tells this story.

'In 1989 my father was in intensive care in a Sydney hospital after a series of cardiac arrests. I had returned home to Brisbane after spending two weeks with him, when word came that he was getting very weak and could no longer even prop himself up in bed. After two phone calls to other Sahaja Yogis in Brisbane, everyone put him into bandhan and gave him vibrations by directing their attention to him.

The following morning a phone call came from my mother to say that the doctors were absolutely astounded, unable to believe it was the same patient as the previous day. My father was sitting in a chair beside his hospital bed, eating breakfast and reading the newspaper. All the medical staff were talking about it with astonishment.'

The following stories illustrate how, by correcting imbalances or weaknesses in various chakras, major health problems can be relieved.

Mooladhara (chakra number 1 on the chart)
This disease is caused by problems in the first chakra.

'My name is Rosaria Tagliacia from Italy. One year before I encountered Sahaja Yoga the doctors said I had a disease called multiple sclerosis. I started Sahaja Yoga and worked on myself with three candles, as was suggested. Some time later I went to the doctors for a checkup. I had an MRI scan to see if my brain had lesions, and they told me that the disease had stopped for the moment. I came back and was so happy. At that time I didn't understand the importance of Sahaja Yoga, so I didn't meditate and didn't do the treatments or go to the collective programmes at the centre. After four or five months I again went to the Sahaja Yoga programmes, but did not do the treatments because I thought I was all right.

Some time later, I again started to have the same problem, but I felt sure Shri Mataji would help me. We came to Cabella and it was the turn of the Italians to help look after Shri Mataji, and I was also helping to tidy up her bedroom and make her bed. I felt such strong vibrations there. After the weekend programme I was asked to wait because I was to take some Indian visitors, friends of mine, to Rome in my car.

They saw Shri Mataji and gave her a rose from me – and made some sort of a poem as they gave it because my name is Rosaria. They said that of all the flowers given, Mother picked out my rose and smelled it and seemed so satisfied with it. I started to cry, when they told me this, because I knew Mother was helping me to get well. Then I did the three candle treatment again, seriously.

Some time later I again went for an MRI and they said it had again stopped, and a year after that when I had another scan they said that even the lesions in the brain could not be seen any more.'

Editor's note: This shows how by putting a flame near the chakra which needs attention, the negativity which is causing the problem can often be removed.

Swadishthan (chakra number 2 on the chart)

Roxana Sindici lived near Shri Mataji's house at Cabella, in the hills near Genoa, Italy.

'My husband Michele had a really bad problem in his back, and we were living near Shri Mataji's house in Italy at that time. He couldn't move at all and was lying in his bed. I phoned someone who could give a message to Shri Mataji. She said to bring him to see her. Two men came, and even though they were both very strong they couldn't move Michele at all. Then they came back with six men and they put him on a door and took him into the dining room at Shri Mataji's house. She came and he couldn't even move to greet her.

"Oh my God!" she said a few times, and began to work on him, to give him vibrations. She put her foot on his side, and started working on him. And someone else was working on him with a candle, moving it around in anti-clockwise circles at the back of his body, and she said to me, "Just put your hand and tell me what you feel." (on your fingers, as to where the problem is in his chakras). She was touching him with her feet, and telling the other man which chakra to work on with the candle flame.

"Now turn!" she said to Michele after about twenty minutes.

"Shri Mataji, I cannot turn," he replied.

"You have to turn," she insisted, so he turned, and she was pressing and pressing with her feet. He was crying out and she was saying that it was all right, not so bad. She went on giving him vibrations, and after one hour said, "You get up now."

Slowly he got up, he stood up and walked out. She said he had to work with the candle two hours a day. He walked out and no one could believe it. He had a hernia and it was a problem of the Swadishthan chakra. It was amazing to see him come in carried on a door and then after one hour to walk out.'

Void and Nabhi (abdomen area and chakra number 3 on the chart)

Savita Arora of Lucknow, India had a problem which concerned her digestive tract. The stomach problem would have been connected to the area of the body governed on the subtle level by the Nabhi, the chakra in the centre of the void.

'Three years before I received my self realisation I was very sick with peptic ulcers as well as other problems. Seven of the ulcers burst and as a result the doctors said that they could not operate as it was in six different places and that I would just have to continue life with them. Continuing life with them was by no means an easy task as I could only eat razgulas, (a sweet made mostly of milk) cottage cheese, ice cream and milk. I was obviously very thin as a result and so bony that I couldn't sleep at night. I was so unhappy and hungry most of the time and had to take eleven different pills daily.

After meditating in Sahaja Yoga for three months, I happily gained weight and energy. I began to feel that I didn't need to take these cumbersome pills anymore. I approached my husband. He was so amazed that I wanted to stop asked me how I would live without these pills. Now I have absolutely no problem. Both the doctor and my husband were so surprised, they couldn't believe it would be possible to be cured only by using Sahaja Yoga techniques.'

This cure from migraines resulted from treating the liver, governed by the right Nabhi chakra and right Swadishthan chakra.

From the age of eleven Ambiga Ramiah of South Africa experienced migraines that got progressively worse as time went on. Her migraines could last up to 48 hours – they used to start and after four hours were at their peak. She was under treatment but the medication did not help when the migraines were at their worst. The only thing she could do was to lie on the bed in a dark room.

In 1997, at the age of 56, Ambiga started Sahaja Yoga because she wanted to experience meditation and not because it could cure ailments. She was placed on the liver treatment* and also to use the ice pack on a daily basis for some time. Slowly, after almost a year, the strength of the migraines subsided and after a year had completely disappeared. It is now eleven years since her last migraine.

Editor's note: for the liver treatment see the Appendix.

Heart (chakra number 4 on the chart)
The correlation of asthma with problems on the right side of the Heart chakra is well-known to Sahaja Yogis and its cause can be a spoiled relationship with the father. The cure, using the vibrational techniques of Sahaja Yoga, fixes both the physical and the underlying psychological problem. Sahaja Yoga treatments are always simple and practical.

This story is from Chris Kyriacou of Sydney, Australia.
'We had a group of four new people coming to our programmes and establishing themselves in Sahaja Yoga. One of the men came with very bad asthma. He used to need six sessions a day on a ventilator using ventiline gas, a brachial dilator used to relieve the constrictions in the airways arising from asthma attacks and relieve the symptoms of asthma and he never left home without ventiline. We told the new people that if they had a problem in their body, they should say, "Shri Mataji please come into that part of my body".

"Shri Mataji, please come into my lungs," he said the next day when he felt an asthma attack begin. He felt the attack subside. For each attack that day, he said the same thing, with the same result each time, the asthma attack was prevented. He now does this all the time and no longer requires the ventiline. The number of the attacks started to diminish as well.

People who are 'rational' and 'modern' do not accept that spirit possession can occur. However, here is a story which suggests not only that such a thing can happen, but can also be resolved. This is taken from an interview of Lt-General VK Kapur, a senior general in the Indian army before his retirement.

'I met Shri Mataji, on 15th April 1995, at a wedding in Calcutta. When I saw her something tugged at my heart. I felt perhaps she would have the answer to my health problems and I requested somebody close to her if he could kindly get me an audience with Shri Mataji. He asked me for my credentials, I told him and he said that he would try. I knew that it was a very important moment in my life and felt that if Shri Mataji would just look at me, my life would just change.

"Beta, (son) what is wrong with you?" she said when I went in front of her.

I told her that when I was in New York, in December 1994, something had happened and my heart had suddenly started beating 200 to 250 times a minute, and I would feel very uncomfortable, but the doctors there could not make out why it was happening. The doctors in Delhi did not have a cure either and told me that I would have to leave the army.

Shri Mataji asked me to put my right hand on my heart and my left hand towards her and repeat after her, "General Joshi! Go and take a rebirth, I am in the very good hands of my mother, Shri Mataji Nirmala Devi."

She asked me to close my eyes, take a deep breath and repeat these words three times and I did it in all sincerity. Incidentally, General Joshi, erstwhile Chief of Army Staff, India, had died in India of a heart attack on the same day and approximately at the same time when I started experiencing this trouble at New York, so obviously a possession had taken place. He was very fond of me and I was formerly his adjutant. He was the one who had sent me to New York, on duty.

"Now you are cleared. This problem will never take place again, if you learn how to meditate in Sahaja Yoga," she said after my third repetition. "The Sahaja Yogis in Delhi will teach you to meditate." When I bent down to do pranam (a gesture of respectful gratitude) she told me to come near to where she was sitting, and tapped me on my back with her right fist.

I returned to Delhi and learnt to meditate but did not feel any vibrations for about 45 days. Anyway, like a good soldier I kept on meditating, morning and evening. In the middle of May, it was very hot and I was meditating at 4 o'clock in the morning and for the first time an intense experience occurred. The chaitanya (cool vibrations) started flowing from every pore of my body, like a cloud burst, from my eyes, ears, nose, hands, feet and head. It was such a wonderful experience, and from that day onwards till today it has been a journey full of joy and love.

Needless to say, I have never had that heart ailment again.'

In India and many other traditional cultures, the feet of very holy, saintly and divine people are the source of many blessings, as was the case with Alex Henshaw from Australia.

'In 1984 Shri Mataji invited me to stay at her house in Brompton Square, London. She learnt that I had a hole in my heart from birth.

"You never told me you had a heart problem," she said.

"No, Shri Mataji," I replied.

"Well, I'd better help you with this."

She sat me down and put her foot on my back over my heart. It was an amazing experience, I felt an incredible blast of vibrations and I could feel the sensation of coolness in my heart blasting the heat out. She went very silent.

"Turn around," she said, put her foot on my chest and went into deep meditation. I could feel incredible coolness and joy. She took her foot off after five minutes. "I had to go back to your previous life to work out some problems, but it's all right now."

The doctors had done some tests on this hole, which was quite big, and had recommended that I get surgery. I had put off going back to the doctors but after my experience with Shri Mataji I went back and they tested my heart. They found that the hole had become a lot smaller. The vibrations from Shri Mataji started the process of the heart healing itself. They still recommended that I have surgery but it was a much simpler procedure, without the need for a Teflon patch as was recommended before. It also meant that I didn't need to take blood thinning medication for the rest of my life. The surgeon was amazed, and couldn't understand it, because of all the previous tests and x-rays they had done showed that the hole was large, and now it was visibly smaller. I attribute it to the vibrations Shri Mataji gave me on my heart.'

Editor's note: Alex is still healthy twenty-eight years later.

Vishuddhi (chakra number 5 on the chart)

Hearing is related to the Vishuddhi chakra and defects can be cleared up by giving vibrations to that centre. This is from Said Ait-Chaalal, a lawyer from Algiers.

'In Lausanne, Switzerland, in 1983, after a public programme Shri Mataji met a Portuguese lady who had lost her hearing. Shri Mataji asked her to come back the next day to the house of a Sahaja Yogi with whom Shri Mataji was staying.

The following morning, we were once again in Shri Mataji's presence, in the drawing room of that house. Mother gave vibrational treatment to several people, leaving the Portuguese lady till the last. This lady had lost her hearing many years previously and an operation had not succeeded in restoring it. Shri Mataji worked on her with vibrations for about ten minutes, during which all communication with the lady was with written notes on scraps of paper, translated on the way from Portuguese to French and then to English. Then, at one moment, the lady started to hear more clearly what was being said. She burst into tears and embraced Shri Mataji. Her hearing continued to improve after this.'

This is Dr. AV Izmailovich from Russia.

'In Kiev, there was an incident involving a lady with a stiff right arm and no strength in her hand. While the Sahaja Yogis were working on her, a scarf which had Shri Mataji's vibrations was tied around her Vishuddhi chakra in the throat area, and suddenly she was able to move her arm and felt strength in her hand. The scarf had been used to cover a chair that Shri Mataji had used in St Petersburg.'

Agnya (chakra number 6 on the chart)
After self realisation we can follow, with our vibratory awareness, what is going on in another person. The different fingers and other parts of the hand correspond to the seven main chakras, as mentioned above. The ring finger is related to the Agnya Chakra, at the level of the forehead. This story is from an anonymous Austrian Sahaja Yogi.

'When I was very new in Sahaja Yoga, in 1986, I went on a bus excursion with some colleagues, who had not had self realisation. In the afternoon many people were feeling headaches. As we sat in a restaurant, one of our tour guides told me of the pain he was feeling. I suggested he take a little Tiger Balm and put it with the right ring finger on the middle of his forehead. This is the place of the Agnya chakra. As he was doing it, I put my attention on his vibrations. I had never felt the Kundalini of others before, but when I put my attention on him, suddenly I felt the cool breeze blowing through my palms.

"Now it is starting to work. You see?" I said to him.

"Yes," he said. It did not strike him as odd that I could tell him the exact time when it started to work. I kept my attention on him and after about half a minute the flow of vibrations stopped.

"Now you are not feeling the effect anymore," I said.

"Yes, that's right," he said again.'

Editor's note: to clear the Agnya, look at the suggestions in the Appendix.

The following report is again by Dr AV Izmailovich, then head of a department of Curatology and Physiotherapy at a government hospital in Russia.

'At a meeting with Shri Mataji some years ago, nine doctors were blessed with their self realisation. Their very good experience prompted them to bring a teenage girl suffering from epilepsy for an experiment with Sahaja Yoga. This child had a problem beyond the control of specialists and had been to all of the best institutions in Russia without any positive results. Shri Mataji blessed this child with her self realisation. Working on her Agnya chakra helped open her heart and, from a closed sick personality, she spontaneously transformed into a fully-blossomed flower. This experience prompted the doctors to arrange another meeting, where thirty-five specialists came for realisation.

In the next meeting, fifteen patients were worked on, using Sahaja techniques, in the presence of the thirty-five specialist doctors and one psychiatrist. The atmosphere was very heavy because of the egos of all the doctors and the negative energy of the patients. However, the attention guided the Sahaja Yogis to give self realisation, first to dissolve the aggressive egos. This time, self realisation was amazingly granted with just the simple prayer from the heart to the photograph of Shri Mataji, 'Please come in my heart.' Some blockages were also cleared when the doctors and patients forgave everyone. It was a tremendous blessing. Their first experience lasted approximately fifty minutes and there were no questions left. During the experience all the specialists were laughing, crying and opening up in the loving security of the Mother. All of the fifteen patients experienced our Mother's love and, as observed by the doctors, there was a considerable improvement in the balance of the various energy levels.

A miracle occurred – the little girl is now cured of 'incurable' epilepsy and her doctors are convinced about the possibilities of Sahaja Yoga. The encephalogram trace of the brain is clear of the characteristic signals of epileptic activity.'

Generally we do not have problems connected with the Sahasrara, but to finish this chapter, here is a nice story about the top chakra by Pradeep Singh Rawat, who lives in India.

'I had been in Sahaja Yoga for a few months, and understood that I had attained something precious. Later in the year we went to the annual seminar at Ganapatipule, south of Mumbai.

On the last night the programme was over at 3:45 am. Shri Mataji was about to leave, we all got up to express our respect and I felt like somebody poured water over my Sahasrara (at the top of the head). It was flowing continuously and I was in a blissful state. The tent was covered and it was not raining; I touched my Sahasrara with my hands but they didn't get wet.'

Chapter 10

Traditional Practices, Untraditional Outcomes

In Sahaja Yoga the mantras that we use each correspond to a particular chakra or a particular aspect of our being and are usually in Sanskrit. Mantras are only effective if one has a connection with the all-pervading power, which occurs when we have self realisation. Otherwise it is like phoning someone when the phone is not connected, or sending an email without an internet connection.

After self realisation, the awakened Kundalini passes through the chakras within us and nourishes them. Each chakra is the seat, or reflection, of a particular aspect of the divine power. As each chakra governs certain parts of our body and aspects of our personality, when we invoke that aspect of the divine power with enlightened attention and due respect, it can help us in many ways.

This story is told by Alan Wherry, a publisher, and his wife Lioudmila.

'In spring 1996, just after Lioudmila came from Russia to live in London as my wife, we spent an evening with some friends at their home in Fulham. On the way, we'd stopped off at a late night store to buy some flowers for them.

When we returned to our flat in Chelsea, I discovered that I'd lost my wallet. I went downstairs to the car parked in a nearby square and searched it, looking with care on the floor, beneath the seats and in the door recesses. Finding nothing, I went back to the flat and phoned my friends, who confirmed that I hadn't left it there. There was only one possible place, the shop where I had stopped off to buy the flowers. Lioudmila came with me. This time we brought a torch and once again, checked the interior of the car and in particular the recesses in the doors. On two occasions I ran my hands down these recesses.

As we drove to the shop, we sang together the twelve names (mantras) of Shri Ganesha. I parked outside the shop on the other side of the street. As I opened the driver's door of the car (a Jeep), just as I was about to jump out, there was a clear rush of air, something simple yet beyond anything either of us had experienced before. Lioudmila, a chemical engineer by training, well used to the disciplines of the scientific method, a very down-to-earth lady, said she'd seen something and asked me to check the recess in the driver's door. When I checked, the wallet was there and it definitely wasn't there on the two previous occasions that Lioudmila and I had looked there.'

Statue of Shri Ganesha

This is by Bogunia Bensaude from Australia.

'Gorai was a beach north of Mumbai, India on a peninsula. We met there for the Sahasrara Puja in May 1983. After the puja was finished many people left for Mumbai but some of us stayed behind with Shri Mataji, who walked down towards the sea. It was a wide beach and the tide was out. Shri Mataji stopped some distance from the retreating tide. She bent down and began to create an image of Shri Ganesha in the sand and then ornamented it with kumkum (red powder). From seemingly nowhere, a man appeared with a basket of flowers and she decorated the image. Then we stood back and admired it, after which Shri Mataji looked towards the sea, a good fifty metres off and dead calm, with little ripples. She told us all to say the mantra to the sea, Samudra Devatur.

After we had said it a few times, the most extraordinary thing happened. The sea came up to the sand Ganesha in a narrow stream about a metre wide, not violently, but just enough to bathe it and dissolve it into the sea water. Then the sea retreated again, back to the main body of water down the beach.'

Suman Mathur of Delhi was also there.

'After I came into Sahaja Yoga, for nearly one and a half years I could not believe in it. I kept saying to myself that if I could have a divine experience, then I would. One day, when I was with Shri Mataji at Goregaon, (Gorai Creek) she asked us to call the sea. At that time the sea was very far from where we were standing. She asked us to stand on both her sides and recite the Samudra Devatur mantra. We did so and after a short while, to my total surprise, the sea came right up to where we were and first bathed the feet of Shri Mataji and then the image of Shri Ganesha that she had made in the sand. I became a true Sahaja Yogini.'

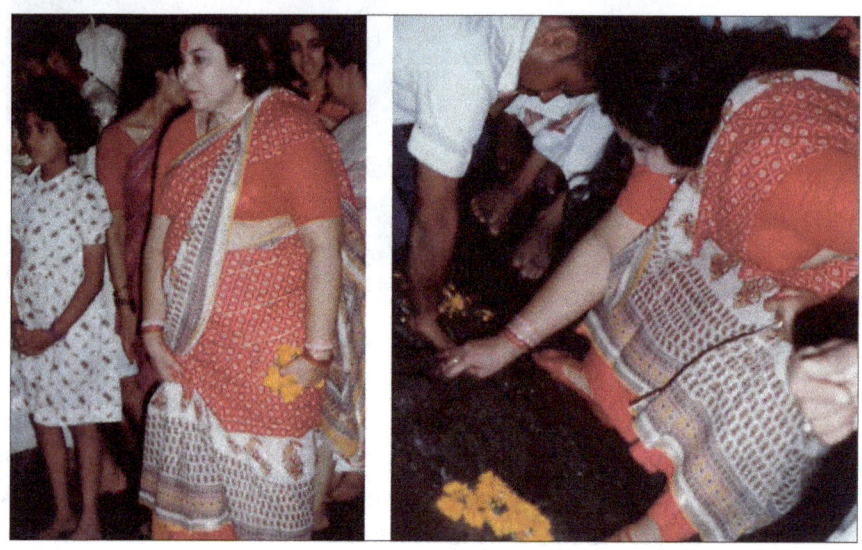

Shri Mataji on the beach at Gorai, with the image of Shri Ganesha

The mantra used by this Sahaja Yogi, from Vienna, may destroy any negativity.

'I was staying at my parents' place and doing some gardening, barefoot. Suddenly, I stepped on a wasp and got stung. The pain quickly started to burn. Then I remembered that Shri Mataji had once said that with the mantra, "Aum twameva sakshat – name of the disease or problem – mardini sakshat, et cetera," we can cure every disease. This was the chance to try my powers. I said the mantra, "Aum twameva sakshat wasp poison mardini..." and the painful burning sensation disappeared the next moment. After a few minutes it came back and continued to burn as before. "Well," I said to myself, "Let's try again." Once more I said the mantra and the pain disappeared, this time for good.'

Editor's note: this really works. I had an annoying recurrent eczema patch on my thigh, and had tried all sorts of remedies, none of which worked permanently. After reading this contribution, I tried it out – Aum twameva sakshat eczema mardini… and within two weeks it had gone, never to return.

A havan is a ceremony where different items such as rice and herbs are offered to a fire. If we have had our self realisation and do one, great things can happen (see also the chapter entitled The World Stage). After the offerings have been made, one can request the purifying element of fire to destroy subtle negativity which may cause problems on a larger scale. Bertrand de Techtermann, from Switzerland, relates an experience he had as a result of a havan.

'For many years I had warts on both hands, which made them look ugly and which made me ashamed of them. One day in mid-1989 we did a havan in our house in Nyon with some local Sahaja Yogis. I was sitting in the front row, with a little mound of rice and herbs in my left hand, from which I would take a pinch to offer to the fire after each mantra that was said. When all the rice had gone, my warts had gone, too, from both my hands, leaving them perfectly smooth.'

Another ceremony which Sahaja Yogis do is the puja, which pays respect to a particular aspect of the divine. Once the all-pervading power of the divine has been awakened within us, by the grace of Shri Mataji, and we start to become aware of its many different aspects helping us, we find these pujas are a wonderfully fulfilling experience.

Mark Mays of the United States experienced pure joy in the form of cool vibrations and inner bliss.

'I had been in India for about four weeks on the annual India Tour, visiting different cities, villages, temples, and public programmes where Shri Mataji was giving self realisation en-masse to thousands of seekers. I was feeling the cool breeze on the palms of my hands fairly consistently, a sign that the Kundalini energy is flowing unobstructed through the subtle system.

The India Tour always ended at Ganapatipule, a secluded beach site about 150 miles south of Mumbai. The vibrations there are absolutely amazing. I had an experience there on Christmas Day that made my entire life worth living. In Sahaja Yoga, we celebrate the various incarnations and deities, many of whom have walked the face of this earth. Of course this would include Jesus Christ, and since the Ganapatipule seminar always took place over Christmas, I found myself doing puja to Jesus, as led by Shri Mataji on December 25th, 1994.

I placed my hands towards her and felt a wave of cool breeze not only on my hands, but over my whole body. These blissful vibrations kept coming: wave after wave after wave. I didn't want to think, didn't want to move - just be. This lasted about 20 - 30 minutes. There is no way my words can capture the depth of joy and sheer bliss of this experience.'

This is from Mrs Lily Rai of Delhi.

'Since I was eight years old I used to suffer from severe attacks of migraine. I would get the attacks almost every week so it was very difficult for me to finish my education. I got married to Dr Umesh Rai, and he visited many Neurological Institutes, to try to find a cure for my migraines, but only temporary medications were offered and I suffered a lot.

In 1985 we came to Sahaja Yoga, and Shri Mataji asked Dr Rai to come to Ganapatipule. We went there and the next day was the Christmas Puja. The day before I had had two severe attacks of migraine, but at midnight the pain stopped. By Shri Mataji's grace the next day I attended the puja and from that day I have never had another attack. I am very grateful to Shri Mataji. It is by her blessings that I could completely get rid of the migraines.'

Editor's note: The Christmas Puja is in praise of the divine power in the form of Lord Jesus and it was just on the dot of midnight, the time when Lord Jesus was traditionally born, that Mrs Rai got better. Lord Jesus is connected to the Agnya chakra, placed in the head.

Gisela Matzer, a retired actress and theatre manager, now runs the Sahaja home for destitute women and children in Noida, near Delhi, India.

'In 1991 I went on the India tour, where the non-Indian Sahaja Yogis would go around various parts of India visiting small villages and towns. At a stop on the way to Mysore, a big agave thorn pierced my hand. It was very difficult to pull it out. For three days I had horrible pain and the hand became swollen. I went to a doctor but he could not help me much.

After the very strong puja that we had in Bangalore, many of us went to the chair, like a throne, where Shri Mataji had been sitting. I also went up and respectfully put my painful hand on it. I prayed from my heart for the pain to go and as I got up, all the pain was gone, the swelling had disappeared instantaneously, and I could move my hand again. '

Chapter 11

Time Becomes our Friend

In the chapter explaining the power of the bandhan, there was a story of a man who managed to catch a plane from Mumbai impossibly quickly. Here are some other stories about time being apparently compressed and extended. The first one is by Jim Thomas.

'I was a seeker for as long as I can remember. When travelling in India I found some books, the Dhammapada, the Bhagavad Gita and the Upanishads, translated into English by a Cambridge University Professor named Juan Mascaro. They not only made the most sense to me but gave me such joy that I could not put them down.

About a year after getting self realisation from Shri Mataji in London, in October 1979, my wife and I were living in Cambridge and attended a lecture given by Juan Mascaro. As soon as he began reciting passages from the Gita and Upanishads in Sanskrit, the whole room lit up around him. When Shri Mataji came to Cambridge for a programme, I arranged for her to meet Mr Mascaro at his house.

An interview for Shri Mataji had been arranged in the morning with the local BBC studio, and it went on much longer than we had anticipated. Afterwards we got caught in a traffic jam, all of which resulted in Shri Mataji's desiring to have a nap before departing for Norwich, a city some sixty miles northeast of Cambridge, where we had arranged another public programme that evening.

"I slept so soundly, it must be quite late," Shri Mataji said when she awoke. I replied that it was, and that we would not have time to go see Mr. Mascaro. "Better go and phone him," she said. I could feel his sadness and disappointment over the phone. When I told Shri Mataji, she said, "Well, he is an older man, better phone him again and tell him I will come." I reported back to Mr Mascaro and I couldn't tell whose relief and joy was the greater – his or mine!

When we arrived at his thatched cottage in a small village about ten miles from Cambridge, he was standing in the doorway with a single, beautiful white rose that he had picked from his garden. To our amazement and delight he began to sing an ancient shloka that we Sahaja Yogis were very familiar with. There were no dry eyes that observed that scene, I can assure you. After presenting Shri Mataji with the rose, he took us inside and the vibrations in the room were so strong that I envisioned the walls of the house collapsing from the power of it. It was as if a long lost son finally had found his mother.

At this point any hope of getting to Norwich anywhere near the scheduled meeting time was so far out of the question that I thought about calling the hall to tell the caretaker to put out a sign saying that the meeting was cancelled. I was resigned to fact that we were going to be very, very late and if anyone did show up they would have left hours ago. The drive to Norwich would normally take between an hour and a half and two hours.

I do not know how long it actually took us to get to Norwich that day, but I do know two things: that the meeting was scheduled to begin at 7 pm and as I opened the door to let Shri Mataji out of the car at the front entrance to the hall, the clock on the church tower across the street began to chime seven times!

"How many times do I have to tell you people that we are not bound by time?" joked Shri Mataji.'

Shri Mataji with Jim Thomas, walking by the river at Cambridge, UK

Heidi Zogorski of the United States recalls a similar incident.

'One time in Los Angeles, a large group of people assembled to see Shri Mataji off and we were waiting near the departure gate at the airport terminal. The person next to me pointed to her watch.

"It's only five minutes until the flight leaves and Shri Mataji is not even here yet," she said.

"The flight is expected to leave on time," I added. Within a minute or so, we saw Shri Mataji walking slowly down the hallway. She greeted the crowd of Sahaja Yogis, which had grown. As she walked, she stopped and spoke to many, many individuals, one at a time, at least thirty people, and was never rushed. She also accepted flowers from many more people, graciously and slowly. Then she walked all the way to the plane, got on the flight and it took off on time. The person who showed me the time before Shri Mataji arrived pulled me to the side.

"Heidi, come here. Look at my watch," she said. It was five minutes later than when I had seen it the first time. We looked at each other and smiled. There was no way to do all that in less than five minutes.'

This airport story is by Wolfgang Hackl from Vienna.

'In the mid 1980's, after a puja at Shri Mataji's house in Shudy Camps, near Cambridge, in the east of England, my plane home was the next day at 10.30 am from Heathrow Airport, west of London. As I was a standby passenger, I had to check-in at 10 am at the latest. I set two clocks to wake me early but both failed and I woke up at 8 am. The vibrations in the tent where I was sleeping were tremendous, as the puja had taken place there the previous day. On one hand I knew that I should rush to the airport, but on the other I thought, 'When the vibrations are strong, we are supported by all the divine forces,' so I sat down to meditate and to enjoy the vibrations.

When I finally left for the airport, about ninety miles distant, it was 8.30 am. We drove straight into the heavy Monday morning commuter traffic as we headed towards London. The closer we got the slower we travelled. I had some important appointments in Vienna that afternoon and it was essential for me to make my flight. I gave a bandhan - it was cool, so I relaxed. At 10 am, the last moment I could check in, we were still thirteen miles from Heathrow and from any human standpoint my last chance to catch the plane had gone. I gave another bandhan, which was again cool, so I slept for a little while. I woke up at 10.18 am at Heathrow and walked towards the crowded check-in counter. They accepted my luggage and I passed through all the counters and controls in what seemed like no time at all, and reached the departure gate, after quite a walk, at 10.29 am. The plane left precisely on time.

This happened when the blessing of Shri Mataji set our Nabhi chakra right. Without effort or worrying everything worked, beyond the bondage of time or space.'

Editor's note: The Nabhi is the third chakra and is placed behind the navel. Its qualities include inner peace, satisfaction, not panicking and having a relaxed attitude to life. An internet distance finder estimated the journey should take well over two hours when done out of the rush hour. It would take longer in the rush hour, and longer still on Monday morning, the worst one of the week.

Wolfgang Hackl's next story took place before the advent of mobile phones.

'I was in Austria and Shri Mataji was in Australia. I had to get a very important decision from her concerning some law case, and was trying to call her.

"Shri Mataji is asleep," they said. Again we tried to reach her, and again they said, "She is sleeping."

I knew she would wake up and then go straight to the airport, and after that it would be too late for a decision. I had to catch the moment when she was coming out. I tried several times, but with no success. Then I just sat back and said to myself, "OK, Shri Mataji, just let me feel when you're ready," so I waited. All of a sudden I was so blissed out, so drenched in vibrations that I almost forgot to call. I pulled myself together and called.

"Shri Mataji is just going out right now, hold on," they said. I was able to talk to her on the phone. She was in Australia and I was at the other end of the world, and just on vibrations I got the ten or fifteen seconds when I could reach her.'

Ajay Arora is from North India and lives in Australia.

'We were in Lucknow, India, at a Sahaja Yoga programme with all the Dehra Dun Sahaja Yogis who had travelled there – a fair distance and some hours on the train. After the programme we were going to board a train back to our town of Dehra Dun, and were sitting in one of the yogi's houses. It was evening and there were a few young people sitting along with their mothers, and we were having a beautiful discussion on Sahaja Yoga.

"It's time to go to the railway station, otherwise we'll miss the train," someone said.

"The train will wait for us, we don't have to worry," suddenly came out of my mouth.

After an hour or so, when it was the actual time for the train to leave, we left the house. When we reached the railway station, they said the train was two hours late, and they did not know why. On top of that, there had been a lot of rain around the railway station and the people waiting for the train were drenched, but not us, because we had arrived late.'

Mr Chavhan's story concerns a cup of tea.

'Some time ago in the 1980's, Shri Mataji and a few yogis went to Kolhapur in Maharashtra, India, for a Sahaja Yoga programme. After a few days, while staying in a hotel, Shri Mataji called Mr Chavhan at about 3 am to ask for a cup of Indian tea, chai. Mr Chavhan said that he would have it ready in about fifteen minutes. He then discovered that the hotel did not have any cooking facilities, and everything in the town was closed at that hour.

He knew of one lady, a Sahaja Yogi, who lived about three miles out of town, so he went outside to find that the whole town was asleep. He was in the empty street, but a three wheeler rickshaw suddenly came around the corner out of nowhere, and gave him a ride to the lady's house, quite some distance away.

When he arrived he found that unexpectedly, at that hour, she was awake and doing meditation. She was worried and wanted to know if there was some problem. Mr Chavhan said that there was not, but that Shri Mataji wanted a cup of tea. So she quickly made a cup, packed it up to keep it hot, and sent Mr Chavhan on his way.

When he went outside, there was no transport so he had to walk three miles. He began to walk, and was somehow there before he knew it. When he gave Shri Mataji her cup of tea, only fifteen minutes had passed!'

Here is a possible explanation for these stories, from Ambar Chatterjee, the physicist.

'The blend of time and space was realised a long time ago by a mind as great as that of Einstein. The perception of time indeed depends on the frame of reference and the frame of reference changes depending upon your state of consciousness. Time could pass slowly and distances could shrink down to nothing if the observer is in an awakened state of awareness.'

Chapter 12

Fire as a Healer

A common treatment in Sahaja Yoga involves the use of fire, or rather a flame. This can be a lamp, a candle or on occasions burning camphor. Kavitha Mohan, of Chennai, India describes an attack of herpes zoster and its cure.

'On the morning of 16th of August 1983, I had shooting pain in my right eye socket, which I supposed was due to watching too much TV. I went to an eye specialist and the family doctor, but the condition got worse, and the pain in my eye became unbearable. I was admitted to hospital and was told that I had an attack of herpes zoster. The right side of my face was covered with blisters and the doctors gave up all hope for the sight of my right eye. For three days I was on heavy drugs in the hospital and was isolated as it was a highly contagious disease. Apart from the pain, the loneliness, the fear of permanent loss of vision and of permanent scars frightened me.

"God is there to take care of our troubles," I said to myself. But the doctors said my physical vision was damaged. When I left the hospital, my right eye was closed permanently. Even a little light made my eyes water and the skin on the right side of my face would start to itch and burn.

Then one day my uncle returned from a visit to Mumbai in great excitement. He had met a great lady who had cured people of leukaemia and he had invited her to visit Chennai, then called Madras. At this time, I was being treated by various skin and eye specialists, one treated me with a lot of antibiotics, another gave me injections inside the eye every two days and another gave me a protective lens. This went on for a year, at great trouble and expense.

In October 1984, Shri Mataji visited Madras and the miracle took place. Mother – as she was called by all who knew her, as she was a Mother to all her children, so gentle and full of love – called me to her and my uncle introduced me. "She will be all right," she said, looking at me. Next day I was invited into her room. She asked me to sit in front of her with a candle in my hand and to look at the palm of her hand through the flame. As I sat there, concentrated on her and inwardly I was begging and praying to be freed from all the physical and emotional pain I had undergone. I realised I could see a glow in her palm, as though my prayers were being answered. Shri Mataji looked at me full of concern and love. She gave vibrations to my right eye, while a visiting Sahaja Yogi raised my Kundalini from behind. I gazed at Shri Mataji through my left eye. After about fifteen minutes, I could see her clearly with both eyes. Then a small lamp was brought, which she held about six inches in front of my eye and swung gently left and right for some minutes. Then I was asked to turn round and the same procedure was repeated to the back of my head. My eye was clear of redness and back to its original size.

Shri Mataji looked at me and smiled and said I was very lucky to have been cured by her. She asked me to start Sahaja Yoga meditation. I stopped my medication, and since then my eye problem has vanished, never to return.'

Editor's note: for details of how to do these treatments, see the Appendix.

This is Graciela Vázquez-Díaz Jimenez of Mexico City.

'It was December 1994, just a few months after I retired from the United Nations in New York. My youngest son, Pedro, who was until then a healthy young man of twenty-one, was hospitalized in Mexico City because of a bad pain in the chest. Pedro had graduated from New York University and was a regular sports player and a non-smoker. He was diagnosed with amyloidosis, a rare genetic disease that had already taken the lives of my sister and brother. The origin or medical cure for this disease is not known.

I faxed a letter to Shri Mataji. That same night, I felt the cool breeze at the top of my head for many hours. During that interminable month, I worked on my son, clearing his chakras with a candle and a camphor flame, and completely surrendered the outcome to the divine.

On the 1st of May 1995, Pedro was received at the National Hospital of Boston, USA. He underwent through intensive medical examination. The cardiologist, director of the medical division, told us that Pedro's medical results were now negative and he was in total good health. The next day, I took a plane to Cabella, Italy to personally thank Shri Mataji.'

John Watkinson from London, again

'I got my self realisation in August 1979. The first strong experience was when Shri Mataji invited some of us to her flat in London a little later. I had been experimenting (taking drugs) with different forms of consciousness and unfortunately it had caused me to hear voices in my head. Shri Mataji got me to put my left hand towards her and the right hand towards a candle flame. After some minutes all the voices in my head stopped and a cool breeze just came blowing into my forehead. It was a lot easier to experience inner peace and inner stillness after that.'

No further need for glasses

'My name is Sharmala Harder from South Africa, but now I live in Vienna. In 1995 I became very ill with Graves' disease, a thyroid problem. I was given radio-active iodine as a treatment and became critically ill. I became almost totally blind in my right eye – ninety per cent blindness.

Shri Mataji came to hear of it and asked us to do three candle treatment constantly. We did this for about one and a half years. My husband worked on me in this way. I had to get special glasses because everything was totally blurred. After some time I began to regain my eyesight but I wasn't sure by how much. I had to go for my Austrian driving licence and was given a retest for my eyes. When I was tested the doctor said I didn't need glasses and why was I wearing them? The test showed that that I was one hundred per cent all right again.

The thing about this eye story which was so astounding is that the doctors initially said that I could not get better and I would probably have to go for a special eye operation, and it might not work and I might have become totally blind forever. The problem appeared in 1995 and by 1997 it was gone, by doing constant three candle treatment.'

Chapter 13

Lost and Found

Bill Hansel from England remembered this incident which occurred some years ago.

'We were in Switzerland in the 1980's, after spending some days with Shri Mataji when she did some programmes there. I was asked by the Swiss to accompany her to Belgium, where her next programmes were to be. Hundreds of Sahaja Yogis gathered at Geneva Airport. Shri Mataji passed through the crowd, speaking to many of them and receiving many flowers. I was hovering not far from her, overseeing her luggage and personal items, making sure they were all intact and on the flight.

A huge crowd had gathered at Brussels Airport, again Shri Mataji passed through the crowd, receiving flowers and speaking to almost everyone. I put all Shri Mataji's luggage and gifts etc into the trunk of the car and also all the flowers. Eventually she reached the car and sat in the back seat. I was just making space for the last of the flowers when Shri Mataji asked for me, from the car window, to bring her the document case and vanity case.

I went to the trunk to search for them knowing full well they were not there, however I emptied the trunk just in case someone had put them in without my knowing. When I had confirmed they were not there I informed Shri Mataji, who said that they had been with her when they had arrived at Geneva Airport, but I had not seen them either at Geneva or Brussels. Shri Mataji asked us to search for them and many of us went in all directions: back to the carousel, lost property, back to the actual aeroplane, all to no avail.

We phoned the Swiss Sahaja Yogis in Geneva, who checked all the places the luggage was likely to be left, without success. Shri Mataji suggested we continued to look and to let her know later in her rooms. The driver had just started to pull away, at Brussels Airport, when suddenly at the very rear of the crowd there was a commotion and I saw a document case being passed over the heads of the crowd to where I was standing. Eventually it reached me and somebody placed it in my arms. I showed it to Shri Mataji who confirmed it was hers. I hurriedly put it in the trunk, then amazingly turned to see a small vanity type case being passed across the heads of the crowd until it reached me again. Shri Mataji again confirmed it was hers then asked me how they had been found. I replied it was a mystery and we did not know.

Shri Mataji then left and I was determined to find out how the cases were found. I made my way to the extreme rear of the crowd and a lady who was connected to Sahaja Yoga told us she had been quietly watching events when a large dark gentleman came to her and gave her the cases, saying that they belonged to the lady in the car, and then promptly disappeared.

Later that day we were asked to go to Shri Mataji's rooms, she was there and on the floor at her feet were the two cases. She asked me if we had found out anything. We related the story of the lady and the large dark gentleman. Shri Mataji commented that she was amazed that the cases should turn up with Air Canada labels on them, because she had never flown with Air Canada. Shri Mataji then fell silent for a short while.

"Shri Hanuman," she said, with a look you could feel melting all your angularities. "Well, you couldn't have carried it anyway."'

Editor's note: Shri Hanuman, the monkey god, was the helper of Shri Rama, who was a king and also a divine incarnation, as related in the great Sanskrit epic, the Ramayana. Traditionally Shri Hanuman can fix almost any problem.

Christina Rosi is a Community College professor in America.

'In 1987 the Sahaja India tour was coming to a close and we began packing for the long trip home. I had bought many lovely gifts and quite a few saris and clothes. At last everything seemed ready, and I put something important, my red jewellery box with the jewellery from my recent wedding in India, in my suitcase, and wrapped it carefully in saris so it was well hidden, in the middle. I later wondered if I should have squeezed this precious box into my carry-on and kept it with me.

After some twenty-seven hours we landed in Los Angeles with barely any time to spare to catch a flight to Boston. They told us our luggage would arrive some time after us. It arrived safely a few days later, but clearly my suitcase had been broken into and some things had been taken, including the red jewellery box. What a blow I felt! Why hadn't I followed my intuition and carried the precious box with me? I prayed to Shri Lakshmi and Shri Hanuman. The next day another Sahaja Yogi from Boston unpacked her suitcase from India. She came to me with my red wedding jewellery box.

"Is this yours?" she said. It had been lying on the top of her case when she opened it. The whole kitchen was filled with the vibrations and everyone could feel them pouring out of the box. I was filled with joy.

Did the thief decide to return my box, but forgot which suitcase he had taken it from?'

This is by Ruth Mattison, a business executive from Cape Town.

'I went to New York for some Sahaja Yoga programmes in September 2005. They were one week apart and we were invited to Canojaharie for the interim. On our arrival we were put into tents - one for women and one for men. During the night it began to rain and the tent leaked so we all got up and moved to drier places. In the morning we heard that Hurricane Katrina had hit New Orleans and heavy rains were on the way. Although the storm never materialized in its full force it was rather damp in the tent and we were continually trying to find a place to dry out sleeping bags and clothes.

In the confusion I lost my purse. It held all my credit cards and cash and it meant that I didn't have any money. I searched right through my suitcase, and all my belongings, to no avail. Everyone looked everywhere. Many bandhans were given. Announcements were made and signs were posted but the purse never materialised. I went to the pond before catching the bus back to New York. As I sat on a rock at the edge of the pond a multitude of flowers came floating over and surrounded my ankles and legs. They were the flowers from the stage in front of Shri Mataji's photograph.

"All the money in the world cannot not buy these vibrations," I heard her voice say to me, and it was a moment of perfect peace, joy and gratitude. I felt blessed and satisfied.

I borrowed some money from a fellow South African and had more than enough for the rest of the trip. When I returned to Cape Town I opened my suitcase and right on top there was my missing purse!'

This is Laxshmi from Vienna.

'When I first got my self realisation in 1988, I did not realise how this would change my whole life. Little by little, with the help of miracles, Shri Mataji, through the all pervading power of divine love, dissolved my anxieties.

Once my husband gave me a ring with Shri Mataji's picture enamelled on it. We were travelling on the highway to Rome. Niraja, our daughter vomited and we had to stop at a petrol station to wash her. In the Ladies Room I realised that I was still wearing the ring and it did not feel right to wash Niraja with it on my finger, so took it off. Later on, when we reached Rome, I realised it was missing and could not find it anywhere. I gave a bandhan and said the mantra to Shri Ganesha, who is the remover of all obstacles, and to Shri Hanuman, who is always eager to help those who have had their self realisation. However, the ring was nowhere to be found.

Three months later, after some time back home, I thought of the ring again and said to myself, Shri Ganesha and Shri Hanuman can do anything. So I said the mantras invoking them again. When I opened my eyes, the ring was lying there on the bedside table. After this experience, I can now see that my whole life is full of miracles.'

Chapter 14

Transformation

'I remember in the beginning, we had six, seven hippies from England. ... These hippies became Sahaja Yogis.'
Shri Mataji Nirmala Devi, 1993, Cabella, Italy

Here are emails from two of those people, in 2008. Douglas Fry (top right in the photo taken in 1976) did a responsible job in the maintenance department of the Royal Free Hospital, London and prior to retirement was given a long service award. Pat Anslow (between Douglas and Shri Mataji) until recently worked for one of the London Municipal Councils, allotting multi million pound building tenders and overseeing building projects. They have both been happily married for over thirty years.

'Before coming into Sahaja Yoga I was quite a heavy smoker, I was also into drugs and as far as drinking was concerned I was virtually an alcoholic. After coming into Sahaja Yoga I found giving up drugs was relatively easy and did so in a fairly short time. Sahaja Yoga also gave me the insight to realise that my drinking was changing from impulsive to compulsive and I managed to give that up fairly quickly too.

By far the most difficult for me was to give up smoking, I had tried a couple of times before Sahaja Yoga, but after a couple of weeks without tobacco I would just suddenly burst into tears and start again. However after Sahaja Yoga with the help of meditation I managed to give up smoking in about three weeks, and that was in 1974 so it seems to work.

I hope that this is of help to you,

Regards, Douglas (Fry)'

Editor's note: for some treatments to help overcome these habits see the Appendix

'There were several ways in which Sahaja Yoga helped me to stop taking drugs. I took them because the world seemed unfeeling and ugly to me and they brought some happiness and magic into my life. I knew they were doing me harm but I was just living from day to day and it seemed worth the risk.

Shri Mataji inspired me to give up drugs by her faith that everyone had the potential to transform themselves. She made me realise that the drugs were destroying me physically, mentally and emotionally and undermining all of the qualities that made me a human being. When I got self realisation in 1975, I felt for the first time that there was a value and a purpose to my life and I could not only help myself but others too.

I could not have stopped taking drugs just to be a good citizen or anything like that. When I started to feel the Kundalini and the chakras working inside me I knew that something real was happening. With Sahaja Yoga I had something I could do instead of drugs which made me feel good and could lead to better and better experiences in the future.

I could feel things changing in myself and in how I saw the world. I started to understand how everything was connected and part of one truth. I realised that the only really unfeeling and ugly thing in this world is the ego and that most of the problems in the world come because we do not really understand ourselves.

Regards, Pat (Anslow)'

This is Joanne Langdon of South Africa's story.

'It has been over twenty years now since I received my self realisation. Looking back it is incredible to see where I was picked up from and how my life changed so dramatically. I was desperately seeking for a heightened consciousness and awareness, and took to drugs and alcohol. I smoked dope in copious amounts for seven years, combined with large volumes of alcohol and packets of cigarettes and then moved on to more chemical drugs such as cocaine and LSD.

One night in Cape Town, going through yet another emotional roller coaster ride, I asked for my self realisation from a friend who had received hers just two weeks before.* I was amazed to see the joyful change in her. For me there was no dramatic experience, but a gentle, warm feeling of having arrived home. And somehow deep down inside I knew that something very special had happened to me, a real treasure to hold onto.

The most incredible thing happened to me, which just shows the tremendous power of the Kundalini. The desire to drink, smoke cigarettes and take drugs completely fell away, and I literally stopped overnight, all of it! I started practising Sahaja Yoga from that day on. It continues to be a beautiful journey and I am ever grateful to Shri Mataji.'

*Editor's note: * Sahaja Yoga is like a candle – once it is lit we can immediately pass on the experience of self realisation.*

Brian Bell of Australia came to Sahaja Yoga in the 1980's.

'I smoked eighty cigarettes a day. I gained my self realisation on a Friday evening and the following day noticed I was not smoking. By the Saturday night my ego was in top gear, saying things like, "What's going on here?" "What sort of hokum is this?" and, eventually, "If you want a fag, you have one!"

In time, the ego scored and I lit a cigarette. It tasted absolutely foul! That was the end of my smoking.'

This is Ingrid B of Vienna.

'While I now generally feel happy and know that my life has a sense, before I suffered daily about everything I did, and my life itself. When I got up in the morning and took my shower, I would wonder for what reason I was doing all these everyday things, like showering, eating, drinking, working, sleeping and even enjoying. It depressed me not to find a sense in it all.

I received self realisation at a programme in Vienna in 1985, at the age of 27. During the programme I did not feel much happening - perhaps some little sensations in my hands, but I was not so sure about them. But after the programme finished and people started to leave, I suddenly felt just above my head a kind of a flame about ten centimetres high, but it was cool and I even heard it clearly. I was so very amazed about it that I walked to the bus station without smoking my cigarette, which was my normal habit after not having smoked for two hours. I was so fulfilled and happy that it was the end of my smoking habit for always. The holy Kundalini did it by rising only once.'

Lydia P, also of Vienna, has always been a sensitive soul.

'Before Sahaja Yoga, I was very afraid of the future and sometimes very depressed because the human race seemed so cruel. That's why I often drank alcohol, which made me forget my problems and all the unpleasant things happening in the world, which I could not change. After having my self realisation and meditating for three weeks, I could not drink beer any more. Something in my body said no. I haven't drunk beer for many years now.'

Sergiy Fadyeyev, from Ukraine, now lives in Vancouver, Canada.

'I started practising Sahaja Yoga meditation in August 1994 in Ukraine. At that time I was, like most of my countrymen, a drinker of alcohol, and would often go out for a drink after a big operation to ease the tension and relax, as I am a vascular surgeon.

Shortly after getting realisation I went to the Shri Ganesha Puja in Moscow, in September, and during the puja I receive a life changing experience. It was of absolute divine bliss, which cannot be compared to any earthly experience.

On my way back home I realised that I wanted this to last forever, and any interference of life's daily pleasures like smoking or drinking alcohol would destroy what I had just received. I was even repelled by the smell of cigarette smoke from a passerby. That was the end of my smoking and drinking career, and I have never again had the desire to do either.'

This testimonial is by Jenny Brown, from the UK.

'I don't usually speak about my past, but feel I must, so my experiences can be of help to someone, somewhere. I had loving parents, spent my childhood riding horses, and enjoying wonderful times. As I grew older I worked behind the counter in stores, but where was the intensity of life? I started smoking dope around 1960 and before long was using heroin and cocaine, with my first husband. He was from an aristocratic family, so everything had an air of respectability; we were 'registered' with a well-known Harley Street, London, doctor. I found the intensity in heroin but knew this was a dead end.

When I was 27, I went to Scotland to a Tibetan monastery, but on returning to London met my second husband and jumped headlong into drugs again. More mad years went by using speed and heroin, and one morning I woke up to find him dead. I was now 42 and put myself into a 'detox' unit, then attended Narcotics Anonymous meetings, but I was spiritually on my knees.

At a Narcotics Anonymous I met somebody and was struck by his happiness – he was always happy. One day he mentioned, "I meditate." "Big deal," I thought, because my experience of meditation had led me to a brick wall. He put a leaflet into my hand: 'Shri Mataji in person at Porchester Hall', close to where I lived.

Shri Mataji arrived, dressed in white, her long black hair flowing over her shoulders, and she walked down the centre aisle of the audience. Everything stopped or faded away and I just saw her. The hairs on my arms and at the back of my neck stood on end and I could feel my heart beating. I thought, 'What's going on here? Who is this?' She spoke such sense, voicing my own thoughts and feelings that I had never been able to articulate. Then she gave the experience of self realisation. We all went through the exercise, then she blew over the microphone.

"How many people felt the cool breeze coming from the top of their heads?" she asked. I looked around the hall, and everyone raised their hand. I felt my bottom lip tremble, as my despair and disappointment began to well up. Shri Mataji's eyes met mine.

"Don't worry, it's alright, if you didn't feel it come up here to me," she said, and although she was speaking to everyone, she was looking at me, in the front row.

"I'm so tired of searching," I whispered.

She asked me what I'd been doing and I mentioned a couple of things. She tutted and shook her head. She held my hand and stroked it for ages. I now know that she was removing heat and negativity within me. She put her hand on my stomach, all the time looking right into me. Suddenly I felt my forehead open up like the opening of a cage; there seemed no top to my head.

"Oh my God, it's true!" I thought. It was wonderful beyond words.

"She's got it," Shri Mataji said. I had 'come home' at last.

All this happened in 1987. My life is now totally fulfilling, although I live quietly and simply with my lovely husband of twenty-five years.'

The brave men and women, such as the next contributor, who were 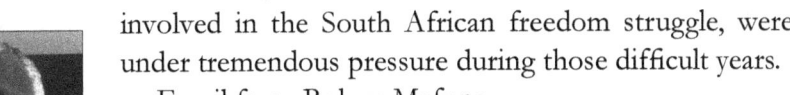 involved in the South African freedom struggle, were under tremendous pressure during those difficult years.

Email from Bokwe Mafuna

I got my self realisation at the Montfermeil ashram, Paris, on the 12th March, 1992. Little did I realise what this would do to change my life. Up to that point it was one of confusion, aggravated by anger with and hatred for the apartheid regime in South Africa, which I was fighting against. I was also drinking heavily.

I started drinking at the age of sixteen in 1953 in Sophiatown, a black township of Johannesburg, and this continued almost unabated throughout my life. I was a trade union organiser, and later went into journalism at the Rand Daily Mail, a liberal newspaper. Drinking was the order of the day for most journalists, and we used to sit after hours enjoying whisky, brandy and beer. This would begin in the newsroom and end up in one of our colleagues' homes, or in a shebeen - an illegal speakeasy for blacks where we could have white people's liquor.

I was into my habits when I went into the Black Consciousness Movement and became a close friend of Steve Biko, who was killed by the security police in 1977 in prison. I was a political exile by then, first in Botswana and later in France, where I was making contact with other freedom fighters to help with our training and other needs. During that time I was working as a free-lance journalist for Radio France International. My drinking took a serious turn for the worse, as frequently I wouldn't return home and find myself in a bar in the wee hours of the morning; or find myself in a blackout on a train not knowing where I was going.

Then came the day of my self realisation. I didn't quite realise what had happened as I had not felt anything really, when I was asked whether I had felt anything. What happened then - and I was completely unaware of it at first until three weeks into the process - was that I stopped drinking altogether. I used to have wine with every meal as is the habit in France. I would also have a beer or two, or even three, early in the morning at the nearest bistro. The evenings were relished with whisky.

Little did I notice after that Thursday evening in Montfermeil how things had changed. It took me three weeks to realise that there was something amiss - and even then it came like a slow realisation: my bottles of whisky and wine were in the cupboard and had been untouched since I was not quite sure when! I couldn't quite come to terms with this. But I didn't try to undo what had happened so subtly, so spontaneously, so quietly.

But I was not yet over the wall. A few months into this bliss, I was present at a cocktail party at the South African embassy in Paris. We were offered drinks - champagne - as we walked in. My hesitation was very short lived, as I took the glass to my lips, wondering whether I shouldn't really be asking for orange juice. However with the first sip, I had my answer: so bad was the wretched feeling I experienced, I thought I was going to vomit in front of all those high society people. My escape was to beat a retreat for the door and the taxi that was waiting outside at the nearby taxi rank. I gave him my home address, and prayed to God I would reach home with my stomach intact.

For over twenty years now, I haven't had another drink since that day. I understood the lesson - and accepted the change that I had been blessed with. That was one of my most significant wake-up calls, and I thank Shri Mataji for it. The drinking problem had been a curse for generations in my family. I was the first to escape from its clutches. After all those years.

I am back in South Africa now, where I am happy to have orange juice without any hesitation. And I am free!

Lucia Coutinho of Brazil has a story of psychological transformation.

'When I first got in touch with Sahaja Yoga, in July 1997, I had many problems. In 1992, divorced after twenty years of marriage, I was living alone in Sao Paulo, Brazil, working to support myself. I was violently attacked in my home by robbers who displaced my lower teeth and broke my jaw. Afterwards I had to go through the terrible experience of going to the precinct, facing the robbers, going to court, etc. Even worse than that were the visits I had to make to the Legal Medical Institute, along with lots of other attacked people, to prove that I had been injured. I went to my mother´s place and stayed in bed for a month with a high fever and many nights would wake up screaming and crying. I started receiving silent phone calls. Sometimes my phone rang thirty times at night while I walked trembling in the dark house. The terror in which I lived affected my heart. Soon my boss started talking about firing me. For five years I had to conceal my heart problems at the office as much as I could and go to the hospital afterwards. Then I had my car robbed and was attacked twice by beggars on the street. Totally desperate, all I wanted was to die.

One morning I saw Shri Mataji´s poster. The next Saturday, I went to the Sahaja Yoga meeting, where I received my realisation. Little by little, my life started to change. Two years after that I had to undergo heart surgery and recovered totally from my heart problems.

With the help of Shri Mataji´s blessings I got over my biggest problems. I´ve started giving realisation to others, and took the responsibility of answering phone calls of the seekers - strangers! - who called for information. Many times when I walked back home alone at night, I remembered the earlier times, when I had to count on the kindness of a Sahaja Yogi to accompany me. I know I owe this miracle to our Holy Mother. I´m totally confident that nothing is impossible for her and trust her completely. My heart is beating smoothly, and I thank her for all this.'

This story was originally submitted in the late 1990's, when this book was started. When the editor sent this story back to Lucia in 2008 to check she was satisfied with it, she sent this email back: 'Hi Linda, at first I thought the story was about another person, so different I'm now. I am retired now and finally moved to the beach, as I always dreamed, and had up to five Sahaja Yoga public programs a week in my new town. Thank you, best wishes, Lucia.'

Chapter 15

When the Five Senses are Enlightened

Smell

This experience, related by Chris Marlow, occurred many times.

'I was with a friend. We'd been out for a pizza in London, England where I live, and we were walking through the back streets, talking about Shri Mataji and the experience of self realisation she gave, which we call Sahaja Yoga. We suddenly got struck by this incredible smell of roses, very powerful.

"Wow, that is fantastic," we said. We looked around to see where it was coming from. We looked everywhere. It wasn't coming from anywhere and suddenly we looked up and realised we were standing right outside Darwin Court, in North London. Shri Mataji stayed in a flat in Darwin Court for a short period of time and she was there at that moment. I told my friend that it was a well-known phenomenon that Shri Mataji's presence was often pervaded with the smell of roses. It was a very intense smell and it certainly wasn't coming from anywhere localized.'

Pamela Bromley was one of the first Sahaja Yogis in Brighton, England.

'Once, in the early 1980's, I was going to a Sahaja Yoga meeting in Brighton, England. I was driving in my car, and was coming near to the place where it was being held. Shri Mataji was obviously there because the fragrance of roses was incredible even though there were no roses around. Many of us had this experience.'

A similar story is related by Paulette Oddo of France.

'For several years following my divorce in the 1980's, I had fallen into a state of total exhaustion and acute mental and physical anguish and was going from bad to worse. But one morning, I woke with a strange premonition that something good would happen that day. I was seized by an immense desire to go to Chartres Cathedral to see the Virgin Mary there.

In the cathedral I prayed before the statue of the Virgin. Immediately I smelled a very strong rose perfume. It was so intense that I turned round to see where it was coming from. I walked around the cathedral and the scent followed me round the whole building. As I left the cathedral and stood in the open air in the square by the entrance, the scent was still there.

Shri Mataji on Brighton Beach in 1980, with some Sahaja Yogis and her grandchildren, and Pamela is on the left of the photo

A few yards away from where I was standing I could see an Indian lady wearing a white sari getting out of a car. She looked at me and smiled, and I felt attracted to her. Suddenly my head emptied of all thought and I could only see this lady, as though nothing else was there. She was still smiling at me. I approached and asked who she was.

"You don't know her? Why are you standing here?" a man who was with her said.

"Because there is such a beautiful scent," I replied. "Roses, can't you smell them?"

"It's Shri Mataji, don't you know her?" he said.

"No."

"She is here for truth and she can protect thousands of people."

I felt an explosion of joy within myself, since I already knew somehow that this lady was very great, and this was what I had been waiting for.

"Why don't you join us?" he went on. I followed the little party into the cathedral. As we walked, I felt a pleasant tingling sensation rising from my feet, through my legs and throughout my body and a feeling in my heart

Shri Mataji at Chartres Cathedral

which I can only describe as expansion or fulfillment. The rest of that day was spent in joy and bliss and, from then on, my sickness and depression simply disappeared.'

Purna Vertunni of Italy had two extraordinary experiences when she was a teenager in the early 1980's, and both were accompanied by the same scent of roses.

'There was a period in my life when there were a lot of problems around me. We were living near the sea, and one day I went in the water. The sea started to take me out deep on some current, and I felt I was drowning. Suddenly I realised that the sea was Shri Vishnu, the principle of evolution, and he couldn't let me die because he was my spiritual grandfather. At that moment I felt a hand taking me, and pulling me out. I could smell that beautiful fragrance of Shri Mataji, like roses or jasmine. The people on the shore could see no one; they had seen me crying for help for a longish time, but I was so far out they could not get to me. They were amazed that I was somehow all right.

On another occasion, when I was going to art school, everything was very difficult, because the school was full of strange goings on. I was already living with other Sahaja Yogis and following the principles of Sahaj, or should I say traditional, morality. I was walking to the school, and I asked Shri Mataji in my heart to protect me, and that Shri Ganesha, who is the principle of innocence and wisdom, should take me through this. Suddenly I again smelt this very strong fragrance of Shri Mataji, like roses, but a very particular aroma. I turned my head, and saw Shri Ganesha actually there, with his arm around me, walking with me and saying, "Don't worry I will always be with you". From that moment I was completely protected and there was nothing that could touch me in that place.'

This experience, from Brigitte Saugstad of Austria, is slightly different.

'In October 1987, Shri Mataji blessed our home in Vienna with a visit. A number of us lived there together. We ladies offered her some rose-oil perfume as a gift. She put some on the back of her hand and told us all to smell the backs of our own hands. We could all clearly smell the perfume coming from the skin on the back of our hands. We were amazed and delighted.'

Editor's note: Shri Mataji, on other occasions, explained this as being an example of collective consciousness, which is our birthright as realised souls, that is people whose Kundalinis have been raised.

John Watkinson of London

'One day three of us came in the front entrance of Shri Mataji's house in Brompton Square, London. It was in the early stages of renovation when the walls were being knocked down and there was a lot of dirt. I had quite a bad blocked nose from all the dust. As we arrived in the front entrance, there was Shri Mataji. We gave her the flowers we had brought and she took my flower and smelled it.

"Mmn!" she said, then offered it to me to smell and I did so.

"I can't smell anything, Mother. My nose is blocked," I said. She took it back and smelled it again and again. Then I could really smell the fragrance, as if she was showing me that on a certain level, we are all one: "I am in you and you are in me," she said. The others standing watching could all smell the same scent too, and we were all laughing.'

Shri Mataji at Vienna Airport, mid 80's

Avdut Pai lived in Mumbai, India, when he was young.

'When I was young I did not smoke many cigarettes, but when with friends, I used to occasionally. In 1980 we were in Dhulia, a town in Maharashtra.

"I need somebody to put his or her hand near my Vishuddhi Chakra, (at the level of the throat) to take vibrations. Somebody who has never smoked in his life," said Shri Mataji.

"Avdut," said the people.

"No, Mother, I have smoked," I said.

"He smoked cigarettes, but he has admitted it in front of everybody," she said.

I spent the whole of the next day with a Sahaja Yogi, certainly did not touch a cigarette, and in the evening we went to a Sahaja public programme. We were standing outside the hall guarding it and suddenly I smelled cigarette very strongly even though there was absolutely nobody around.

"From where is it coming?" I said, then realised it was coming from my right Vishuddhi finger (the index finger). "My God!" I said and showed my friend. "You are the proof. I did not even touch a cigarette today."

"It's true," he replied.

We were staying in the same house as Shri Mataji. As soon as we reached there I washed my fingers with a lot of soap but the smell was still there and would not go away. She was in her room and I knocked on the door.

"Shri Mataji, there's a problem. There's a smell of nicotine on my finger," I said.

"Yes, because this morning you told me you smoked a cigarette, I'm trying to clean you, but you should promise you will never smoke again."

"I promise." She took my fingers in her hand for some time and the smell went away. I never smoked again.'

Touch

This example of collective consciousness is told by Kristine Kirby.

'In 1983 Shri Mataji came to Boston, USA and stayed with us. At one point about fifteen of us were listening to music with her in the living room.

"Let's have some nice music," she said. We wanted Shri Mataji to listen to a jazz artist who we thought might be a realised soul. I put that tape into the machine and pressed the 'play' button and it just wouldn't go. I couldn't figure out what was wrong because the tape machine had been working so far.

"Let me try a different tape," I said. The other tape was some Indian flute music by a realised soul and immediately it worked.

"This is beautiful music," Shri Mataji said, so we listened, and sat in a semi-circle around her. "Whatever is happening in the atmosphere, whatever is happening in the universe is reflected in my body - even the rhythm of this music."

She had me put my left hand under her foot and a very complicated rhythm was pulsing on the sole of her foot corresponding to the rhythm of the music, that of the tabla that was playing with the flute. I felt it with my own hands.

Shri Mataji had us link hands so that my right hand was holding the left hand of the person sitting next to me, then they took their right hand and put it into the left hand of the person next to them. In this way we all linked hands and because we were in a semi-circle, it finally went back to Shri Mataji.

"Now everybody can feel it," she said.

My left hand was under her right foot and everybody felt the rhythm of the music. We sat in that way for about five minutes, experiencing something really amazing.'

Mary Heaton, on a visit from England, had this to add.

'"See, feel the vibrations flow around the circle," said Shri Mataji. We could feel the vibrations flow around the circle. There was a lady there who was pregnant and she could feel the baby dancing to the rhythm. Shri Mataji was in the circle, at the beginning and the end.'

Hearing

One of the first Sahaja Yogis in England, Douglas Fry, relates this experience.

'In the early 1970's when there were just a handful of us in Sahaja Yoga in London, we met a few times with Shri Mataji in a house just over the road from Kings Cross Station. It was here that we had one of the first experiences of actually hearing through the Sahasrara chakra at the top of the head.

"Put your hands over your ears and cover them up completely and you'll still be able to hear me just the same," she said when talking to us one time, and we could. We had our hands over our ears and we could clearly hear what Shri Mataji was saying, exactly the same as before, because we were hearing through our opened Sahasraras. That was perhaps the first amazing experience, apart from feeling the vibrations, we all had.'

This similar story is related by the editor.

'There was a programme with Shri Mataji in 1988 just outside Munich, Germany. One evening there was music, an Indian musician playing a santoor, which is rather a quiet instrument. There must have been three or four hundred of us in the tent, and I was right in the very back row. At a certain point the electricity broke down and obviously the sound system stopped working. The musician went on playing, and the music was very beautiful. I noticed after a few minutes that I could still hear, just as well as when the sound system was functioning. The volume was exactly the same. I couldn't understand how I could hear at all, from right at the back.

It came to me that this man was like Pundit Tanzen, the great Indian musician at the court of the Moghal emperor Akbar in the sixteenth century, who purportedly had power over the elements through his music. At that moment the electricity came back on, and a little while later the musician finished his piece.

After he had done so, Shri Mataji spoke. She firstly asked if those of us at the back had been able to hear when the power was off, and a whole row of us put our hands up, to say we could. Shri Mataji explained that we had been hearing through our Sahasraras. Then she said exactly what had been in my mind, that his playing was so beautiful that he was like Tanzen, and spoke a bit about this famous man. I was in Shri Mataji's presence at hundreds of programmes of Indian classical music and never heard her comment on Tanzen at any others.'

This story is from Derek Ferguson.

'In the public programme in Exeter, in 1982, Shri Mataji got off the stage and started to help all the new people. There was a man who was deaf when Shri Mataji started to work on him and cupped her right hand, placed it on his Sahasrara, then started to talk to him through his Sahasrara. He said he could hear her talking to him, and it was very moving. My eyes were welling up with tears to see a deaf man start to hear again.'

Taste

'Some years after I had my realisation, I went to stay in a house in Scotland which some Sahaja Yogis were running as a bed and breakfast facility. Two ladies arrived from the south of England, and stayed a few days, and we cooked all their meals, not just breakfast. We vibrated all the food, as was our habit, and gave it to our visitors.

After a few days one lady asked us what we were putting in the food, and we were a bit nervous, in case it had made her ill. But it turned out that she had a chronic digestive complaint, and for the first time in years, since eating our food, she was able to digest everything normally. We told her that the only thing we were doing was one of our Sahaja Yoga techniques. They became interested and received self realisation, and learnt how to do it for themselves.'

Patrick Anslow

Editor's note: for instructions on how to vibrate food see the Appendix

This story is told by two sisters from Switzerland, who were in Portugal at the time.

'We were in a small village called Cintra. A few of us went with Shri Mataji to an inn, which was at the top of a hill, and sat around a rectangular table. She was at the middle of the table and on the table there was a basket of bread and some grapes and we were all waiting there to have our supper. We nibbled at some grapes on the table, but they were somewhat tasteless. We were about to take some more grapes and she just put her hands on them for a while.

"Now you can take the grapes," she said. We had a taste of the grapes before she had put her hands on, and they had no taste. After she put her hands on them, they were absolutely succulent, full of a lovely nectar flavour. Then Shri Mataji put her hand on the basket of bread.

"Now you take this bread and share it among yourselves," she said. We did, and I was amazed at what was going on here because I could recall a scene that had happened two thousand years ago.

"You see, when Christ shared the bread among his disciples," Shri Mataji explained, "he could say, "take that because it is my body," because this very bread was his own body, because it was full of vibrations and as he was full of vibrations, he was pranava. He was the vibrations himself. He could convey that to the bread and, obviously, when the disciples would eat this bread, they would eat his vibrations.'

Antoinette Wells

The same incident as recalled by Antoinette's sister.

'One night in Portugal in 1981 we were at a small restaurant, just four or five of us. My elder sister asked Shri Mataji to explain the Holy Communion. I remember that Shri Mataji looked so beautiful at that time, with her long dark hair over her shoulders, and her red shawl around her.

She took a large piece of oval bread in her hand and held it for some time. Then she started to give a little piece of the bread to each one of us.

"That's it. That's all," she said.'

Marie-Laure Cernay

Chapter 16

Coming to Terms with the Weather

The first weather report is from Geoff Godfrey of London, England. 'In October 1993 I accompanied Shri Mataji on a two week trip around America. On approaching every airport, we were informed of low ground temperatures, 5°C or similar, by in flight announcements. In each instance, Shri Mataji just smiled, raised her left hand up her right side*, and upon landing the temperature had eased upwards. Often dull days turned suddenly into bright sunny ones.

"Just give the sun a bandhan," she suggested.

It was the same when we returned to London. Coming into Heathrow Airport in late autumn, Shri Mataji gave vibrations to her the right side, which is associated with heat, and within seconds I was perspiring and we stepped out into a bright sunny morning.'

*The right side of the body and the subtle system is associated with the power of the sun, therefore heat.

Shri Mataji at Stonehenge

'On a trip back from Stonehenge in the late 1970's, we had been having some forest fires in the south of England, which had been going on for quite a long time, because it hadn't rained recently. One of the Sahaja Yogis in the car with Shri Mataji was expressing his concern that we were going to lose these wonderful forests. Being tree lovers, we were a little concerned and he was telling her that it was a shame that this fire had been going on for so long.

Shri Mataji looked out of the car window and in the distance there were a few clouds in the sky. She just looked at them and all of a sudden they began to move from the right hand side of the car, over the car, towards where the forest fire was raging many miles away. We heard on the news that night that there had been rain over the fire and it had been put out.'

Bala Kanayson

'In 1983 one of the yogis mentioned to Shri Mataji when she was visiting us that it would be a great blessing if Australia could be drenched with a heavy rainfall as the whole country was suffering drought. As a result bush fires were causing havoc in many parts of Australia because of the heat and dryness.

It was decided to have a puja at the seaside the very next day. We were only about fifteen Sahaja Yogis at the time and we found a wonderful quiet beach where we could see the city of Melbourne in the distance. Shri Mataji was seated on a flat rock and everything was silent. The sea began to react to the vibrations and started to rise and she waved her hand.

"Calm down, calm down. It's all right," she said, and with that, the sea was still and calm. She then started drawing an image of Shri Ganesha in the sand and slowly kept shaping his form over and over again. Everything was peaceful and silent – just the gentle ocean lapping the sands. Shri Mataji offered the image flowers, kumkum, turmeric and rice.

"Now, after this puja, the whole of Australia will not suffer from drought," she said joyfully.

About a week later, on the 20th March 1983, while we were preparing the garland of flowers for her sixtieth birthday, suddenly the sky exploded with a crack of thunder and there it was – rain – torrents and torrents of it and it went on for days.

"You see, your prayers are answered," Shri Mataji announced.

Even the newspapers were headed with a full front page 'Miracle Rain.' The whole of Australia, including Ayer's Rock, was blessed with rain.'

Gauri Mehrani-Mylany

Here are some more rain stories, from Frances Henke, a journalist from Australia.

'When Shri Mataji first came to Melbourne, she did a sea puja at Shoreham, a beach near where we live, to help resolve Melbourne's water problems. This was in 1983, and that year we had bad fires, and then right after she did the puja the rain came. As we left her press conference at the Windsor Hotel, the first drops of rain fell there too.

My husband and I moved on to Sydney to help with PR there, and in Sydney we told a nurseryman, from whom we were buying plants for the garden at the Sahaja Yoga Burwood house, where Shri Mataji would stay, that it was going to rain. He told his friends and they just laughed. Then it rained. He was flabbergasted and relieved.

Frances Henke interviewing Shri Mataji

Before we went to the UK, we had one last programme at our Sahaja centre in Woolahra, and as everyone was leaving rain was falling in the valley and right up to our doorstep - an amazing phenomenon. We described it to Shri Mataji and she said it was ritam bara pragnya, a blessing of nature - the one that skips houses with good vibrations during bush fires.

And one last: we were doing puja at the Sahaja Yogi's ashram in Surbiton, London, UK and a cloud came over. Rain began to fall and we started to stand up. "It's only a head bath," Shri Mataji said.

"Stay there!" and sure enough it was just a light shower.'

Shri Mataji spoke many times about the late Mr. Koli, a fisherman. This was written by his son Raju Koli.

'It was the rainy season in India - the monsoon, when we have very severe storms and no one can possibly go on the sea. My father had been in Sahaja Yoga for some time, and had heard Shri Mataji telling people to use their vibrations, their pure desire and their surrender to the divine all-pervading power for many blessings.

One day he arranged to do a programme of Sahaja Yoga in a village on an island because he had heard that Shri Mataji wanted us all to spread Sahaja Yoga to the villages as well as in the towns. Unfortunately when it was time to go it was raining very heavily; the wind was roaring and the lightning flashing, and it was impossible to take the boat out. Then he asked, in his heart, for the storm to stop so he could get to the island. He gave a bandhan and immediately the weather calmed down even though it had been a heavy monsoon storm.

He took the boat to the island and gave self realisation, and then left, not even thinking about the weather. It took him three or four hours to get home again - we lived on the seashore - and the moment he stepped inside our house the storm and rain started again just as heavily as before. All of us at home were delighted to see the rain coming again - because we need the rain in India, but not a storm when my father was on the sea.'

This story is by Lev Doronski from Turkey.

'When Shri Mataji was here in Istanbul, in 1999, at the public programme, the tent which was supposed to be for about fifteen hundred people was overfilled and we estimated the total number of people to be about two thousand.

As soon as Shri Mataji entered, it started raining and was raining almost till the end of the programme. Shri Mataji gave self realisation in a very simple way. She just asked people to put their hands towards her, like in namaaz that the Muslims do, and to feel vibrations. While giving realisation, she was blowing in the microphone. As soon as she started, we heard a long and powerful sound of thunder which lasted as long as she was blowing. The sound was very similar to the sound of blowing so they merged into one. It was magnificent.

I subsequently heard a story of one lady who was late for the programme. She saw the tent from the outside, and everywhere it was raining, but no rain was falling on the tent - as if there was a huge umbrella over it!'

Claire Nesdale also has a rain story.

'In 1992 we had built a hangar at Gidgegannup, our property near Perth, Australia, but the centre of the roof hadn't been put in. Shri Mataji started to talk and about ten minutes later big clouds came over and rain started to pour down.

Nobody was moving because it would have been impolite. Shri Mataji looked up and saw what was happening and cut through the air with her hand and immediately the rain stopped. It seemed to stop in mid-air and just didn't come down any more. Everybody looked to see what had happened because nobody could quite work it out. At the very same time, a wind blew up and blew the clouds away within minutes. The big rain clouds had gone and there were just soft fluffy white clouds in their place and fine blue patches of sky.

The Sahaja Yogis talked about it for years afterwards. New people, who had only been in Sahaja Yoga a year or so, couldn't believe what had happened because one minute you were being drenched with these heavy drops of rain and the next minute it was just cut in mid-air.'

Helga Adams from South Africa was only in Shri Mataji's presence once.

'I went to a Sahaja programme in Tyrol, Austria right up in the mountains, in about 1990. The miracle happened after the programme that was held in a big tent. It had been pitched by the side of a river which was coming down the valley.

Towards the end, a terrific thunderstorm started. The rain was pouring down and was coming in on the side of the tent where some ladies were sitting. Some of them tried in vain to right the tarpaulin to stop the water, but Shri Mataji just waved her hand and the water ran off the side. As Shri Mataji rose to leave, she made us promise not to go outside the tent for the next half hour, but just to sit in quiet meditation. We heard the thunder and did not see much of the lightning, as the tent flaps were closed.

The next morning, we were told by our landlady at the pension where we were staying, never in her lifetime had she experienced such a storm with such terrific rain and thunder, and the lightning actually rolled down the main street, to the utter amazement of the local inhabitants. They all were very worried about our big tent on the banks of the river and came to help us, but could not believe that the river had not come high enough to touch us. The place where the large tent was pitched was the flood plain which was always under water when the river came down after such a downpour.'

Two Australians, Kay McHugh and Cheryl Bradshaw, reminisce over an experience in India.

Kay: Do you remember that village called Karuse in Maharashtra? It was an amazing experience because the villagers had come from miles around. We were way out in the countryside and it was a very simple village. They had a simple bullock cart with palm trees over the top of it and a bullock driver who slowly took Shri Mataji through the village. We danced in front of it and all the villagers played their music and came when she gave a programme to give them all self realisation.

Cheryl: It was outside Pune, a very dusty place and all the village people came and they were sitting on roofs and walls. They were just everywhere. The programme was held outdoors.

Kay: It was in the middle of the day and there were people hanging out of the trees and on the tops of ruined walls and everywhere. It hadn't rained there for such a long time and they were destitute. Shri Mataji gave a short talk in Marathi. As soon as the talk finished the skies opened and the rain came down. We all had to run for cover, and there were thousands of people.

Cheryl: It just poured, for about an hour. It had not rained for nine months and the Indian people were totally over the moon, more so, because this was not the rainy season and it almost never rains there at that time of the year, even in a good year for rain. They danced, sang and ended up covered with mud. Because there had been no rain, it was very dusty and when the rain came it became very muddy. It was a really joyous occasion.

Traditionally, when an honoured guest arrives at your house in India, you do 'aarti' to them. A tray is prepared with little lamps, made from cotton wool soaked in butter and lit. The tray is waved in an arch around the guest's head and then a garland is offered. Rachel Ruigrok tells this story.
'Shri Mataji came to Holland in the summer of 1992. The moment she got off the plane it started to rain. It was pouring so much the driver could hardly drive the car. As she arrived at our house, the rain just stopped as if someone had switched off a tap.
Shri Mataji got out of the car and the whole sky was lit by lightning even though there was no rain. She walked up the path with lightning and thunder going all the time we did aarti to her. Every time the aarti tray went round in an arch over her head, the lightning flashed and the thunder crashed. She walked in over the threshold and the moment she was inside, the rain came down again as if a tap had been switched back on as I put the garland around her neck.'

Phil Ward tells of the great snowfall of February 1985, in Geneva, Switzerland.
'Shivaratri is a celebration and worship of the deity Shri Shiva, who is said to live in the snows of the Himalayas. He represents the pure spirit within all of us. In Geneva, the day before, we were preparing everything and thinking how apt it would be if we could use melted snow, as this is the purest natural form of water. We had had a little snow earlier that evening and we thought we might be able to trap some in two bowls, if these were left out overnight. So they were put out in the garden and we went to bed, giving a bandhan that there might be some snow. It was quite a mild evening with a cloudy sky.
Next morning there was no sign of the bowls. Everything was hidden under two to three feet of fresh snow and more was falling as we gazed through the curtains. Eventually, we found the bowls, after some poking around in the snow. They were placed in some shallow hot water in a bathtub to melt their contents.
Meantime, the snow continued to fall. Geneva had the heaviest snowfall of

the century, and the weathermen had completely failed to predict it. Amazingly, it was confined to the Geneva area and even in Lausanne, fifty miles away, only a few centimetres fell.'

This is Silvi Moodley from South Africa.
'It was in March 1998 at Shri Mataji's birthday celebration in Delhi. We were sitting waiting for Mother to come in and it was very hot. I was looking at the people near me and they were also suffering and perspiring. Suddenly, we felt a change and it was as if a mist just floated in. I thought, 'This is just me seeing this.'

"Look at this mist," said the girl next to me, a schoolteacher who lived near Delhi.

It became so icy cold that all of us put our shawls on. At that moment Shri Mataji arrived and we stood to welcome her.'

Graciela Vázquez-Díaz tells how Shri Mataji solved a weather problem in South America.
'We were eleven Sahaja Yogis travelling with Shri Mataji from Bogotá to Medellín, in Colombia. The small plane made a stop and we went with Shri Mataji to greet some yogis who were at the airport. The pilot was nervous because the fog was coming down and it was going to be difficult and dangerous to take off.

Sitting in the plane behind Shri Mataji, we could see the pilot and the fog that was already down on the earth. She did a bandhan towards the fog and the pilot and, just as Moses saw the sea open to cross to the other side, we saw the fog open and our plane took off.'

Shri Mataji in Colombia

Martin Purcell is a construction consultant.

'In April 1989 we Sahaja Yogis were traveling from Perth to Melbourne, in Australia, by car. It is more than two thousand kilometres across a vast open desert, the Nulabor, in the outback. There is little human habitation along this road, whose side is marked by relics of travellers who did not reach their destination. After several hours, we stopped in a small town called Ceduna for lunch.

The lady managing the cafe put down her knitting and made us steak sandwiches. She told us of the very difficult situation she found herself in. She was unable to work her farm as it had not rained for five years, so that now the soil was blowing away. If it would just rain a little she would be out in the back planting some seeds for a new crop. To make matters worse, she told us that she had an opal mine in the north that could not be worked either, as it had been flooded out by rain! A shame, we agreed, and really felt for her, out there in the baking hot dry land.

The conversation shifted to other topics and we eventually paid for our meal and got up to leave. We opened the front door to find it was absolutely pouring with rain.'

Rosie Lyons of Australia explains how the elements showed their magic.

'One day about five of us Sahaja Yogis went down to the sea in Australia, on a very stormy day. We started to make a Shiva lingam, a column like shape which represents the power of Lord Shiva, reflected within each of us as the spirit. We also made a big aum sign on the beach.

As soon as we put the last stone and offered flowers to the Shiva lingam, the storm completely calmed and the light opened out through the clouds and streamed down upon us. It was incredible, from a really big rough storm to this total calm.

Another time, Shri Mataji was going to come to Cambridge, England and we were all collecting poppies. It started pouring with rain and no one got wet. The rain was pouring down all around us in these huge fields full of red poppies, and we did not get wet at all.'

The editor, then in South Africa, tells of a weather related incident.

'At the end of the 1990's all the weather experts around the world said the current El Niño was going to be the worst ever. One evening the newsreader on the TV news in South Africa gave a long warning: farmers who lived on marginal land should not bother to plant maize that year, as there would be a very serious drought. The papers were also full of gloom and foreboding, because droughts were bad for the economy and catastrophic for the poorer people who lived at subsistence level. In the past serious El Niño conditions invariably meant bad droughts in Southern Africa.

Sahaja Yogis can give bandhans, and there is also a song which we can sing. All around the country we did bandhans for normal rain and sang 'Bathe in the waters' a lot, a song which often produces rain when Sahaja Yogis sing it. That was about October. In December I went to India, and flew back into Johannesburg in January. As is usual for the time of year, there were thick clouds everywhere, and when we flew below them to land, the landscape was verdant green and it was raining. I asked some friends how the rains had been, and they said they had been very good: heavy but no flooding. Some time later the newsreader apologised for getting the predictions wrong.

There was a bumper harvest and the only problem was the availability of storage space for all the grain. Was it anything to do with us? Who knows?'

'One time,' related Douglas Fry, 'in the 1970's we were with Shri Mataji outside her house at Hurst Green, Oxted, doing a havan. It was cold and overcast outside as it was late in the year, but as we did the havan, the sky opened up just above us, like a great big halo over the house. The sky was quite dark, but there was a whole light patch above where we were.'

Marie-Laure Cernay contributed this story.

'In July 1984 Shri Mataji was in Switzerland and saw a postcard of the Matterhorn.

This mountain is a 'swayambhu'* of Shri Ganesha," she said. "We should have the Ganesha Puja there," so the same year we had the puja in the village of Zermatt. It is in the mountains and when we were there Shri Mataji showed us how we could see the profile of Shri Ganesha in the mountain.

After we left, even though it was only the very beginning of September, the whole village was completely closed because it snowed for two days non-stop, although at that time of the year it never snows there. There was no train or anything. We told Shri Mataji, who said Shri Ganesha wanted to enjoy the vibrations emitted by the puja, and to be quiet and have peace. If you see a map of the area, it is as if there is a 'swastika'** dropped on the earth.'

Editor's notes: *A swayambhu is a place on the earth which naturally emits vibrations, or sometimes a statue or rock which has spontaneously appeared from the earth and has vibrations, such as the Kaaba at Mecca. Occasionally the term is applied to a sacred structure, like Stonehenge.

**The swastika is an ancient and auspicious symbol found in a number of traditions, representing the four petals or aspects of the Mooladhara chakra, the first and lowest one. The word Mooladhara, meaning the 'support of the root', as has been mentioned before, is associated with Shri Ganesha, the wise, innocent, child god."

Shri Mataji in front of the Matterhorn

Phil Ward and several Swiss Sahaja Yogis went to the same place without Shri Mataji in the summer of 1986.

'We had come together for a weekend Sahaja Yoga seminar at the foot of the Matterhorn in the Swiss Alps. This mountain is a swayambhu or natural manifestation of the principle of Shri Ganesha, the elephant-headed child god of Hindu mythology, and we had been able to see the form of an elephant's head in the profile of the mountain. We established that the mountain emitted cool vibrations by holding out our hands to it. The sun was shining and we decided to meditate together in the open air, facing the mountain and with Shri Mataji's photograph in front of us. We uttered the mantra of Shri Ganesha and the cool breeze grew within us and gently took us into a state of deep meditation.

In spite of the cool breeze, the sun was beating down on us all the time and someone suggested that we should pray that the sun would recede and allow us to continue our meditation. Within a few seconds a fine layer of cloud formed and veiled the sun, reducing the heat but maintaining the light. For some of us who were new in Sahaja Yoga, it was amazing to see how the elements could listen to us and help us. But more was to come. The clouds started to dance in the sky, forming different shapes. We could see the swastika, which is a symbol of Shri Ganesha, the tear-drop associated in India with the Goddess, the three and a half coils of the Kundalini and an elephant's head which seemed to emerge from out of the summit of the sacred mountain. At the same time, through the vapour, a rainbow was forming a bandhan, symbol of the divine protection, which appeared to surround the mountain.

We were transported into joy and a few Sahaja Yogis had the presence of mind to photograph some of these manifestations.'

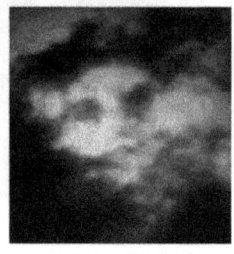

In one the face of Shri Mataji appears and one can see a similarity between the photo and the image in the clouds.

Shyam Etchepareborda, from Nyon Switzerland, tells of his experience.

'Some years ago I had to leave a Sahaja Yoga seminar in England in a great hurry to report for military service at a barracks in Switzerland. I had to quit the paradise on Earth and was transported to a fair approximation to hell. However, the last words of Shri Mataji, as I left, boosted my morale tremendously. She said we should absolutely have confidence in ourselves, and even the elements would obey us.

On my second day in the army I had to do some exercises lying in some grass under the intense August sun and Shri Mataji's words came back to me. I prayed within myself, 'If we really have power over the elements, please let the atmosphere cool down.' At the instant I finished uttering these words, I felt a great gust of breeze arise and pass over my cheeks, followed by more, one after another. I was in a state of shock, but I felt myself filled by a great joy and tremendous confidence. By the end of the afternoon, the sky was completely covered with clouds. Throughout my four months of army training, whenever I had problems I looked at the sky and felt I was well looked after.'

Gisela Matzer has a story from India.

'In December 1993 my daughter Siddhi got married. She was only eighteen, and after the marriage, we went to Pune to her new family. For me, she was still an innocent child and it was difficult to leave her. Before I left India, we went to Pratisthan, Shri Mataji's house.

As we drove away, I looked up to the sky and immediately asked to stop the car. Siddhi, Rahul (Siddhi's new husband) and I saw the same thing. The sky was like a bright and colourful mosaic made out of spots in all rainbow colours. In the middle was a small white cloud. It was shaped like a girl holding a lotus flower above her head. Immediately, I remembered how Siddhi, as a small girl, had danced for Shri Mataji in Austria and offered her a lotus flower. Suddenly, the cloud that looked like a girl brought down its arms, spread them out as if it would give blessings, got a trunk and was like the elephant headed Shri Ganesha, two of whose qualities are innocence and auspiciousness, and who traditionally blesses marriages.

We drove further, but I could not take my sight from the sky and looked in the direction of Pratishthan. Again I saw a small cloud. First it had the head and hands of an Indian dancer, but suddenly, the head split into three heads, all the same, with a crown on top. It was Trimurti (God in the form of the creator, the maintainer and the destroyer). After this experience, it was easier for me to leave Siddhi, for I knew that there was a divine power acting.'

Another remarkable cloud formation, photographed by Brijbala Samii

'I was at Pratishthan, Shri Mataji's house near Pune, India, and showed her some photos I had taken on the India tour of 1989/90. We were on the banks of the Krishna River, and all the Sahaja Yogis were standing there, while the sky was dramatic with both light and dark colours. This was the reason I took it for her to see.

"Look, this is Shri Shiva with his hair in a knot," Shri Mataji said, and showed me the image in the clouds.'

The enlargement, below, shows where the image of Shri Shiva can be seen in the cloud on the left hand side, above the men in white kurtas. Shri Shiva is the aspect of the divine who represents the pure spirit, and is the witness of the entire play of creation. He is often portrayed as an ascetic with his hair tied in a knot on top of his head.

Claire Nesdale relates a magical experience which took place in a village in India.

'We were in Maharashtra, in the middle of the Sahaja Yoga India tour. We were way up on the plateau at a very isolated village. It seemed quite ancient and Shri Mataji had organized that we should have a procession through it. She used to ride on a bullock cart. We waited for about an hour in the broiling sun and were all getting quite hot. Then Shri Mataji came, on a bullock cart, and some musicians. She led us with the musicians through the village to a pendal (tent-like structure). It had a back side – three open sides and a top that covered us so that we weren't in the sun. There was a stage with a backdrop. Shri Mataji sat on it and the musicians played.

She tried to get all the Westerners in out of the sun but only about half of us could get in and she was quite concerned. The sky was totally blue and you could see for miles; there were low mountains in the distance. Shri Mataji looked out from the stage to the centre point of the sky and concentrated very hard on it. There was not a cloud to be seen anywhere, even on the horizon. She concentrated hard and then looked at the musicians and us. A few minutes later she looked back at the sky.

Right in the middle of the sky where she was concentrating a grey cloud was starting to form from nothing, quite thickly, a heavy sort of cloud. It and it grew from the centre outwards. She stopped looking at it and looked back at us. Within about ten minutes it covered the whole sky. It spread out in a circle and we were completely covered in shade and were protected from the hot sun.'

One can never be sure of the weather, especially in England – a story from Grazyna Anslow.

'My husband Pat and I went to work on Shri Mataji's house at Shudy Camps, near Cambridge, England, when it was first bought in 1986. The whole place had to be refurbished including the roof, which had to be completely replaced. The work on the roof was taking a long time but the builders were hoping that the good weather would hold on. We completed the work on the roof by the end of October and the weather was perfect until that day.

"I told everybody that it would not rain until the roof was finished. There were even bets in the village," proclaimed the local postman, who was very friendly with the Sahaja Yogis and who often dropped in for a cup of tea with us, being as Shudy Camps Park House was the end of his round.'

Derek Ferguson was also there.

'While doing the work on the roof of Shudy Camps house, the weather was very good and it did not rain for about six weeks (almost a record in the UK). The postman told us that the village people were very happy and were asking when we were going to do some more outside work so that the weather would again be good.'

Chapter 17

Power over the Elements

Air

'One day some of us went to meet Shri Mataji at Heathrow Airport, London. Shri Mataji was coming from America with Hari Jairam. As we were approaching the airport, we noticed that the sky looked extremely unusual. It was sunset, but not a sunset I have ever seen before. The sky was of so many different colours, with such breathtaking intensity, that we were stunned. The colours kept changing very fast and they were in front of us, behind us and just everywhere. It was a feast to the eye and a masterpiece of artwork.

Hari told us later on that when the plane was circling above the airport, Shri Mataji was playing with the sky.

"Should I add some pink here and some yellow there? What do you think?" Hari said Shri Mataji was moving her hands and the colours were changing all the time.'

Grazyna Anslow

Fire

'Once in Shri Mataji's house in Brompton Square, London, she was walking around and directing people who were helping out. It was a mess to begin with. One always has to make a mess to create a house.

One day Shri Mataji was wearing a highly inflammable synthetic nylon sari, blue and white, and walking around amid the rubble and dust. Some other people had been working in the room too and someone had left a blowtorch burning, pointing into the middle of the room. Shri Mataji walked in towards the blowtorch and did not appear to notice it. As she passed very close to it, the flame leapt right out of nozzle and went completely around Shri Mataji two or three times, at the height of her knees, forming a blue ring of fire a few centimetres away from the sari, then back into the torch.

While all this was happening I was horrified and took a dive across the room to move the torch. I landed in an undignified heap on my stomach in a pile of chalky dust at Shri Mataji's feet, having grabbed the blowtorch in order to point it away from her. When I realised what had happened, I looked up in amazement to find Shri Mataji smiling down at me.

"I am the fire, how could it hurt me?" said Shri Mataji. "The fire is just doing aarti to me."

She calmly went on her way to supervise putting in some pipes in the next room.'

The Editor

The synthetic sari

Another story from Wolfgang Hackl of Vienna

'When I had only been in Sahaja Yoga a few months, I went to work in a summer camp for children. On the afternoon of the last day, there was a festival with a huge fire in the centre of the camp. That evening I was passing the place where the campfire had been and I noticed that nothing was left of this great fire, no smoke, not even the slightest glow, just cold ashes. I sat down on the beach nearby. A colleague approached and sat down and started talking. The conversation quickly turned to Sahaja Yoga and we talked together for about an hour and a half. The only word I knew in French to name the Kundalini awakening was 'illumination' – enlightenment. The very moment I held my hand above her head and I felt the coolness emanating from it, indicating her Kundalini had risen, her face shone suddenly with a strong ruddy light. I turned and saw the fire, previously inert, burning brightly, flames leaping one or two metres in the air. This lasted not even a minute and the flames disappeared without leaving any signs of a fire.

Like me, my colleague was completely stunned.'

Sue Sutcliffe, from South Africa.

'I had been in Sahaja Yoga for about seven months. It was August 1990, another cold, Cape of Good Hope winter and my husband and I had been out for the evening. Upon our late return we noticed the house alarm flashing. As we cautiously opened the front door, we were overwhelmed by plumes of swirling, thick, black smoke.

We had a spare bedroom where I kept a huge photo of Shri Mataji and meditated there regularly. One and a half walls were curtained with heavy lined curtains, highly inflammable. We also dried the washing in front of the asbestos heater, and in error, my husband had left a damp bath towel draped directly over it. A raging fire had started, but then it had mysteriously gone out. Great black webs of soot clung down from the ceiling, the wooden clothes-horse, and its load of wet washing had burnt to a cinder, the carpet had burnt right through, the lampshade had completely melted, but amazingly enough the new curtains, just behind the washing rack, were not burnt.

The whole room and nearly everything in it were covered in black balls of soot and ash and my eyes fell upon Shri Mataji's photo, upon which there was not a speck of soot or ash. As I looked, her whole face changed; she smiled at me; a beautiful, mischievous, knowing smile.

The following morning I called my father, a very practical man who was an insurance assessor specialising in claims for fire and theft, and told him what had happened.

"You had a miracle in that house last night," were his words. "Fires of that magnitude don't just go out. If the occupant is out, they lose the house. I've been in this business for forty years and you had a total miracle."

At the time a yogi was visiting our collective and shortly thereafter was in Shri Mataji's presence. He told her about this and she said something along these lines to him. "Sahaja Yogis must be very careful with fire. This is something I can't always help you all with, especially when they rage totally out of control."'

Water and Light

'In the early 1980's, seven Sahaja Yogis and I went with Shri Mataji to do a public programme in Ratnagiri, Maharashtra some way south of Mumbai. After the programme was finished, we were to catch a ferry back to Mumbai, but it was very late.

I told Shri Mataji there was a Ganesha temple close by, on the sea shore, at

Ganapatipule, so we all packed into cars and went to see it. This temple is at sea level and sometimes the sea enters it at high tide. Shri Mataji entered the temple, where the swayambhu was, to check the vibrations and told us this swayambhu was very powerful. A swayambhu is a stone, or statue, which has come out of the earth and radiates vibrations naturally.

The elephant's head swayambhu on top of the hill

Shri Mataji spoke about the swayambhu and then we went to paddle in the sea, which helps to clear the lower chakras within each of us.

"Now I am going to show you a miracle. Look out over the ocean and tell me - what you see?" said Shri Mataji.

"We see the waves all coming in our direction."

"Now watch. I will change the direction of the waves," said Shri Mataji. She walked towards the south and the waves all went in that direction and followed her. Then she walked north and the waves all went that way. When she stood still, the waves also stood still as if waiting for the next instruction.

"You may be having doubts, and thinking that the wind is doing this, so I will show you again."

She then did everything all over again. After this we went back to Jaigad to wait for the ferry, and by this time the sun had set.

"Now I will show you all another miracle," said Shri Mataji. "The Ganesha

Miracles of Shri Mataji | 115

temple is in that direction," she pointed. "Do you see anything over there?"

"No, we can't see anything," we all said.

Shri Mataji asked us to look again. As we looked, we could see, slowly appearing, a huge cylindrical circle of light, as if thousands of volts were coming out of Mother Earth and going straight up into the heavens.

"There is no other light around here, and that light is coming from the Ganesha temple," said Shri Mataji. "This light will not stop until I tell it to. It is coming from the swayambhu of Shri Ganesha and I am taking it out."

Shri Mataji then asked us if we all had seen this light, and if so she would stop it. When all the Sahaja Yogis had seen it Shri Mataji said she would stop it, and it did stop. It was there for about ten minutes.'

P.D. Chavhan

This story is told by Bogdan Shehovych, an Australian doctor who lived for some time in Russia.

'In the summer of 1991 a few hundred Sahaja Yogis from the city of Togliatti, in Russia, came together for a seminar on the banks of the Volga River. On the Saturday afternoon after our arrival, we all sat for meditation in the open air on the bank of this great river.

The next day we saw in the local newspaper, which regularly reported this information – the Volga being normally extremely polluted – that the concentration of active bacteria in the river flowing through the city had suddenly dropped by an unprecedented thirty percent, and that was since our collective meditation.'

Earth and Water

Stories of the South East Asian tsunami, December 2004

'Over a hundred and fifty Sahaja Yogis lived on the Andaman Islands, near the epicentre of the earthquake. About twelve were at the Christmas celebrations in Pune. On the way home to Madras in the train we were shocked to read about the disaster in the newspaper. Then one yogi said, relaxed and peaceful, "My house is about 300 metres from the seashore. My mother and sister are there." Another said, "I live one kilometre from the beach." Soon the news came: everything and everyone is okay. The rest of us were sure that they would have been wiped out.'

Gudrun Ortner, Chennai (Madras)

Email: Thursday, 6th January, 2005 (shortly after the tsunami)

The Andaman and Nicobar group of islands of India have suffered around

3000 deaths and little over double that number reported missing. The leader of the Andaman and Nicobar Sahaja Yoga group, Mr Manoranjan Saha, is based in the capital, Port Blair. His attention is always towards the Mother Earth or Shri Mataji.

On calling him up yesterday morning he said that all 150 Sahaja Yogis in the group are safe. He informed me that one had a house at the jetty. The waves crossed the jetty's wall but stopped at the wall of this house. You may have seen in photographs of areas along the coast in south-east Asia that all structures along the coast were completely destroyed. This house is not.

On asking him whether he needed any help he seemed very hesitant to ask. Here he was in a land torn apart by tsunamis and in one of the worst affected places of India, being asked how he and the other Sahaja Yogis could be helped. His only regret was that he had wished to donate some land and build an old age home, but the water has now gone over this land. A number of islands have gone under water completely or partly.

More on the miracle – though in Sahaja Yoga it is not a miracle but a known fact of the divine protective powers. The Sahaja Yoga centre in Port Blair is on a hill so not flooded, and had many photos in frames of Shri Mataji. They all fell down because of the earthquake but not a single one was broken! The public address system too is intact. It had cost Mr Saha quite a sum to purchase this for public programmes. They had a couple of televisions and everything is intact. Most other buildings around are destroyed and people are saying that this building remaining, and that too with all its contents intact is a miracle.

I just had a phone call from a Sahaja Yogi in Chennai (Madras) in South India – of course all the Sahaja Yogis there are safe there as well!

A Sahaja Yogi from Pune

Malathi Menon, from Kuala Lumpur, Malaysia also had a tsunami story.

'My family and I were in Penang, an island in Malaysia for a holiday in December 2004. We arrived on the 23rd and stayed in a hotel on the beach road. On Christmas Eve I was walking on the beach and found a group of about eighty schoolchildren who were learning martial arts, staying in a hall on the local Devi temple premises. I approached their teacher, asked whether I could teach them to meditate, he said yes and on Christmas morning they and their teacher all experienced the cool breeze and learned about meditation.

The next morning, at around 9.00 am or so, I was in the hotel room and felt a powerful force slowly spiraling up my spine, then everything in the room started shaking: the glasses on the counter, the lamps and the furniture.

"What is it?" my husband asked.

"It's an earthquake," I replied in a matter of fact way. I had never experienced one before and it was as if someone else was saying it. I was strangely calm and felt very protected. We had a leisurely breakfast and thought there was nothing to be worried about.

We checked out, drove along the beach road at no great speed and exited it. The earthquake we felt caused the tsunami and while we were on this road, the tsunami was heading towards it. It killed fifty-two people in Penang, and some were picnickers by that beach road. The waves washed boats onto the beach road, and cars were washed with mud and sand very soon after we exited it.

My heart tells me that the powerful feeling I felt was Mother Earth herself, communicating through my Kundalini.'

Power over matter is shown in this story of a wooden statue.

'I was very fortunate to be invited to stay with Shri Mataji at her house at 48, Brompton Square, central London, in 1984 and I witnessed many miracles when I was there. At the bottom of the stairs there was a statue of an Indian boy playing the dholak. One day Shri Mataji walked down the stairs and noticed that this sculpture was not formed properly and was anatomically incorrect.

"I need to fix this," she said when she saw it.

I was standing in one place and another man was a little lower, and we were both watching from different angles. What I witnessed was pretty amazing because Shri Mataji started giving it vibrations and I saw the shape of the wood change. It was as if the shadows became more defined, along the scapula at the back; she was giving vibrations and it became like plastic before my eyes.

Suddenly the other person there said, "Yes Mother, I can see! I can see it's changing!" He was pretty excited. When Shri Mataji had finished, the actual form and shape of the sculpture had changed. There was more definition around the back and the muscles at the back were correct.

"That's much better! That looks better, doesn't it?" she said. "Vibrations have the power to transform matter." She explained that through vibrations we can change matter, and that the matter responds to vibrations.'

Alex Henshaw

Something had happened.

'Another miracle concerned a handsome wooden figure of a kneeling African man. This was on the banisters at the bottom of the stairs. My husband

David and I went to the house one afternoon, and the Sahaja Yogis pointed out this figure that had recently arrived and, at Mother's instructions, they had placed it on the newel post at the end of the banisters. It certainly was a fine piece of work, but the rounded back of the man hadn't been carved and was completely flat and smooth.

A few days later we were again called to the house and this time Shri Mataji told us to go and look at the kneeling figure, as something had happened to it. It certainly had! The back was no longer plain and smooth, but you could count all his vertebrae and see his muscles. The yogis told us Mother had raised its Kundalini, and then all the muscles had appeared.'

Patty Prole

Here is a similar story from Hong Kong.

'In November 2003, Shri Mataji spent three days in Hong Kong. The collective rented a suite in the Park Lane Hotel near the Sahaja Yoga centre on Hong Kong Island and we decorated it with vibrational items: Chinese silks, statues and other things of beauty. One of these was a jade statue of Kwan Yin, the Goddess of Mercy, the Chinese incarnation of the Adi Shakti, which I had hesitated to buy because the expression on the face was extremely severe. However, despite the stern frown, the vibrations were so strong from the statue that I bought it anyway. It was a great joy to me that it was placed in Shri Mataji's bedroom, on a shelf at the foot of her bed.

On the day of Mother's arrival, I was ironing my sari ready to go to the hotel. It was about 5.30am. As I bent down to unplug the iron, I looked at my left palm and noticed it was mottled, covered with very red markings in places. Then the spots changed and formed a small face that looked like Shri Buddha. As I was looking, the mouth, which was very serious, a straight line, changed into a really sweet smile.

I forgot all about this incident until I was cleaning and rearranging the altar at home on Friday morning, the day after Shri Mataji's departure. I put the jade statue to the side of her photo and after being in her bedroom, the vibrations were really amazing. I picked it up to have a closer look and I recognised the face! It was the one that I had seen on my hand and I suddenly remembered my experience on Monday morning. I looked at the mouth and it was totally different. Instead of the cross expression there was a sweet smile just like the one that had appeared on my hand. Shri Mataji had changed the mouth to make Kwan Yin smile.'

Madhavi Fordham

Here is another story, this time concerning a liquid, again from 48, Brompton Square, London.

'One day my mum, Magda, had been invited to help at Shri Mataji's Brompton Square house. Shri Mataji was always very hands-on in all aspects of her housing projects. No detail was too small to escape her attention – even down to the quality of the products being used. Shri Mataji handed my mum a small bottle of 'very good varnish' and asked if she could varnish a little wooden bedside cabinet. Magda looked at the bottle and then at the cabinet and thought, there's probably just enough to cover it. When the cabinet was finished Shri Mataji returned, inspecting the work she declared it a job well done.

"Good job! It is really good varnish, isn't it Magda?" she said. Full of enthusiasm, Shri Mataji decided to join in with the varnishing, getting a new brush for herself. "How about we varnish this chest of drawers as well?"

My mum looked at the little bottle, and looked at the big chest of drawers, thinking - we'll definitely need to get some more varnish soon. However, she knew better than to put in her tuppence worth. Alongside my mum, Shri Mataji started painting that lucky piece of furniture, giving it a rich, glossy sheen. Every piece of furniture in the room received the same loving attention from Shri Mataji; and each time one varnishing project was finished she would playfully proclaim, "What wonderful varnish!" And they would both laugh.

Finally, when everything had been painted, Shri Mataji handed back the little bottle to mum who rested it on some newspaper. As she placed the bottle down, a little bit of the dark liquid bubbled out of the top.

"Maybe we praised it a bit too much!" and then said: "You see Magda, whatever you praise, increases," Shri Mataji glanced at the spillage, smiled and commented.'

Danya Martoglio

This is Patti Prole, a retired TV actress, who tells a similar story.

'It was a wonderful time for all of us when Shri Mataji was renovating her house in Brompton Square in Knightsbridge. One day she asked two of us to clean the marble in all the bathrooms. We didn't know what to use.

"Try this," she said, handing us a tin of liquid furniture polish. There wasn't that much in the tin, probably about a quarter full. This was a very pleasant job, and we worked for some hours, finally arriving at the top of the house to finish the last bathroom. It was Sir CP's, Shri Mataji's husband's. She was with us and my friend remarked how amazing it was that we had cleaned all this marble, and yet there was still polish in the tin. Shri Mataji agreed and we all looked at the tin, marvelling that the polish had lasted so long. At that moment, the polish overflowed out of the tin and made a huge stain on the beautiful new pale yellow carpet. We were amazed and shocked.

"Oh, we must have praised the polish so much, it has overflowed," she said. As for the stain, she told us to sprinkle some water on it, gave it a bandhan and told us not to worry about it.

The next day I went to the house and was asked to arrange some things in Sir CP's room. I could not find any evidence at all of any stain whatsoever. The carpet looked just like new, not a single mark on it!'

Chapter 18

Animals, Fish and Vibrations

The following stories show how animals, birds and all nature are part of the universal consciousness, and respond to the vibrations. Humans, especially modern, 'civilized' humans, have often lost that sensitivity, but we can regain it, and go further, because whereas for these living creatures it is a spontaneous unconscious awareness, for us it can become a conscious recognition of what in Sanskrit is called sat chit anand – meaning truth, enlightened attention and inner bliss and joy. These three qualities describe the awareness of the spirit awakened within us, experienced physically as a cool breeze.

Trout

'There is a photo of Shri Mataji with her husband, taken at Loch Rannoch, Scotland, where she was fishing for trout on the bank of the loch, at the end of the garden. She was sitting on a rock and had a fishing rod, and was very amused by this activity. Someone else caught a fish but she did not. What did happen was that about a hundred fish suddenly came to the surface, bobbing up as if they wanted to be caught. They just appeared out of nowhere. These fish started appearing spontaneously and when she left they all vanished again.'

Kevin Anslow

Loch Rannoch, Scotland, 1979

The Crown of Thorns Starfish

'The Cairns Sahaja Yogis told Shri Mataji about the plague of the Crown of Thorns starfish that was occurring in Queensland, Australia, in the early 1990's.'

Claire Nesdale

'Shri Mataji went to the Great Barrier Reef in a jet boat, to Green Island, just off the coast. This is a boat that allows you to see the reef and fish. The reef looked beautiful and a great sea turtle swam close to the boat; she smiled and said he was attracted by the vibrations. The day before we told Shri Mataji how the Crown of Thorns starfish was in disproportionate numbers and was eating the reef away. Later, after Shri Mataji had left, there was an article in the paper saying they just didn't know where all the Crown of Thorns starfish had gone to, but they just disappeared.'

Kay McHugh

Shri Mataji on the beach at Cairns, Queensland,

'We talked to Shri Mataji about the problem of the starfish when we were on the beach and she looked out to sea with a very focused gaze for some time and then changed the subject. Up until this point the Crown of Thorns starfish were completely devastating the reef and scientists had no idea what to do. In the newspaper story, they said it was a mystery where they had gone.'

Sno Bonneau

Corals outgrow starfish damage

This article from the local Cairns paper is about the disappearance of the starfish and the regeneration of the reef. Quote from the article: 'it was a mystery where they went or what made the starfish reach plague proportions.'

'After this Shri Mataji flew to New Zealand. On the way back from there she wanted to watch the news on the internal flight video. The first item was that thousands of Crown of Thorns starfish had been found floating dead off the Great Barrier Reef. The Crown of Thorns starfish had gone back to pre-plague numbers. This happened about twelve days after she had been there and put her attention on it.'

Claire Nesdale

Big Game

'In 1981 Shri Mataji took some of us to a game park near London. As we were driving around the game park, I recall two things. Firstly, we were going past some giraffes, which were not too close, and as we drove past they turned their backs to us. Shri Mataji explained that the animals felt the vibrations as a cool wind and, in the way of animals, turned their backs to shield themselves from the cold. Mother said animals are one with the universal consciousness, whereas unrealised humans are split off from it in their egos and superegos. As realised souls, we should be one with it again.

Mother also said that when she first married, they went to her husband's family palace. The family owned some elephants and, as this was in India, that was not unusual at the time. What was unusual was that when they saw Shri Mataji, they all knelt down out of respect for her.'

Auriol Purdie

Birds

'One night in the early 1980's some of us stayed at Shri Mataji's house at Brompton Square after working there late. I had slept a night in her flat at Ashley Gardens and on both occasions noticed the same thing. Often if one wakes early in London in the summer, before the traffic noise drowns out everything else, one can hear the birds singing. But in all my years in London – over ten in all – I only heard the birds singing all through the night on two occasions, both when I was staying in a house where Shri Mataji was at the time. I asked her about it.

"Yes, they feel the vibrations," she explained. She has often told us to meditate in the early morning, just before the sun gets up, because the vibrations are very strong then. This is the moment when birds generally start to sing. The birds felt her vibrations all through the night, however, and started to sing as they would have normally done at dawn.'

Linda Williams

Dogs: two rabid, one lost, one friendly and one sick

'I met Shri Mataji in Bucharest, when she first visited Romania in October 1990. As she came through the gates of the airport, she had such an incredibly warm and radiant smile! That evening Shri Mataji invited us to the house where she was staying and I joined the twenty or so others in spending an unforgettable couple of hours with her. At that time I couldn't understand what was being discussed, but felt tremendous vibrations in my hands, as if a thick blanket of vibrations manifested, floating just above the floor.

My closest friend and I left in a state of total bliss and walked on the street very late that night. I told him that I felt so high that I could walk through fire without hesitation. At that moment a test of this appeared in the form of two rabid dogs that started to bark at us and eventually attacked us. We continued to walk in silence, our attention in the Sahasrara, and I felt shudders go up my spine as I saw one of the dogs jumping at me, but it was unable to reach me. It was really amazing to see the dog leap and then fall down as if there was an invisible wall between us, and he was never able to touch me.'

Calin Costian

This is one of the most bizarre stories in the entire book, from Mitesh Gandhi, an optometrist.

'I lived in the suburban town of Greenford in London and there were only two people who practiced Sahaja Yoga there. This is how my story begins. A local lady had been walking her dog early that morning in the park, but on this particular day, the dog suddenly went AWOL and ran off. After searching frantically for the dog, she gave up and went back home.

Later, I had woken up and was getting ready for work. Through my bathroom window, I noticed a dog panting and clutching a ball in its jaw, sitting at the end of my garden. I had never seen this dog before and certainly didn't recognise it as being from our neighourhood. Soon it was time for me to leave for work, but the dog was still there, nicely settled, so I approached it and noted down the telephone number on its collar. I quickly rang the number.

"Excuse me, have you lost a dog? It's been here for a while now. We have one in our garden with your phone number on its collar," I said.

"Oh yes, Mitesh, I'll come and get it now. It's my mother's dog and she's so worried."

I was stunned, because I thought I was phoning a stranger. He hung up and I just stood there in bewilderment. There was something really weird going on, because how did this stranger know my name, and seem to know me?

Soon a car drew up and it was Steve, the only other Sahaja Yogi in Greenford. Steve's mother was not involved in Sahaja Yoga, but Steve lived with her. After running away from the park, the dog must have felt similar vibrations coming from our house, and recognised it as being familiar. Otherwise, why did it choose our garden out of all the other thousands of houses in Greenford? It did not know me and had never been to our house.

I went to work that day wondering about the subtlety of vibrations and how animals are amazingly sensitive to vibrations and positive energy.'

Mitesh Gandhi

Editor's note: Steve later explained that Mitesh's house was difficult to find, even for a human who knew where it was. The front door was down an alley and had a gate into the garden.

Joanne Moore is from the UK.

'In the spring of 1985 Shri Mataji came and spent a weekend with us in Birmingham. We met her at the train station on the Friday and she was going to spend the afternoon at a Sahaja Yogi's house before going to the public meeting. When we got to the house the yogini was worried about the dog being a nuisance and had put her upstairs.

"I like dogs," Shri Mataji said simply.

After we had eaten lunch, one of the Sahaja Yogis travelling with Shri Mataji asked the lady who owned the house to let the dog down as Shri Mataji wanted to see it. We were all sitting in the living room in a big circle, Shri Mataji in one of the armchairs, some of us on the floor, others sitting on the settee. The dog came in and did a whole circuit of the room, ignoring everyone, including its own family members until she reached Shri Mataji's chair, where she sat down and put her head in Shri Mataji's lap.'

'A couple of years ago my dog, a large Rottweiler, was experiencing a strange and crippling internal pain. We didn't expect her to survive. She could barely walk, and would often collapse in on herself with a yelp of pain. The vet had a look, and said it was definitely internal, possibly bleeding, but couldn't tell without tests. Vets are very expensive, so my husband said no, it's a dog.

As a last desperate measure, I put seven lemons and seven chillies, a 'matka', beside our dog's bed in our closet at night. The next day she woke up cured, completely. She was walking like her young spry self again.'

Shannon Shapovalov

Editor's note: instructions for using the matka are in the Appendix.

Chapter 19

Responsive Plants

The story of the totally dead flowers
'In May 1987 Shri Mataji visited Australia. For the Sahaja Yogis, the height of her visit was a weekend programme in the Snowy Mountains, in the town of Thredbo. Everyone had gone to a great deal of trouble to have a flower to give to Shri Mataji when she arrived on Saturday night. This was not easily done, as florists are few and far between in the Snowy Mountains, but we'd all managed somehow. We had our flowers ready, but Shri Mataji went straight to her room without taking them. When she came out she went directly to the meeting hall and spoke to us for quite some time. Then we had a musical programme, after which she spoke to us again. By this time, most of us had been holding our flowers for three or four hours.

"I see you have some flowers for me. Would you like to give them to me now?" Shri Mataji very sweetly said, as was leaving.

So, torn between the horror of offering these dead flowers and the longing to give something to Shri Mataji, we gave the dead blooms even though they were hanging down and completely finished. They were completely dead, not just slightly dead, but utterly dead. Shri Mataji went back to her room and after a while asked for the box of flowers to be brought in.

"Bring them into the bathroom," she said. "We're going to have a miracle. You'll see. Fill the bath with very warm water just as if I were going to have a bath." As the water was running, Shri Mataji put her hand into the bath, vibrating the whole thing. "Now put all the flowers into the bath," she said. "Make sure all the stems are down in the water." When all the flowers were in the bath, she said: "See, they're already looking better." And they were. "You wait and see in the morning. We'll use these flowers for the puja." Next morning all the flowers were fresh and blooming.'

Matthew Fogarty

Jeremy Lamaison tells a story of a lemon.
'When we were in Rome some years ago, Shri Mataji called us to the leader's house. She called for a lemon because she wanted to work on one of the people there. There was only one lemon there. Shri Mataji explained that when you work on somebody you really need a fresh lemon. She took a lemon which was dark and had lost its shine and was wrinkled. She carried on talking

to us and was massaging this lemon the whole time. After about two minutes she took the lemon, and it was literally shining. It was bright yellow, as if it had just been plucked from the tree. I've never seen such a bright shiny lemon.

"This is how the lemon should be!" Shri Mataji said.'

Editor's note; a lemon can be used to absorb negativity. The editor has personally seen people who were suffering from incontrollable shaking, or who were crying out involuntarily, relieved almost instantly with this treatment. See Appendix for details. Please note it may not always work and should not be used instead of normal medication.

This story is told by Ursula Doring from California.

'I am a flight attendant and was working on the aircraft, preparing to leave on a seven day trip from the USA, in 1988, when my husband came to the plane to present me with my favourite flower, a beautiful peony. He had driven for over an hour to surprise me. The crew noticed the sweet gesture, but by the end of the first long flight, to Tokyo, without water and with the dryness of the cabin, the peony was completely wilted. Once in the hotel room, I placed it in vibrated water and kept it next to my picture of Shri Mataji. I honestly felt the flower was a lost cause, but was too tired to be overly concerned.

The next morning, as I opened my eyes, I couldn't believe it. Although I had seen the miracle of the flowers at Thredbo on Sahasrara Day in Australia, the year before, when Shri Mataji vibrated extremely wilted and dying ones so they became beautiful enough for puja, here was my own personal demonstration. It was absolutely beautiful and its fragrance filled the room. When it came time to leave Japan for Manila, I carefully tied the cellophane and ribbon back on and reported for my flight. The crew actually came rushing up to comment that it couldn't be the same flower. They were amazed and wanted to know more. This went on for days, in and out of water, flying to and from Manila twice, the same flower, each day still full fragrant and beautiful and the crew more and more interested in Shri Mataji and Sahaja Yoga. Even I was amazed it could last so long.

On the seventh day, our flight home, again I came down through the hotel lobby with my flower in my hand. It was finally showing some wear. Just as I walked out of the hotel to get onto the bus, all the petals fell off, right in the garden entrance. It seemed a most fitting end and in its final moments, it spontaneously blessed and vibrated the Japanese countryside.'

Anyone who is a gardener knows it is quite difficult to get cuttings to take root at the best of times, and few people would try to grow rose bushes from a bunch of formerly half dead rose stalks.

'In the early 1980's we had a programme at the Temple of All Faiths, Hampstead, and afterwards a lot of flowers came back to Shri Mataji's house at Brompton Square. I filled up a couple of bathtubs with them but there were quite a few bunches of roses that had drooped over and were dead.

"Give me some of those roses," Shri Mataji said. She took some of the roses and put the stems on the palm of her hand. "We can bring these back to life with vibrations," and she showed me how to do it.

There was no immediate change in the roses, but I put them into the water and the next day they were upright and blooming. When they had finished flowering she told us to take some cuttings so we got some pots and soil, and then Shri Mataji put the stalks into the pots.

"Because we have given them vibrations, these roses will turn into rose bushes." So every single cutting that Shri Mataji put in took root. She showed me how to put vibrated water there, and they turned into beautiful bushes with blooms of all different colours.'

Alex Henshaw

The gallant sunflower that defied the English winter

'One year, 1981, Shri Mataji stayed in London for Christmas. In the summer we had planted a sunflower outside the kitchen window at Chelsham Road and, as the months went by, it got taller and taller, like Jack's beanstalk in the fairy tale, but did not form a flower. It got even stranger, because sunflowers are frost-tender and are usually dead by October or November and this was before the climate change started and it didn't die. By mid-December it still wasn't dead and started forming a flower head - again, quite extraordinary in the dark, cold depths of the English winter.

On Christmas morning it blossomed, even though it was snowing, and had been snowing since the previous evening. We picked it and put it on the top of the Christmas tree in the room where Shri Mataji came for our Christmas celebration - one moment of glory for a gallant sunflower. Shri Mataji had often passed the flower when it had been growing, as in those days she would come to our house at 44, Chelsham Road, in South London, once a week or so.'

Auriol Purdie

Guillemette Metouri's story, from France, might be of interest to farmers everywhere.

'In May 1983, my father had just met Shri Mataji for the first time, in Paris. He was a simple countryman, a very deep and loving soul. That year, Shri Mataji invited all the new French Sahaja Yogis from different parts of the country, about thirty, to come and meet her in her room. She addressed a nice word to each individual.

"I would recommend," Shri Mataji said, "each of you to take some vibrated water from the puja we had together and sprinkle it in your houses and everywhere around, where you feel there is some negativity. It will clear things out."

My father went back to Brittany with a tiny bottle of vibrated water. The following morning, he decided to give a special treatment to the field he had planted with potatoes. A common disease called mildew had developed amongst the plants, by which the leaves were turning yellow. If nothing was done, the crops were at risk. That morning was foggy and we couldn't see two metres ahead of us. Following Shri Mataji's advice, my father added some vibrated water to the product he prepared to sprinkle around the field. At about two or three in the afternoon, the sun came out and the fog disappeared. My father came running to me.

"Come quickly, this is extraordinary! Come and see! This is Shri Mataji for sure!" I rushed to the field and discovered the leaves of the potatoes had turned green again (normally it would take a few days before they could get back to their original colour). Most incredible of all, they had grown by four to five centimetres within a few hours! Our neighbour, a rather gross farmer, was shouting in a strong Breton dialect.

"How come? I don't understand! This morning your potatoes were yellow and now they're green! On top of that, they've grown!"

Added to this, a couple of months later all the village farmers were intensely busy discussing the amazing size of our potatoes compared to theirs.'

Dr. Hamid Mehrani-Mylany, from Iran and now settled in Vienna, is a specialist in agriculture and forestry. At the beginning of 1985 a project was undertaken near Zwiesel, Germany, to monitor the effect of vibrations on spruce forests dying from acid rain.

He used vibrated water on trees damaged by acid rain and his research showed that the vibrated water helped the trees considerably. Before the project began all spruce trees in the forest were deteriorating at a uniform rate. The improvement began from the tops of all the spruce trees and most of them also improved in the crowns after treatment with vibrations. The 'control' trees, which did not have vibrated water, generally did not fare as well; the greater the percentage, the poorer the health of the trees, on the graph below.

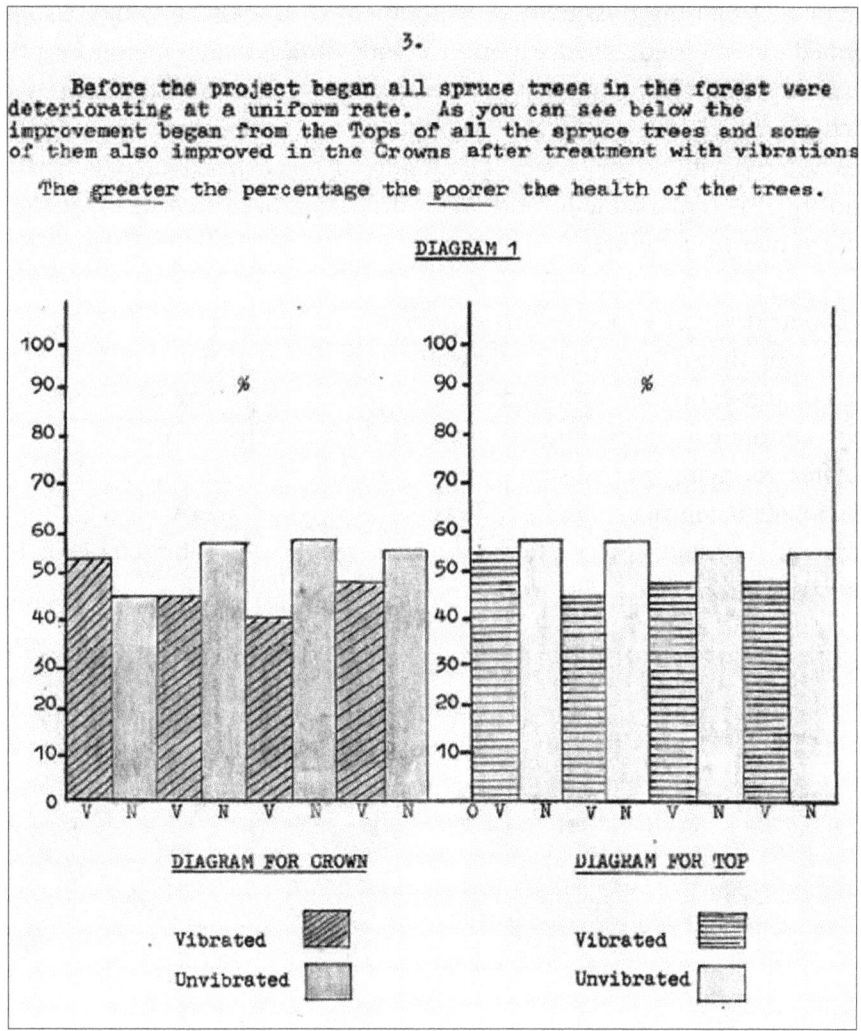

Here is an extract from a talk he gave on other work he did with vibrated water.

After getting my self realisation in 1982, I met Shri Mataji and was astounded at her knowledge of every subject. She told me that the all-pervading power has created everything, that it nourishes everything, generates everything and controls everything efficiently. It organizes, it thinks and above all it loves.

She taught me how to use vibrations. I tried to establish divine vibrations, which is the all-pervading power, (and make them) visible through an experiment. At this time I was working in an International Plant Breeding Company. I had the possibility to experiment with a lot of things, also with vibrated water. I tried a small experiment with vibrated water on tomato plants. It was surprising to find out that the tomatoes watered with vibrated water were much bigger, a better colour and even the taste was excellent compared to the ones watered with normal water. The results of this experiment developed my curiosity. It is remarkable to note that Shri Mataji has given vibrated tomato seeds to many people free.

The next time I expanded my experiment to an aeroponic system. In this system one doesn't use soil - only water with different nutrients added. The result of this experiment showed the same pattern of growth which persuaded me to continue my great interest in vibrated water experiments.

After receiving permission from Shri Mataji, I decided to do a field experiment using maize and sunflowers. I sowed an area with 6 repeats of maize and 6 of sunflowers and did the same for the non-vibrated block. Each area was approximately 2 sq. meters.

Sunflowers

The plants that were given vibrated water are on the left side of the green cards, the ones given non-vibrated water are on the right.

I sowed the field on 27th May, which was much later than the farmers in this area. I didn't have a lot of time to irrigate daily so I made up an automatic irrigation system. This had several advantages in that it was independent from me, if the field was watered by someone they could give more water to vibrated crops. So as it was run by computer the crops received water at exactly the same intervals.

The automatic watering system

The results of this experiment were that the vibrated field produced much greener plants and were about 1 ft. higher. Sunflowers grown with vibrated water on left, with nonvibrated water on the right. The average weight of the plants was 25% heavier.

With the sunflowers we measured the diameter of the flower to be 2 inches more than the non-vibrated. The vibrated plants are shown in the left hand photos.

The maize cobs from the plants watered with vibrated water are in a heap on the left, those from the plants using nonvibrated water on the right.

Shri Mataji experimented with sunflowers at her farmhouse during research work in Pune and produced sunflowers tremendously big, more than twelve inches in diameter, very heavy and gave on the average 250 mm. of oil. This was reported in the newspaper.

Shri Mataji with the outsize sunflowers grown at her house at Pune, India

Chapter 20

Chance Meetings

This is the classic story of a chance meeting in Sahaja Yoga. Such encounters show the sychronicity of our lives, the ways in which we are connected. In this case Guillemette Metouri of France and Ruth Eleanore, living in Rome at the time of this story, met in an extraordinary way in Sicily.

Guillemette: I am French, and in 1981 I went to Sicily, where I had previously lived, and gave my friend Mariella self realisation. At that time there were no Sahaja Yogis in Sicily and only two that I knew of in Rome. Unfortunately not many people seemed interested in Sahaja Yoga in Sicily. On the 15th of August, I was invited to a friend's house for the Catholic feast of the Assumption of the Holy Virgin Mary into the heavens. After lunch I went alone outside to the back of the house, where the white peaks of the mountains stood above the wooded hills.

"What's happening? They don't take me seriously. I cannot do anything on my own!" I burst out.

A week later we went for a meal in another village called Castellana where our host had come on holiday from Rome.

Ruth: I had had my realisation two weeks earlier and went to Sicily with some Italian friends. We stayed in a little village in the mountains. After some time the family decided to invite some guests and I was introduced to one who was French, because I am French speaking.

"Are you French?" the lady asked.

"No," I replied.

"So, you're on holiday in Sicily?"

"Yes, I live in Italy because I work in Rome." I told her what my line of work was.

Guillemette: "Really? I know someone who is also in that field there. His name is Gregoire," I replied.

"Of course I know him!" said Ruth. "But how do you know him?"

"Well – in fact, we practise the same yoga."

"You mean Shri Mataji's yoga?" enquired Ruth with a large smile.

Ruth: "Well, then you are doing Sahaja Yoga," I said, and three minutes after we had met we fell in each other's arms. We could not believe that we were both doing Sahaja Yoga. She told me the other lady with her was Adriana, who was also practising Sahaja Yoga.

Guillemette: Our friends were flabbergasted!

"How did you decide to come to Sicily?" I asked.

"That's strange, too," Ruth said. "I was going to go on safari in Africa, but then, without knowing why, I decided to come to Sicily."

"When did you take your decision?" I asked.

"Just after the 15th of August."

Another bomb exploded in my heart! Seeing this, our friends thought it might be worth trying Sahaja Yoga. The following day about ten of them got self realisation.

This is Patrick Redican, from Canada, now living in India.

'In 1982 I came to India for the first time, a little before the other Sahaja Yogis. One day the plane carrying some others was supposed to be coming in from Canada, my country. I went to meet the plane and it turned out it was going to be delayed by more than twelve hours, so I came back into town from Mumbai Airport on the bus and got down at the wrong stop.

I had very little idea where I was in this vast city of many millions of people and didn't know Mumbai at all. Then I realised I was round the area of the Jaslok Hospital and remembered that Shri Mataji's mailing address in Mumbai was somewhere in the large area of the Jaslok Hospital. I went into the reception area of the hospital, where completely by chance I met Shri Mataji, and she took me home to where she was staying.'

Nirmala Verma set off into rural India knowing she would meet up with Shri Mataji.

'Shri Mataji told me to visit Rahuri, a small place in Maharashtra, when she was there. Once when I was visiting Mumbai I told my brother that I wanted to go to Rahuri.

"Where is Rahuri?" he asked.

"I don't know. I'll just go the State Transport Bus Station and get on a bus for Rahuri," I replied.

In the bus I made the conductor's life miserable by asking him how far it was, every five minutes. He got fed up and said he would let me know when we reached there. We arrived at midnight, having left Mumbai in the morning at 8.00 am. My daughter was with me. The conductor said there were three bus stops in Rahuri: the Sugar Mill, the Patil's House and the University, and where would we like to debus?

Something guided me from within and I told him, 'Patil's House'.

As we got down from the bus I smelled a very strong fragrance of roses. The conductor was also very nice to us. He put us in a tonga (horse cab) and told the driver to take us to the Patil's House. As we reached it, Raol Bai (Shri Mataji's helper) also arrived there in a jeep. She told us that Shri Mataji had asked her to go to the bus stop as the guests from Delhi had arrived there. I asked Raol Bai how Shri Mataji knew we had arrived and how to find us, when I myself did not know where we were.

"She knows everything," she said simply.'

A chance meeting in Germany, as remembered by Mara-Madhuri Corazzari

'This story is from 1987, when Shri Mataji was staying with us in Munich. I opened the door to a man who had been knocking. He said he was a journalist and had long wanted to interview Shri Mataji but had never been able to arrange it. I asked him how he had managed it. He told me that in the morning he had been in the Marienplatz, the Square of Mary and, although the day was very hot, because it was the middle of August, he suddenly felt very cool. He turned round and there was Shri Mataji in front of him, and he immediately recognized her. There were a few people with her because she was shopping. He was so surprised, and went up and asked if he could interview her.

"Of course," she said, and gave him the address to come to. He was writing a book about the Virgin Mary, the mother of Lord Jesus and recognized the qualities of Mary in Shri Mataji.

Shri Mataji came downstairs and was happy to see him. The interview was beautiful and was for the magazine he was working for. Shri Mataji spoke to him as if she had known him for a long time. He had a problem on his leg and all the time he was interviewing Shri Mataji, about two hours, she gave vibrations to his left knee and helped it.'

Christine Sweet had a great desire to be close to Shri Mataji.

'We were in Milan, north Italy, in 1988. Shri Mataji had been doing some programmes there and we were supposed to go further north to the next one, in Switzerland. My car broke down and I had to take the offer of a friend to go in her car. She had to go via Arezzo, which is way down south of Milan, in central Italy at a distance of over four hundred kilometres. She wanted to visit someone there, but promised we would be in Switzerland in time for Shri Mataji's next programme. During the drive down to Tuscany, in central Italy, I suddenly developed a very strong desire to be with Shri Mataji. I couldn't see why I had to go down to Tuscany, if Shri Mataji was going north, to Switzerland.

At Arezzo we got out and sat down in a coffee shop and to our amazement, suddenly a car drove past with Shri Mataji and her family in it. We walked towards the car and found Shri Mataji at a square called the Square of Mary.

"What are you doing here?" she said, and we didn't know what to say because Arezzo is a long way south of Milan.

"You come shopping with us," she said.

Shri Mataji went to a popular shop which dealt in semi-precious stones, and white horses carved out of stone and that sort of thing. She was buying things, ordering things and so on. It was all very quiet and Shri Mataji was sitting in a chair with a Coca-Cola. When Shri Mataji stood up to go out of the shop, four and a half hours had passed. Then Shri Mataji spoke to Helga, the driver of our car.

"What did you buy?" she asked. Helga said she had bought an egg of semi-precious stone. Shri Mataji said the egg was very auspicious, then walked towards me and took both my hands in her hands and pressed them.

"This is the desire," she said, meaning that we had found her because our desire was that. We had been wondering how this could have happened. When Shri Mataji pressed my hands, something so beautiful happened. I felt overwhelmed with joy for hours afterwards. I don't know how to describe it.'

Whether in Italy or South Africa, the editor found the people she needed to, quite easily.

'In 1989 I was going to live in South Africa with my eight year old son, and broke my flight from London in Italy to go to a collective Sahaja programme with Shri Mataji at Sorrento, near Naples. After this there was a public programme in Naples. My luggage was put on a truck and left for Rome but my son and I somehow got left behind, alone, at Sorrento. I hoped I would be able to find the public programme, because it had been well advertised, but was a little concerned, as I had become parted from my luggage, had a child with me, did not know the address of our ultimate destination near Rome and had a plane to catch to Johannesburg the next day.

I had heard things about Pompeii, the city buried by the eruption of Vesuvius in AD 79, which did not attract me to it, but the railway line to Naples went past there, and something prompted me to get off the train and go and look at it. We reached the ruins, bought tickets and started walking through the many streets, not having any plan. It is a large area, but after a few minutes who should we meet but Shri Mataji and the Sahaja Yogi group. I had no idea they would even be there. We joined them, and then all had lunch together, after which I was given a lift to Naples and later Rome.'

I duly went on to Cape Town and some months later drove to Pietermaritzburg in Natal, well over a thousand miles away, to meet the other Sahaja Yogis in South Africa. I drove alone, stopped for a nap now and again, and reached Pietermaritzburg in the early morning, at about seven o'clock, having been driving on and off for over twenty-four hours. I had never been there before and with the help of a map reached the right suburb, but did not know how to find the house, although I had the address of Dr Siva Govender, who was to be my host. I stopped at the beginning of the suburb and saw a car driving towards me along the totally empty road, stopped my car and waved at the oncoming one to stop. He did so, and I asked if he could direct me to Munireddy Road.

"Oh, you must be Linda. I'm Siva, and our house is ... (he gave me directions). I'm going to work now but I'll see you later. The family are expecting you."'

Vera Pinheiro of Brazil tells of a prayer, a messenger and an unexpected gift.

'I met Shri Mataji in 1989. Soon after that, my father died and I passed through a bad period. One night I started to cry and sat in front of Shri Mataji's photo and asked, "Please, Mother, I'm suffering and I need to know that you are with me. Please, I need an answer, something real that I can touch."

At 8 am I heard the phone ringing, answered it and heard a voice I didn't recognize. The lady on the phone said she had something for me from India. At 2 pm we met at the main hall of the Cidade da Paz, where I worked, some distance from Brasília.

"Vera, Shri Mataji sent you this sari," she told me, handing a beautiful red sari. I started to cry with joy. "I am on my way back from India," she explained. "I arrived at six o'clock at Rio de Janeiro airport. I had to take the connecting flight to my home town, and heard that the flight would stop in Brasília, so decided to stay some days here."

What a coincidence! I was so glad that I forgot all my troubles.'

Chapter 21

A Perfect Sense of Direction

It is said that in the future, humans will be more interested in inner, spiritual knowledge than the outer manifestation of physical cause and effect. Anyone who has got this far with this book is already going in that direction, and may be asking themselves, "Is there some logic, some pattern, behind the fact that the people mentioned in the last chapter found each other?" In this chapter are some stories of how Shri Mataji navigates her way around towns she has never visited before. Perhaps the answers to this and the above question are hinted at in these quotations.

'The first centre (the Mooladhara) is very important. It is of innocence, which gives you the magnetic powers in the sense not only that you are attracted, but you attract people. But magnetic means that you know whether you are moving to the north or to the south. Birds have this power in them.... that's how they fly from one place to another because they can feel the magnet within and the person who is pure at that point, he never gets lost because he knows which side is moving. I have never had a problem like that, I move either to the left or to the right or forward and my husband who is dealing with shipping says 'I have never met a better navigator than my wife' and it's so spontaneous. I don't have to think. I know for definite that you are moving in the wrong direction or in the right direction ... they have got all the maps and everything and immediately I know that you are going to the wrong direction, because the magnet immediately turns round, so the magnet is placed within you there but it's to be awakened.'

Shri Mataji Nirmala Devi, Public Programme, Houston, Texas 1981

'The power of Shri Ganesha's greatness is auspiciousness. It's a formula we can say, in scientific language, that emits auspiciousness. It's a magnet in the Mother Earth. The same magnet is within you, which is Shri Ganesha. You leave me alone and I can tell you which is the north, south, east, west. Close my eyes, still I'll tell you.

You know there are so many birds who fly out all the way to Australia, to Siberia because they have that magnet with them. They have that innocence with them. There are so many fish, which have got an actual magnet placed in them.'

Shri Mataji Nirmala Devi, The Ganesha Principle, San Diego, USA, 1986

Here are some examples of Shri Mataji finding her way round the cities of the world. This is by Marie-Laure Cernay.

'Let me tell you a story which shows the power of Shri Mataji. For example in 1982, at the first public programme in Spain. At that time I lived in England and we were a little group who came to Madrid to prepare and organise that programme.

The Indian ambassador organised a reception for Shri Mataji in his home, before the public programme. There were no Sahaja Yogis in Madrid then, so we had to drive Shri Mataji and I found myself driving her car. My sister-in-law Marie-Amelia had just come from Portugal with Shri Mataji. My sister-in-law and I decided to drive to the ambassador's house the afternoon before, because we had never driven in Madrid before, but when we went in the evening, with Shri Mataji, we got completely lost. We were talking in French and wondering where to go, and didn't dare to say anything to Shri Mataji.

"Keep right – turn left – go straight," Shri Mataji suddenly said, and she directed us perfectly to the house of the ambassador. It was absolutely amazing, because she had never been to Madrid and had never been to that house before.'

'We were in Dorset, and got in the car to take Shri Mataji to catch the train to Bristol, from Yeovil, England, in the early 1980's. I had come to give directions as I knew the area, but halfway there I could not remember how to get to the railway station. Soon I relaxed as I realised that Shri Mataji would know the way, even though she had never been there before. After a bit, when it was clear that I could not give any directions at all Shri Mataji spoke up in a decisive manner.

"We'll try and go this way," she said, and directed us in a very matter of fact manner through this town, previously unknown to her. We ended up at the station fine and although we were expecting to be a bit late, the train hadn't even come in. So there was plenty of time to stand on the station and talk with her.'

Felicity Payment

Trupta de Graaf, originally from Paris, tells a similar story.
'In 1987 Shri Mataji came to Paris and gave a programme in the centre of the city. Before she arrived we had carefully studied the way we would drive her through the city, so as to go the fastest way possible to the programme

hall. On the evening of the programme I was in the car beside Shri Mataji and a Sahaja Yogi who lives in Paris was driving. At one moment, just before we  were going to cross the River Seine, Shri Mataji told us to go right, while we had planned to go left as it was the shortest way. Unfortunately we both answered Shri Mataji that the way was left, and we went left. However, after a few hundred metres some traffic problems appeared, and we got stuck for a long time.

"You see, I told you to go right," Shri Mataji said.

Because of this we arrived late at the programme. All the seekers were waiting for Shri Mataji, as the introduction had already been done.'

'We were in Salvador, Brazil, in 1989 and went to the Raul Chaves Auditorium in the university. The room was completely full and there were also people standing. I gave a long introduction while waiting for Shri Mataji to arrive. The person who was driving Shri Mataji's car lost sight of the car in front of him that was supposed to be showing the right way. After a bit of a drive around, Shri Mataji herself directed the driver of her car to the hall where the programme was being held, even though it was a town of three million people and she had never been there before.

· The public meanwhile were waiting patiently, and with interest. Shri Mataji entered from the rear door and walked up the central aisle to the stage between the rows of seated people. A Sahaja Yogini who was there for the first time said that the moment Shri Mataji entered the hall, in spite of the great heat there, she felt a fresh cool energy coming from behind, to the point that it made her turn round.'

Duilio Cartocci

'The first year Shri Mataji visited Thailand, in 1990, at the time of her 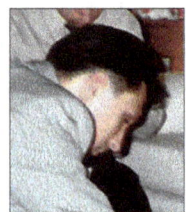 departure, I left early for the airport with her luggage and passport to arrange for her check-in. I got onto the highway, which was the fastest way to reach our destination, but experienced heavy congestion due to a traffic accident. To my utmost surprise, when I reached the airport, Shri Mataji had reached there almost twenty minutes before, although she had left the house much later than we did.

As soon as Shri Mataji left the house, she asked in which direction the airport was. She was told that it was towards the left but that they needed to turn right first to get onto the express way. Shri Mataji told them not to worry and that she would guide them via another route. She indeed guided them and they reached the airport much faster than they ever thought they could. This new road was completely unknown to the people who lived in Bangkok, but Shri Mataji somehow knew about it.'

Prakash Sreshthaputra

Editor's note: Shri Mataji was not familiar with the city of Bangkok.

Chapter 22

Things Just Work Out

'Now all the miracles you have described I have seen; I mean there are so many still to be recorded. It's just a play of this power which thinks, understands, and cooperates. It coordinates and loves and looks after you, and is at your disposal. Wherever you go the connection is maintained. It's like a governor travelling - you see the security travels with him. So they are all around, not only with me but with you also. You are already booked there. And they know you are the one they have to look after.'
Shri Mataji Nirmala Devi

A story from Liselotte Wiehart and her husband Herbert
'In 1983 we wanted to go to Nepal. We asked Shri Mataji for her advice and she gave our project her blessings, remarking that we absolutely should not worry about money.

After some time in Kathmandu, some money which was supposed to be coming from Europe had not arrived and we were running out. One day we had only five rupees left, but we trusted in Shri Mataji's words. Two days later, a Nepali gentleman knocked at our door. He had heard that we cooked very well and asked us to run the newly-built restaurant in his hotel. We were delighted, but told him that we had no money at all and would be unable to advance three months' rent, as would be normal. He was silent for a little while.

"I want a foreigner to run my restaurant. Whatever you need, I will lend you," he said.

Two weeks later we started the restaurant and from the first day it was full. After some time the high season was about to begin, at the end of the month of Ramadan. The Muslim butchers who supplied our meat were all celebrating and not working, so we had no meat. About the same time our deep freeze broke and we could only stock about sixty kilos of meat in our fridge.

My husband started using the meat we had and after a week we had already consumed seventy-five kilos, but the fridge was as full as ever. The second week, the Muslim's celebrations were still in full swing and again there was no meat delivery. We kept taking more and more meat out and still the amount in the fridge did not diminish. In the third week, the plane which flew up from Calcutta with the meat broke down, so again we had no delivery.

"I feel a bit strange, taking more and more of the meat and still there is plenty left in the fridge," said Herbert.

"Shri Mataji is doing this for us," I said, laughing.

After that the normal supply resumed and the fridge emptied in the normal way. When we calculated how much meat we had used in those three weeks, we had taken two hundred and eighty five kilos from the fridge, whereas we knew for sure that it contained only sixty.'

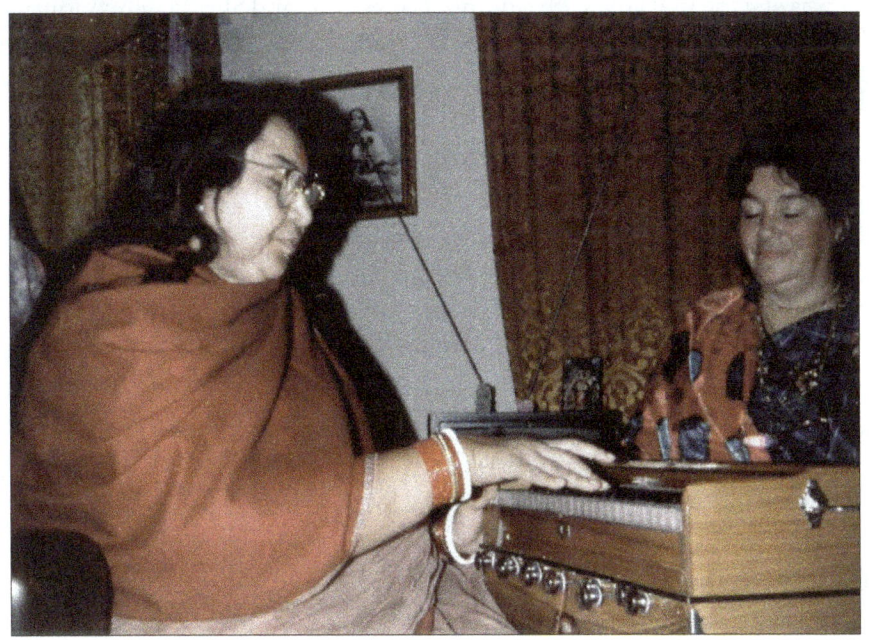

Shri Mataji visiting Liselotte in Nepal

Andrea Cousins of New York was a hard working young mother at this time.

'When I was a journalism student I found it quite difficult to complete my homework assignments, with my six month old child. Our professor asked us to attend a court session and report on the details of the proceedings. If that proved impossible, the alternative was to read a police blotter, which details daily police activity and reports on a crime. I could not go to the court, but rushed off, child in arms, to the local police station for a look at the blotter.

"I'm sorry, you can't read that. It's not for the public," the officer told me, and I left disappointed. The assignment was due in the following day, so I put the matter in bandhan and picked my husband up from work. As I put my young daughter in her car seat, I inattentively placed my wallet on the car's roof. I got in the car and drove off and only when I arrived home did I realise my wallet was missing. The phone was ringing as I opened the door.

"Are you missing something?" the voice asked. Within minutes, the wallet was returned and, as I chatted with the day's hero, learned he was an off duty policeman. He shared his police book with me and before long I got an 'A' for my homework paper.'

A magical cup of tea

'I was staying in Rome with a number of people and Shri Mataji. A journalist came to see her and I was at the back of the room trying to keep my lively son quiet. Shri Mataji however called me to the front as the journalist wanted to talk about the damage inflicted by false gurus, something I had suffered badly from. I was a bit worried as the journalist didn't speak much English, and I had to try in my very rusty Italian. I had learnt some when doing an Art History degree but had not spoken it much for fifteen years and I am not very good at languages.

I sat at Shri Mataji's feet and she gave me a cup of tea, I was very grateful and it settled me. I looked at her pleadingly, wondering how to ask for an interpreter, but she encouraged me to try in Italian, and it was amazing, after that cup of tea the Italian just flowed out. I even went down to Rome with the journalist in a Sahaja Yogi's car that afternoon, and continued to talk effortlessly and at length with him on a number of aspects of Sahaja Yoga. He complimented me on my near perfect Italian. I used words I did not even know I knew, thanks to that magic cup of tea!'

Linda Williams

The param chaitanya – the all-pervading power, sometimes plays little jokes.

'I have had about thirty Premium Bonds for fifty years now, from when they first came out in the 1950's to today, 2012. These are a kind of government lottery and statistically one can expect to win something now and again. However, in all that time I have only once won a prize, of the then minimum fifty pounds.

I had been living in India for six years and returned to London to my home, which had been rented out while I was away. After a couple of weeks I discovered there was to be a puja, or Sahaj programme, to the Hamsa Chakra, which is between the eyebrows and governs our sense of discrimination. I knew mine was not good and really wanted to go, as it might have helped, but did not have the money for a flight, as it was in Germany. The time drew closer and it did not seem possible to go, and one morning a letter came through the door with 'On Her Majesty's Service' written on it. These buff envelopes are what tax demands come in and I couldn't bring myself to open it. "Oh no, the Inland Revenue has caught up with me already, and I've only been back here a few weeks," I thought.

Eventually someone else living in the house persuaded me to open it on about the last day I could make a plan to go to Germany for the weekend. It was a cheque from the Premium Bond Department and was just enough to get me to the puja. My discrimination was so bad, I nearly didn't make it, despite the windfall. It got better after that programme in Germany.'

Linda Williams

Pamela Lewis, from Brisbane, Australia also had a windfall.

'Several months after our move to a new town, my husband's employment situation was still resolving itself. Each time I went shopping, the many items we needed for our baby would come to my attention, but I would put off buying them 'till next time,' when, we hoped, the money would be flowing freely. After a while, time was running out, things were becoming increasingly difficult, and my husband told me to have more trust in the divine power, and to go and buy them. So, I did, gathering all the items together with the regular food shopping at the local supermarket. As the checkout girl tallied them up, a young woman approached me, dressed in a uniform with the logo of a large pharmaceutical company printed on it.

"Congratulations. I see you are purchasing several of my firm's products for your baby," she said, "and you have been chosen to have the full amount of your purchases here today refunded."

I laughed with joy, to the surprise of the people around. Not only were we provided with the baby needs, but also our weekly shopping bill was taken care of.'

Gisela Matzer from Austria also tells a story involving money. Shri Mataji  told us time and again that we should not worry too much about money, although she also warned us not to get into debt by borrowing heavily.

When I went to my second puja with Shri Mataji in Eastbourne, England, I did not have any money, and I had decided to make the trip to England with an overdraft on my account.

"If you really want to go you will somehow get the money for it," said my friends. As I came home from England and opened the letterbox, I found a letter from my landlord. At first I got a shock because I thought I had to pay back a lot of money, but after reading the letter carefully I saw that for years I had paid too much money and now I was getting back a sum of 10,400 Austrian schillings, which was exactly the amount I had spent on going to England. '

Greg Turek from Australia relates how he avoided bankruptcy.

'When I first came to Sahaja Yoga in the 1980's, I was a member of a business partnership which had invested in a small passenger aircraft. We got into difficulties due firstly to a recession, and secondly because of the bankruptcy of the company which had leased the plane from us. Then the Australian dollar dropped 30% against the American dollar, and as our loan was in US dollars we immediately owed another million Australian dollars. We seemed completely doomed and at this point I prayed and surrendered the whole problem to the divine.

Within a couple of days, I received a call from our lawyer, saying the finance company who had provided the loan had unexpectedly found a 'hedge clause' in the loan documentation. This was an insurance against currency fluctuation. We were very surprised, because when we had taken out the loan the Australian dollar had been so stable it had been considered unnecessary. We double checked, and found that none of the twenty or so other virtually identical aviation partnerships that had been set up at that time by the same company had a hedge clause – so why ours?

Our fortunes were reversed, because our debt was reduced by a million dollars, and we almost immediately found an airline who leased our plane at a very high monthly fee. Within one year we were well out of trouble, and even had a lavish dinner to celebrate our 'windfall'. To this day no one knows how the 'hedge clause' found its way into the documentation.'

Deepali Bandakar is an alternative therapy practitioner and Sanskrit scholar, and is usually very efficient and organised.

'I am a Sahaja Yogi and live in Mumbai, and one day I left my flat to go to the bazaar, where I had to pick up my watch which had been repaired. When I was on the street I remembered I had left the gas ring burning in the kitchen so went to turn it off, but when I got there, somehow it was not on. I went out again and this time could not find my purse with my money in it. I assumed

I had left it in the flat. I went back a second time and it was not there, but discovered it was in my bag all the time.

Eventually I got to the bazaar and a man came running towards me. He explained that a big truck loaded with sacks of rice and wheat had fallen from the flyover onto the very shop that I would have been in, if I had not taken such a long time to get there.

There is a shloka (sacred saying) in Sanskrit, which goes: 'Ya devi sarva bhuteshu bhranti rupena samsthitha namas tasye'. This means – 'I bow to the goddess who exists in all beings in the form of error'. She saved my life that day with those errors!'

Shri Mataji was a great cook, in many ways.

'Shri Mataji did a lot of the cooking for us when she came to our house in Scotland and had a seminar there with about thirty of us, some very new to Sahaja Yoga and many of us with bad problems. Shri Mataji explained that if she cooked for us, her healing vibrations in the food would help us in many ways.

The strange thing about the cooking was this. We had a big catering-style fridge and Shri Mataji made a chicken stew type dish which we didn't finish, so we put the leftovers in the fridge for another day. Then after she left, about a week later, I made another chicken stew and also put it in the same fridge and forgot about it. About three weeks after this we suddenly remembered the two stews, but whereas my stew had gone completely rotten, Shri Mataji's was as fresh as the day it had been made, almost a month before.

There was another small and subtle miracle which Shri Mataji did at Caxton Hall in London. She was invited to dinner at 10, Downing Street by the then Prime Minister, Mrs Thatcher. It was a Monday and Shri Mataji came to the programme at Caxton Hall looking beautiful and ready for the dinner, but she had insisted on cooking a meal for us. That morning we had gone to the meat market and bought chicken legs. We bought eighty portions, that is forty big chicken legs which were divided into two. Shri Mataji made a delicious chicken dish and we took the pots to the programme and served it out after she had left for Downing Street.

I was serving the chicken and went on counting the portions as I was concerned there might not be enough. I got to well over a hundred and ten, and just kept on dishing out the chicken legs even after that. There were just enough for everyone.' – Linda Williams

Shri Mataji dressed for 10, Downing Street

'I was living in Finland and had been in Sahaja Yoga for six months when I met a lady who was planning to go to Italy, Cabella, for Shri Mataji's puja. I immediately got a strong desire to go too, but I didn't have any money. At that time I was a single mother and a housewife, living on social security. I was visiting that same lady when suddenly my mobile rang. It was the social security office, telling me they had paid me too little money for quite a long time and had decided to return that lacking money to me. It was almost exactly the amount I needed for the travel and the puja.

The next thing was to get a flight. The lady called a travel agency and they told her they had absolutely nothing left. I made a bandhan and another flight, the perfect itinerary and a lower price suddenly appeared out of nothing into their system so we booked it.

In Frankfurt, where we were supposed to change planes, we found out that the entire airport staff at Malpensa Airport, Milan, Italy, were on strike. No more flights would leave that day, maybe the whole weekend. We made another bandhan and sang the mantras of Shri Hanumana, the protector of travellers, and Shri Ganesha, the destroyer of obstacles, and as we got back to the desk, the Malpensa staff had decided to go back to work and we got seats for the next flight.

That whole weekend was one big miracle and everything worked out smoothly, despite the obstacles.'

Hanna Rentola

Making curtains can be a tricky business, but sometimes things just work out perfectly, as Rosemary Maitland Hume relates.

'We were making curtains for the hall at Shudy Camps, Shri Mataji's house in the English countryside. Shri Mataji had purchased the right amount of material for the large windows in the main hall. She had bought that kind of brocade which has a very big repeat pattern and had asked an expert to give her the right amount of material to allow for this large repeat pattern. We had seven metres extra for this.

So there we were in the hall at Shudy Camps with our trestle tables and scissors and tape measures and this enormous roll of fabric. We started measuring and rolled out the fabric and marked it each time at exactly the right measurement. We then rolled it out again and we had to match these huge pattern shapes so the curtains would hang true. We were expecting to have at least two thirds of a metre of extra fabric for each drop, so we could get the patterns to match, but every time the fabric matched exactly. Every time we rolled out the fabric this happened. It felt so natural. At least twelve lengths all matched perfectly without any wastage at all, and we could make another whole set of curtains out of what was left over. Amazing.'

Nea Alanen from Finland has a beautiful memory.

'I was eleven when I was at one of the first Daglio summer camps for young Sahaja Yogis in Italy. I was running around the girls' dorms and suddenly I stumbled into a barrier and fell down, hit my left arm on one of the beds and fell on the floor. I couldn't move my hand at all. My thumb was probably broken and there was definitely something very wrong with one of the ligaments in my arm. I cried and went to tell an auntie.

After a short discussion the aunties and uncles decided to take me to Shri Mataji's house. They came with me. When we arrived they made me sit in front of the doors of her rooms. I cried and there were several yogis giving me vibrations, massaging me and correcting my posture. They told me that Shri Mataji was sleeping.

After an hour or two suddenly I could somehow move my thumb again. My hand and arm were very sore but the thumb wasn't broken anymore. I felt the deepest calmness and the cool wind blowing through my Sahasrara was like a strong pillar. I heard Shri Mataji laughing and talking in Hindi very joyfully in the next room with some yogis. I sat there and listened to that beautiful sound that I would never forget.'

Things definitely worked out for this girl, after she got her realisation.
Email, June 26th, 2012.
Dear Friends,

I am a volunteer for Children in Kenya. In January 2012 I took Mercy (12 years old) to a hospital in Kenya for her eye problem, a squint , where a doctor disappointed me badly by telling me that nothing could be done because she was too old. It should have been done before the age of five, he said. The next day in the classroom, together with some Indian Sahaja Yogis from Nairobi we gave realisation to all the children and teachers in the orphanage at the Samaritan Children's Centre.

After the realisation exercise, we asked the children to tell us what how they felt. Mercy stood on a chair next to me and said she felt very nice and was praying to God that I and the other volunteers from Cyprus would help her correct her eyes. I felt a very deep pain since there was no way I could help, and I was just hoping for a miracle.

In April 2012 I went to Kenya again with a volunteer doctor, and we took Mercy to another eye specialist who directed us to the top eye surgeon in Nairobi. We raised the money and a miraculous eye operation was performed last week. It was a great success and Mercy's first desire after self realisation was fulfilled.

The feeling of happiness is so great and I thank with all my heart all those who have contributed towards this miracle. What a blessing. I am so happy for this very clever, beautiful and now realised child, Mercy. She deserves the best.

Thank you God!
Regards, Stavros Neofytou

Chapter 23

Technology Enlightened

Robert Ruigrok of Belgium tells a story about an unusual pay phone, with a gentle moral.

'We were preparing Shri Mataji's visit to Belgium in 1985. From a telephone box, I telephoned her in London to ask for some details about her trip. At one point she spoke some beautiful and totally unexpected words of encouragement:

"You are my eyes, my arms, my hands," she said. Suddenly, the phone was interrupted as it ran out of money. I had to change paper money and got about fifteen Belgian twenty franc pieces, about twelve dollars. I rang back, Shri Mataji came on line again and made some comment about how phones take all your money.

After the conversation, I put the phone down. To my great surprise, like a jackpot in a slot machine, the phone released an avalanche of Belgian twenty franc coins. A continuous stream of coins came out and I had to hold my hands together to catch them all. It was against all the normal laws of nature and definitively not how phone boxes operate in Belgium. It was an incredible and immediate confirmation that when we work for Sahaja Yoga and use our own money, the rewards do not fail to come to us quickly.'

Dr. Jadunandan Prasad of Delhi explains how he overcame various little problems, some common to those who know India.

'In May 1994, just two months after I had received my self realisation, there was a Sahaja Yoga function at Hyderabad in my house, in the south of India. It was scheduled at 9.30 am for an hour or so, and there was always a power cut in that area from 9.00 am to 10.00 am. This would have meant the function would be without power, not a happy situation. I tried talking to the electricity board officers to get exemption from the power cut for that day but without success, so went to the sub-station to ask for help, where the officer told me that the power cut in my area would be changed from that day onwards. The transformer supplying power to my area had just burnt down and they had arranged power from another one, whose cut was between 11.00 am to 12.00 noon. Needless to mention the function went very well.

In December 1995 we were recording Shri Mataji for a Doordarshan (Indian National TV) programme at Ganapatipule. The recording was set up near the tourist bungalow on the sea shore where she was staying. When we were about to begin, the sound engineer informed me that the sound quality was not at all clear as it was picking up a lot of ambient noise from the nearby sea shore. I told him not to worry and we would deal with it during the editing.

This conversation took place in Shri Mataji's presence, although we were quite far away from her and she could not hear us. However, to our utter surprise she asked some time later if there was any disturbance in the sound recording and if we removed this disturbance with filters. I answered in the affirmative and was impressed by her knowledge of sound recording. When we edited the programme there was no disturbance of any kind; we did not have to use any filters and the sound was very clean.

My friend and I always take our private chartered bus to our weekly Sahaja Yoga programme in Delhi. It reaches our stop at about 5.10 pm. On one occasion when the bus had still not turned up at 5.30pm I phoned someone who would know whether it was coming, from a booth at the bus stand and heard this person's wife, Mrs Gunraj, saying, 'The bus is reaching you any minute,' after which the phone was disconnected. At that moment the bus arrived and we went to the programme. A few days later, I saw Mrs. Gunraj and told her about our phone conversation on the 9th January, at 5.30 pm. She replied that she had not received any phone calls that day because their telephone was out of service until two days later.'

Mobile phones have one shortcoming - they need to be recharged.
'At the first follow up programme in Istanbul, in 1999, one lady told us that when she came to the introductory programme in Shri Mataji's presence, the battery in her mobile phone finished and the phone switched off automatically. After the programme she decided to turn the phone on (normally, in such a situation it can work for maybe one minute, so that she could make one fast call). To her surprise, the battery was fully charged, so we all witnessed direct transformation of the power of vibrations to the electric energy. Later I heard that a few other people had a similar thing happen to their mobile phones.'
Lev Doronski

Zuhra Dunderski from Kazakhstan is a concert violinist now living in Vienna.
'In the summer of 2001 some friends invited my son and me to stay with them on a lake in Austria. Before we went away I had a feeling I should insure the contents of my apartment, so an insurance person came round, but somehow instead of talking about insurance I gave him self realisation. I

told him that Sahaja Yogis are always saved, for example in the big earthquake in Turkey in 2000, when many people were killed, there were quite a lot of Sahaja Yogis in that area, but not one was hurt, and not one of their houses was damaged. I felt certain nothing would happen while we were away, and he had to go because it was late. We decided to do the insurance business when I returned from my holiday.

Two days before we returned to Vienna from the lake there was a big storm. When we got home we noticed the automatic garage door was stuck open and the light was not working. This part of the house was the common property of all the tenants. When we got to our own front door, we went in and turned on the lights. A lot of paper was stuck in the fax machine which I had left on, but the machine was fine, and still working.

I found an electrician and he said that very near our house two trees had been badly struck by lightning during the storm and all the electronic things in all the apartments had been affected. Everyone's telephones, computers, fax machines and so on were hopelessly damaged. The lightning had gone down through the roots into the electrical cables. Mine was the garden apartment and should have been the worst hit as I was the nearest to the tree, but there was absolutely no damage of any kind.

By coincidence, somebody had given me the German Sahaja Yoga magazine to read while on holiday, and in it was an article about another Sahaja Yogi who had had a similar miracle.'

This was the story Zuhra refers to.

'In 1995 I spent nine months in America in order to write my doctorate there. I lived as a housekeeper for a man in Kansas City, Missouri a region known for violent storms, often the forerunners or byproducts of tornadoes. One night our house was shaken by the loudest and most violent storm I had ever known. Lightning struck the trees and the earth. It went on all night and was very frightening. At 4 o'clock in the morning, the storm was still raging in its full force, and I got up to meditate. I prayed to the all-pervading power in the form of Shri Vishnumaya, who governs electricity and lightning, and begged her to keep us safe.

The storm abated during the morning, but was followed by heavy rain and it was still so dark outside that we needed lots of lights in the house. I finished the usual jobs, made breakfast for myself and my landlord, washed up and sat in front of my computer to carry on working. The telephone rang. It was a neighbour who asked whether we had our own electricity generator. I said that we didn't and had power from the city grid just like everybody else.

"How is it that your lights are on?" she asked. The electricity was off in a quarter of the town and our house was right in the middle of this part. I said that I really did not know why, but we had electricity.

She then asked whether she could put a few things into our fridge. Within a couple of hours it was filled with the contents of other neighbour's houses as well. My landlord in the meantime called from his nearby office to ask if we still had power. He said that the electricity was off everywhere and he even phoned the power company to ask whether it was possible that we could have power. He was told it was absolutely impossible because the power grid in this part of the town had completely broken down. He asked me whether I had done some sort of Sahaja Yoga magic. I told him that I had not done anything except to pray for protection. The power was off until the evening, but we had the lights burning and my doctorate work was safely backed up.

Nowadays mobile phones are standard, but not in 1986.

'In 1986 there was a New Year Puja at Alibagh, on the coast north of Mumbai. A miracle took place in our house. Shri Mataji reached there around 7.00pm from Ganapatipule, and many other Western yogis too. When Shri Mataji stepped out of the car she was surprised.

"This place is so beautiful. I always wanted to come here," she said and went into the bedroom. "I must tell Sir CP (her husband) about this place and so he can come and visit it."

She asked one of the yogis if she could use a phone as she wanted to call Mumbai. Since it was not a developed village there were no phones. Then she asked my father, Mr Koli, for a coconut. He asked Shri Mataji if she wanted to eat one and she said she did not, but wanted a fresh one from the tree. A village boy climbed up and got one in ten minutes and gave it to her. She went into her room and closed the door.

Many Sahaja Yogis were sitting in the hall outside, and later one of them said that Shri Mataji was using the coconut as a phone and they had heard her speaking to Sir CP for nearly an hour.'

Lena Koli

Email: Thousands got self realisation thru Radio FM from Nairobi, Kenya
DATE: Thu, 17 Apr 2003 06:47:11
From: Kapil Goyal kapilgoyal_in@...
Dear All,
Yesterday we got permission to air our presentation on the No.1 FM Channel of East Africa, East FM. Today morning they allowed us more than

an hour to speak about Sahaja Yoga, a live interview, and replying to the queries of listeners. The anchor lady, a very versatile Kenyan Muslim, made us feel so comfortable before the programme.

We spoke about the Kundalini, Shri Mataji, the global practicing of Sahaja Yoga, etc. There was a flood of phone calls and some seekers asked how they could get their self realisation. We told them to remove their footwear and put their feet on the Mother Earth, to keep both hands open and think of Shri Mataji Nirmala Devi. Then we gave a Sahaja audio cassette to the anchor lady to play.

Needless to say the Kundalini of thousands of listeners found its way to their Sahasraras and they felt tremendous cool breeze, even while sitting before their radio sets. So many phone calls and SMS messages flooded in the studio to tell us!

During this we were in the studio listening to the Jogawa song, which is a Marathi bhajan, asking the Kundalini to rise. My Kundalini was dancing and the whole of my body was chilled, the studio room became like a refrigerator, as if Shri Mataji was present there, working out countless Kundalinis through the ether element.

Here is a story concerning music.

'We have been practising Sahaja Yoga since 2001 in Hyderabad, India. On one occasion we moved house, and could not go to the Sahaja Yoga weekly meeting. I was singing the song Vishwavandita, a song in praise of Shri Mataji, along with the rest of my family. My son Anil and my daughter Sowmya provided the music – percussion with plates and spoons. In between we suddenly heard some music, the melody of Vishwavandita, spontaneously accompanying us, and we enjoyed it. After we had finished the song we noticed that the music came from the keyboard, which was packed up in a bag. My son took it out and played it and got the same tune. We were surprised, since no one had played that tune on it before.'

C. Ranganayakamma

What follows, taken from Nirmal Fragrance, by Rabi Ghosh of India, has been included in this chapter because one needs a fair amount of technology to see the form of the carbon atom. Even if it seems obscure, the reader will no doubt grasp that there is an exciting and profound connection between matter, spirit, all the different divine personalities of the different religions, the symbols connected with these and the Kundalini placed within each one of us.

In the carbon atom the electrons occupy four tear drop shaped clouds in a tetrahedron-like arrangement. These clouds represent the areas in which the electrons spend most of their time. They move so rapidly in this zone that they form a cloud rather than a specific flight path. Recently a number of researchers have suggested that within these clouds exist specific zones that the electrons favour. These zones form a spiral around the surface of each of the teardrop shaped clouds.

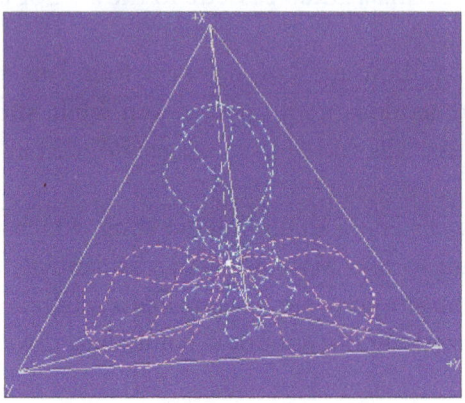

'... the Mooladhara (chakra), you will see swastikas, because it is made of carbon atom. If you see from the left to the right, you can see Omkara. And if you see from down upward, it looks like Alpha and Omega. In those days Christ said, 'I am the Alpha and I am the Omega.'
Shri Mataji Nirmala Devi, Christmas Puja 1992, Ganapatipule, India

'... Her Holiness Mataji Nirmala Devi made certain revelations based on her divine vision to a very renowned scientist of United States, Dr. Vinod Ram Rao Worlikar of Cerritos, Los Angeles, about the carbon atom. The details of that are mentioned below in his own words.
Dr. ... Worlikar ... in a communication said that ... 'It was difficult to believe at the first instance. However, on my return to Los Angeles (Cerritos), I tried to verify it in my laboratory and to my surprise it was absolutely the same as she told me.'
Medical Science Enlightened, Prof UC Rai, 1993, p.150

When this configuration was viewed from certain angles the physicist was surprised to find that the spirals formed recognizable symbols. In the first view a 3-dimensional Omkara could be seen.

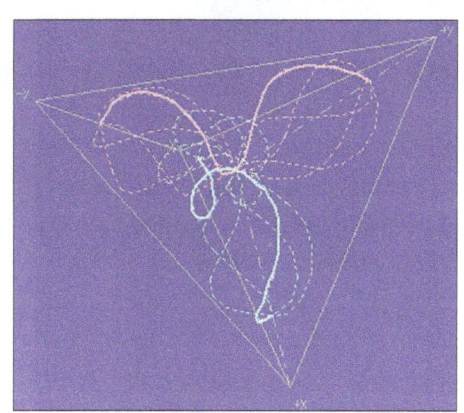

Part of the OM sign, the Omkara

From a different angle the Omkara became a flat, 2-dimensional Swastika. The Swastika, he concluded, was actually 2-D representation of the 3-D Omkara.

Swastika

Rotating the model to another angle shows those symbols change into the Greek letters Alpha and Omega.

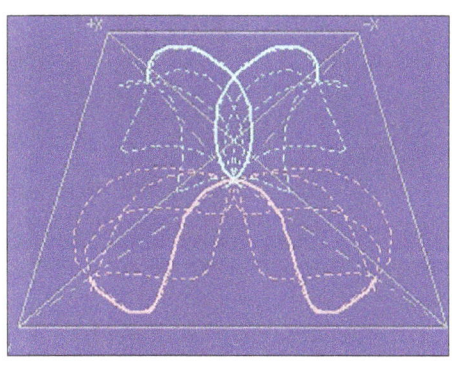

Alpha and Omega

At a cosmic level, the symbols of Eastern Spirituality, the Omkara and the Swastika, are different aspects of the same spiritual truth that is also represented by the symbols of Western spirituality, the Alpha and Omega. The carbon atom, by containing within it these universal symbols, demonstrates that matter is a manifestation of the same divine consciousness experienced by the saints and sages of all history. The universe does not exist separately from the universal consciousness; it is a direct expression of it. Living matter, which is carbon based, must have a unique role in this expression. All people, objects and even energy itself are expressions of the same divinity.

The Alpha and Omega are traditionally ascribed to Christ, whereas in India Shri Ganesha presides over the Swastika and the Omkara. The chakra associated with Shri Ganesha is the Mooladhara, at the base of the spine. The word Mooladhara means 'the support of the root,' the base of the Kundalini. Shri Ganesha, like Christ, was created from his mother. Christ, whose great qualities of forgiveness and resurrection, and transformation into that which is subtler, are qualities of the Agnya chakra, which is placed in the brain. This chakra is the support of the Sahasrara.

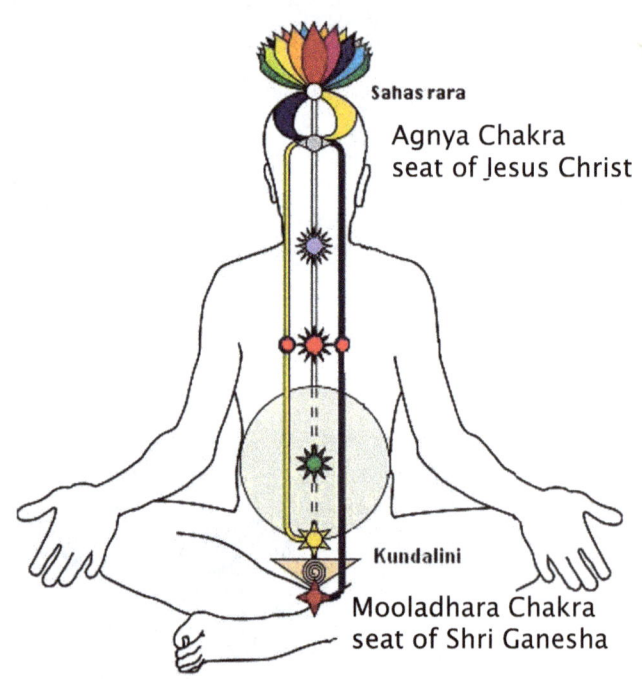

162 | The Breeze of Sahasrara

Chapter 24

Simultaneous Appearances

On a number of occasions Shri Mataji appeared to people when she was, in the normal course of events, somewhere else. Many of these people were nothing to do with Sahaja Yoga and often did not even know who she was.

In October 1982, Shri Mataji was visiting Bedford, England, where she spoke at a public programme. Her photograph had appeared in an advertisement in the local newspaper, the 'Bedfordshire Journal,' earlier in the day. While Shri Mataji was speaking at the programme, a road accident took place some distance away from the hall, in which a young man, Jason, was injured. Only a day or two later did he recognize the photograph in the newspaper as the lady who had come to his aid, as Journal reporter Ross Francis related under the front page headline, 'GURU AND THE MIRACLE BOY.'

Jason was not 'seeing things,' according to the man who is arranging the present whistle stop tour for the lady Guru. He said it was quite probable that Jason had seen a 'mystical vision' of Shri Mataji.

He said there were many cases known to the movement of people who had witnessed the vision of the woman who, it is claimed, can cure serious illnesses by the touch of her hands.

'It's quite possible Jason had such an experience connected with this lady. Strange things have happened that just can't be explained rationally. I don't discount what he says at all.'

Jason came off his motor scooter after colliding with a car in Cauldwell Street, Bedford, last Thursday at 9:15 pm. He had finished work for the evening and was riding home. At the same time, Shri Mataji was at a meeting in the Guildhouse, Harpur Street. She didn't leave until 11pm.

Jason said, 'I was just laying in the road in pain. People were standing about saying, 'Don't touch him – he may have broken his back.' Then I was aware of this Indian lady over me. She put her hands on my head, my shoulders, my arm and my body. As she took her hands away from each spot, the pain just vanished. I thought I had broken my arm, but she said I hadn't.'

He didn't see the lady after that and minutes later was taken to hospital in an ambulance. Bruised and shaken, he was allowed home later in the evening after his worried parents called to see him.

Two motorists concerned in the accident said they had remained at the spot until Jason was put into the ambulance. Neither had seen the lady. The ambulance crew which took Jason to hospital and police officers who attended the crash also said they had not seen her.

BEDFORDSHIRE Journal — North Beds Edition

A strange happening in Cauldwell Street

GURU AND THE MIRACLE BOY

Exclusive by Ross Francis

AN INDIAN faith healer and a jobless teenager from Bedford are at the centre of a bizarre miracle mystery.—

As motor scooter rider Jason Haynes, 17 lay in a crumpled heap after a crash, he says a woman spiritualist came up to him and eased his pain by simply laying her hands on him.

But at the time of the crash on Thursday night, "Holy Mother" Mataji Nirmala Devi was a quarter of a mile away at a public meeting in Harpur Street.

Yet Jason was not "seeing things", according to the man who is arranging the present whistlestop tour for the lady Guru.

At his London home, Mr Gavin Brown, a devotee of Shri Mataji's Sahaja Yoga movement for the last 11 years, said it was quite probable that Jason had seen a "mystical vision" of the spiritualist.

He said there were many cases known to the movement of people who had witnessed the vision of the woman who, it is claimed, can cure serious illnesses by the touch of her hands.

"It's quite possible Jason had such an experience connected with this lady. Strange things have happened that just can't be explained rationally.

"I don't discount what she says at all.

Jason came off this motor scooter after, colliding with a car in 'Cauldwell Street, Bedford, last Thursday at 9.15pm.

He had just finished his part-time job at Sainsburys and was driving to his home in Barkers Lane, Bedford. At the same time, Shri Mataji was at the meeting in Guildhouse, Harpur Street.

She didn't leave until 11pm.

Jason said: "I was just laying in the road in pain. People were standing about saying 'don't touch him'. He may have broken his back."

"Then I was aware of this Indian lady over me. She said: Do you have faith in me? I said, 'Yes'.

She put her hands on my head, my shoulders, my arm and my body.

"As she took her hands away from each spot, the pain just vanished. I thought I had broken my arm, but she said I hadn't."

He didn't see the lady after that, and minutes later was taken to hospital in an ambulance.

Bruised and shaken he was allowed home later in the evening after his worried parents called to see him.

Two motorists concerned in the accident said they had remained at the spot until Jason was put into the ambulance.

The ambulance crew which took Jason to hospital and police officers who attended the crash also said they had not seen the woman.

Mrs Maria Smith, of Irchester, Northants, was at Thursday's meeting in Bedford.

She said the faith healer stayed at her home that night.

Her husband Harry was in the car that took the guru to their home after the meeting.

"The car didn't stop and no one got out to help or a road accident," she said.

When told of the strange events this week, Shri Mataji said: "It's marvellous to think that such occurrences are happening in this country and it is a blessing".

Jason's mother, Mrs Margaret Haynes, said, "I would love to meet the woman to thank her for whatever happened.

"I never really believed in faith healers before but now I'm not so sure.

"It is like a miracle."

And the final word from Jason: "I definitely saw this woman and she helped me.

"There was only one spot that she didn't touch, my lower back, and that is still hurting."

The couple with whom Shri Mataji was staying after the programme and who drove Shri Mataji home said that her car had not stopped and no one had got out to help at any accident. But when told of the strange events this week, Shri Mataji said, 'It's marvellous to think such occurrences are happening in this country and it is a blessing.'

Jason's mother said, 'I would like to meet that woman to thank her for whatever happened. It is like a miracle.'

And the final word from Jason, 'I definitely saw this woman and she helped me. There was only one spot she didn't touch, my lower back, and that is still hurting.'

Brian Bell of New Zealand added some points to this story.

'During the 1983 tour of America, Shri Mataji, while she was in Los Angeles, did a radio interview. We were waiting with her for the studio to become clear. This was shortly after the incident which happened in England, the so-called 'Bedford boy'. Shri Mataji was talking about this incident, and a Sahaja Yogi asked her, "Shri Mataji, were you conscious of that? Were you conscious of being with that boy at the accident?"

She answered something like this, "The Divine is always transmitting. The message is always going out from the Divine. Whether it is picked up or not depends on the quality of the receiver. If the receiver is good, then the divine message is picked up."

Presumably the boy in Bedford was a good receiver.'

The editor corroborates the same story.

'I was at that Bedford programme, but because my baby was crying, I took him out and sat in the back of my car with him. Shri Mataji's car was near mine in the car park, just outside the door into the Town Hall. No one came in or out while the programme was on. I was watching the door intently all the way through, waiting for Shri Mataji to come out when she had finished the programme, and her car, which was parked near mine, did not leave the car park. She finally left the hall at about eleven o'clock, accompanied by the other Sahaja Yogis. The Bedford boy incident had happened much earlier.'

Annette Haines tells of a tree that unexpectedly stopped shedding flowers.

'This happened when I was living in Sydney, Australia, in 1986. It happened in a Royal Australian Naval townhouse. Our neighbours were friendly, with some ladies looking after their children by themselves while their husbands were at sea. I was about three months pregnant with our second child and was threatened with a miscarriage. My friend came by one day to give me vibrations, then left me alone. I went into a deep and blissful state. I felt that Shri Mataji started to come out of her photograph, and I saw flashes of a golden ribbon being flung around, like a gymnast dancing with long ribbons. The Heart chakra was full of very powerful love.

After a while, things came back to normal and I went downstairs and lay down on the sofa in the sitting room, facing outwards into our little garden with its enormous coral tree overhanging it in flower. I started to relax and, before my eyes, a ray of sunlight came down through the tree and suddenly Shri Mataji, dressed in a white sari, was walking casually down the path towards our front door. She entered the house and changed into a heavenly golden light which enveloped me. My body became like a hollow golden instrument or pipe, not dense like particles slowly increasing and decreasing, golden and brilliant as I looked down into it. I was part of the whole vision, a drop in the ocean of joy of the universe.

My neighbour had swept the path to our front door that morning to remove some dropped flowers, but the coral tree did not shed any flowers for about a day afterwards, as it normally would continuously during flowering. Our daughter was born a happy baby, very wiry and strong about six months later.'

Sandeep Gadkary, originally from India, tells of 'a wonderful defence'.

'There is a story which is well known by the Mumbai Sahaja Yogis concerning old Mr Pradhan, who has now passed away. He was one of the early Sahaja Yogis, from the seventies. Mr Pradhan was an advocate, and often had to go into the courts to defend his clients. On one occasion he had a rather important case on the following day.

Shri Mataji asked him if he could spend the next day with her, as she needed him for some reason, and without hesitation he accepted. The day after he went into the courts, hoping that somehow things would have worked out with the case he was supposed to have defended.

Some of his colleagues came up to him as he entered the court and congratulated him on having given such a wonderful defence on the previous day. He could not exactly say that he had been with Shri Mataji all day!'

In Austria Sahaja Yogis such as Elizabeth Schulz often give self realisation to people they meet in their daily lives.

'This is a story about a newspaper seller. I gave him realisation on the street in, 2002, and he was very happy. Then I gave him an invitation to the follow up programmes which we have every week in Vienna. He said he would come but the next week I didn't see him and thought maybe he had lost the piece of paper I had given him so I went and found him on the street again. I asked him why he didn't come and he said he didn't have time that week, but he wanted to come because, apart from anything else, he had met Shri Mataji and had promised her he would come. I had given him a picture of her and he was quite certain that this lady had come and talked to him. He said he had also met her on the street and she had also told him to go to a programme.

At first I didn't believe him and said it couldn't be true because she was in India at the time, and anyway she did not walk around the streets of Vienna like that. He was absolutely sure that it was the lady on the photo I gave him who came and talked to him. She told him that she was always there in the programmes in Vienna, in the collective group.'

Mirriam Oweke of Kenya, now working for the UN in New York, tells a sweet tale. 'Mine is a short one. When I was going to have my second baby, I saw Shri Mataji in a green sari the night my labour started and she was beside my bed not saying anything. Later when I was in hospital, the doctor was wondering why the contractions were so controlled. I did not feel any pain at all throughout the whole birth!'

Didier Goven has another story from Kenya.
'We went to Kiweze in the south a few years ago, near the Tanzanian border. We gave self realisation in this little village for three days and on the last day went to the father of one of the men. His father was a very old man and he came out of his little hut and we didn't know what to say. We just showed him the picture of Shri Mataji and when he saw it he immediately went into meditation. There were lots of kids, and the three of us, and he was looking at Mother's picture and after some time he started to speak with his son in his own language.
"This lady came here last night. I know this lady," he said. We were very surprised, because we had never showed him the photo of Shri Mataji before. "Yes, she came here last night and came in," he went on. "I was not frightened and she was just smiling at me. Then she tapped me on the shoulder and said "Wake up now," and left the hut laughing. She was black, but it was this lady!'

The hospital visitor
'My name is Theresa Biara and I come from Ivrea, Italy. I was recovering in hospital, and I had a photo of Shri Mataji on the bedside cabinet. I told the people there this photo would be good for my health.
There was a young lady, a nurse, who was working there at the time, and a bit later she discovered about Sahaja Yoga, through a friend, via the internet, from Rome. When she saw the photo of Shri Mataji on the internet, she said, "I have seen that lady. She was at the bedside of Theresa when she was in the hospital. The lady was wearing a sari, and she came to see Theresa."
But officially, Shri Mataji never came to see me! I had no idea that Shri Mataji had come to see me - I never saw her. As far as I was concerned I had her photo by my bed, and that was all.'

A transcript of a tape recorded interview.

'This is Marylin Leate from Rome and I want to talk about a miracle that happened to my father. He was seventy five, and was going into hospital for a tiny operation in London, but I had a feeling, from the vibrations, that it was going to be serious. I prayed that if it was his time to go, then all right, but if possible could he survive the operation, and especially if he could realise about Shri Mataji and her blessing of Sahaja Yoga in some way.

On the day of the operation I phoned my mother and discovered that the doctors had discovered an aortic aneurism which was about to burst. They were doing an emergency operation and there was very little chance. I rushed to England and when I got to the hospital I realised his Kundalini was very strong and his vibrations very cool. He was in a coma for several days but he recovered, much to the amazement of the doctors. Once he came round he started speaking about love, and caring. Before he had been typically English and found it hard to express his feelings. He had never been like this previously. He seemed very changed.

One day I went to visit him in the hospital and he told me he had had a wonderful visitor, a young Indian doctor, who came and sat on his bed and hugged him and said she had saved his life. He explained that it was miraculous he had survived and I wanted to thank this lady. He said she looked exactly like a young version of Shri Mataji. There were no doctors like that there.

He had also given up smoking, and he had smoked since he was twelve. After that he spoke all the time about caring and loving, and lost all the racism which he had from being English and of that age group. After all this, he kept Shri Mataji's photo with him, and said that one day he had some pain, and the moment he touched the photo it all went away.'

Raju Koli of India tells of their efficient security guard.

'This happened during the construction of Shri Mataji's house in Alibargh, where we live. This is near Mumbai in India and was in 1984. When one is building a house, the raw materials, sand, cement, steel and so on, are always all over the place. Since it was in a small village we did not have a security guard. But one night it so happened that one man, who had been sent away for several years for not obeying the rules of our village, came to rob the steel. As he got there and was about to start stealing it, someone came after him with a big stick. The next morning he came to see us and asked how we could keep a security guard who was a woman.

We told him we did not have one, least of all a woman. He did not believe us, and saw our photographs of Shri Mataji which we had in the house. He immediately said the lady in the photograph was the security guard who was after him with a big stick. He said she had been wearing a white sari and had a blanket on her shoulders. He was not afraid that we might punish him for stealing our materials, but wanted to know who the great lady was that we had guarding our building site.'

Devibehn Kalam lives in Rylands, Cape Town, South Africa, in a beautiful house and she runs a catering business from her home. One of Devibehn's customers knocked at her front door and went into the house.

"Who is that lady in the red sari who I saw outside?" she said to Devibehn, "She had such a lovely smile and I felt so warm and comforted, it was as if it was my own mother smiling at me." Then the visitor saw the photo of Shri Mataji which Devibehn had in the house.

"That is the lady I saw outside!" she said.

"Are you sure?" asked Devibehn, who went to have a look, but there was no one there. Then she told her visitor how special Shri Mataji was, but that she had never been to South Africa. Devibehn said the visitor was so lucky to have seen her outside the house, and the lady said she had often seen Shri Mataji walking round the house as if she was looking after it.

Alice Abergal lives in France.

'My daughter Daphné was nine years old and she went to a week-end with the scouts. They played in the woods and their coordinator gave them an itinerary to follow and walk alone in the woods, saying when they would meet a cross point in the woods, they would turn right and everyone would meet up. She walked for a long, long time alone and didn't remember where to go. Then she thought, "Oh God, where am I to turn now?"

Shri Mataji appeared to her in a red sari and told her, "You go there." She followed Shri Mataji's instructions and soon found the others. She was so surprised. She didn't tell me, but instead told this story to a friend of mine, who told it to me.

My son David was eleven years old, and I was meditating in his room, because Shri Mataji's picture was on his desk.

"Mama, can't you take away the picture of the lady from my desk?" he said.

"Why?" I asked him.

"Each time I enter my room she blows towards me," he answered. He thought she was angry but in fact the photograph was blowing vibrations on him.'

The surgeon mentioned here knew nothing about Shri Mataji or Sahaja Yoga.

'My son Kiran had a very serious operation to remove a tumour from his brain. It was as big as a fist with tentacles all over in very delicate areas. On the day of the operation, the operating theatre personnel agreed to keep Shri Mataji's photograph on the drug stand during the surgery.

The operation began in the morning and at 2:30pm many of us Sahaja Yogis in different places, who had our attention on him, felt the vibrations went very hot and pricky, and at 4:45pm I was told things were not looking good. I told myself, 'Let me surrender this to the Divine.' Suddenly at 5:55pm, Prof Fagan, the head of the team, called us up.

"All went well," he said. "Now tell me, who is this lady you sent into the operating theatre with me?" he asked.

My husband Prem and I were stuck for words and I wanted to explain more about Shri Mataji, but the surgeon was too tired and just wanted to know her name. We then said, Shri Nirmala Mataji and the vibrations were just everywhere.

"It is funny," he said, "this lady in the photo was telling me which direction to go and she guided me when things were not looking good."

All the doctors in the operating team said that Kiran's recovery was miraculous and they felt the Divine powers had a lot to do with his survival. He is now recuperating at home and although he is not yet completely cured, everything is looking very hopeful, five years after the first operation. In one more year he will be completely out of danger.

Sheena Sivaprasad

Editor's note: Kiran is now out of danger.

An answer to a mother's prayer

'I live in Switzerland, and my daughter and I had had our self realisation, but she had not been involved in Sahaja Yoga for very long. My daughter, then sixteen, went to Canada for a visit and I prayed she would be alright. On one occasion she went to a club with two young friends she had known from childhood, and had a very brother/sisterly relationship with them. When they were there, one of them went to the bathroom and she was alone with the other. Suddenly two very fierce punky looking men came up, attacked the boy with her and threatened to hurt her with a knife. At that moment an Indian woman with long dark hair down her back, large strong arms and wearing a sari, appeared from nowhere in front of her, between her and the punk, and stopped him from attacking my daughter. It seemed that the Indian lady was holding the punk's arms to stop him troubling my daughter.

Somehow she knew it was Shri Mataji even though she had never met her. Then the police came and everything was all right. When my daughter told me this story, I felt so much cool breeze – vibrations – flowing all around me, and knew that it was true, and felt very grateful. It is said that when a mother prays for the safety of her son or daughter, the prayer is often answered, and so it was.'

Meera Szegvary

Agam Gupta, a young man who is a Sahaja Yogi from Pune, tells the following story.

'On the 5th May 1970, Shri Mataji sat under a certain tree (photo below) at Nargol, on the seashore in southern Gujarat, India, and experienced the opening of the cosmic Sahasrara, as was recounted earlier.

The tree under which Shri Mataji sat on 5th May 1970

Shri Mataji passed away in February 2011, but in some ways is very much still here. As has been the practice for a number of years, thousands of Indian

Sahaja Yogis often have a collective gathering there, on this occasion for a seminar at Christmas in 2011. The following incidents were reported.

Firstly, a young Sahaja Yogi told us that one month earlier, when they were preparing for the seminar in Nargol, a local woman who sold coconut water near the tree asked him about Shri Mataji's badge, which he was wearing.

"She is Shri Mataji Nirmala Devi," the boy replied.

"We see her here every day, busy doing some work, near this tree, many times, in a white sari," the coconut seller said.

Secondly, at the seminar they had brought in caterers from outside who were not Sahaja Yogis. When they saw the photo of Shri Mataji, one of these caterers said, 'This lady comes here daily in a white sari and tells us, "Make tasty food for my children."

Chapter 25

Collective Awareness

In Sanskrit, a rough translation of collective awareness is 'ritam bara pragnya'. Kristine Kirby of Boston, USA gives an example.

'We were driving to an interview with Shri Mataji in Boston, USA, in 1983. On our way there she described the power of ritam bara pragnya, where, as I understand it, you can, by just speaking something, work it out. You can make it come true.

Very shortly thereafter, she was discussing Japanese gardens for some reason, but as we were discussing it, we passed by a corporation and in front of their property someone had made a Japanese garden. As she was speaking about this we looked out of the window, and there it was, a Japanese garden.

"That is ritam bara pragnya!" she said.'

Douglas Fry gives another example.

'We were painting various bits of Shri Mataji's house in Hurst Green, near London, in about 1974. One evening Shri Mataji went out with Sir CP Srivastava to a reception. He was at that time the Director General of IMCO, International Maritime Consultative Organization, one of the offices of the United Nations. We were cleaning a wall and painting it and about half way through the evening we all suddenly got a terrific headache and felt really strange, but we just carried on working. So it passed. Shri Mataji came home and asked us how we were.

"I got this really terrible headache half way through. I didn't know what was happening," I said.

"We were at this reception and somebody, by mistake, gave me a glass of wine and I drank it," she replied.

What happened was we felt the effects of the wine that Shri Mataji drank. Because it had an effect on the collective consciousness, we actually felt it from her.'

Robert Ruigrok tells of an incident in Belgium.

'The public programme in 1985 was in the big hall in the Shell Building, Brussels. It got so full that we had to arrange for a second hall in the same building. Engelbert Oman headed a second self realisation programme, simultaneously with Shri Mataji's, but next door.'

Richard Payment of Canada continues the same story.

'At one point the lobby of that building in Brussels was to me more like a train station. We simply hadn't expected that large a crowd. As I looked from one room to the next, it was obvious the same meeting was happening in both places. Shri Mataji and Engelbert, in the second hall, were speaking on the exactly same topics, and at precisely the same time, even though he had no way of knowing what Shri Mataji was saying in the main room.'

Marilyn Leate of Italy took her friends to meet Shri Mataji.

'My second visit to Shri Mataji's home in London in the late 1970's was with two friends, one who was completely new and the other had just been to one public programme, and had never talked to Shri Mataji personally. She was having emotional problems because she was breaking up with her partner. Shri Mataji entered the sitting room to meet us.

"I don't know how to greet you," my friend said to Shri Mataji.

"Greet me as you would greet your mother." So my friend threw her arms around Shri Mataji and gave her a big hug, which, of course, Shri Mataji returned.

To the other friend, Shri Mataji exhibited her powers of understanding everything, for she outlined the situation the girl was in without any of us having opened our mouths about this subject. Shri Mataji went into accurate detail. She explained with great care what this girl should do to ease her emotional pain and how to save the relationship, all said in such a gracious, easy, humble, grandmotherly way.'

Anthony Visconti of Italy tells of a letter which did not need to be delivered.

'A lady in our group had done Sahaja Yoga for a few years, but she continued to have a problem with obesity. She tried everything but was not getting over this problem. Eventually she asked me if I would take a letter to Shri Mataji. The next day we went to see her off. I asked someone if they could give the letter to Shri Mataji, but was told it was not the right time. So I had the letter in my pocket, and then unexpectedly the plane was delayed for an hour or so. We all sat with Shri Mataji waiting for the plane to leave but I was too shy to give the letter to her.

All of a sudden Shri Mataji started talking about the problem of obesity in women, for no rhyme or reason. She said that the problem of obesity in women comes when they are overactive as children, especially around the age of twelve or so. They become tomboyish and right-sided. Then when they grow up, their metabolism is overactive and this can lead to obesity when they slow down. So it is important that girls don't do sports that are men's kind of sports and should not be too right-sided. She said that these women should take an ayurvedic medicine called ashokeri. She repeated at least six or seven times that this was the medicine to take. I never gave the letter to Shri Mataji, but she gave the answer there and then.

A few weeks later I went to India so I bought the medicine and gave it to this lady. She took them and experienced the benefits.'

Mark Williams, a journalist from Australia, relates an incident.

'Shri Mataji sometimes takes on your form of speaking when she is with you. When I first got married we were at Pratishthan, Shri Mataji's home in India, and it was the first time I had ever met her. We were standing in the kitchen and peering out into the backyard and she was sitting in the garden. She saw us and waved at us to come out, so we did, and sat down.

"What do you think of the house?" she said.

"Shri Mataji, it's a palace. It's absolutely fantastic," I said.

"Yes, it's just one of my crazy ideas," she said. I say that all the time. The people said they had never heard her use that turn of phrase. She was catching my thought.

I had the opportunity to ask Shri Mataji on a similar point. I was in a rickshaw in India with an American and he was scared. It was getting near sunset and the rickshaw driver didn't appear to understand where we wanted to go. I put it in bandhan and the vibrations were so cool I thought: "Forget it. We'll get there." However, after about five minutes I thought, "This driver is completely lost. He doesn't know where to go. We're never going to get there." But I was in such a nice state, I thought, "Forget it." Suddenly the American guy grabbed my arm.

"We're completely lost," he said, in a panic, "we're never going to get there. This guy doesn't know where we are going."

I realised I had been thinking his thoughts. When I saw Shri Mataji, I mentioned that this had happened.

"That's exactly what happens," she said. "We do actually catch the thoughts of each other." She explained that that's how one can change the world, because although sometimes people catch negative thoughts from each other, they also catch good thoughts from us. "That's the hundred monkey theory. When there are a hundred monkeys, one will do something, then another, then a few more, then suddenly all the monkeys do the same thing without quite realising why."

Chapter 26

Traumatic Events

Mrs Nirmala Verma first met Shri Mataji in 1971, on a social occasion.

'Shri Mataji invited us to tea at her residence, Jeevan Jyoti, on Napean Sea Road, Mumbai. My husband, my brother, who was a criminal lawyer and I, went to her place in my husband's car. As we were about to reach there, a small girl fell under our car. My husband picked her up, I started crying and we walked into Shri Mataji's residence. Shri Mataji, who was watching us from the first floor balcony, came down. The child was bleeding so profusely that my husband's shirt was soaked with blood. Shri Mataji sent for some water, washed the child and told us that she would be alright.

My brother insisted on making a police report. He and my husband went to the nearest police station with the child. On seeing my brother the police officer refused to write the report. My brother suggested that they took the child to the hospital. On reaching the hospital, a doctor examined the child and asked my husband what he wanted the child to be treated for as she had no wounds on her body. My husband showed the doctor his blood-soaked shirt and asked the doctor to examine her properly. The doctor emphatically told them that as there was nothing wrong with the child they could take her home.

When my husband and brother had gone to the police station and hospital, I had stayed back at Shri Mataji's place. I was feeling very embarrassed as we were overstaying her hospitality. Every now and then Shri Mataji would place her hand on my shoulder and tell me not to worry as everything would be alright. Whenever she touched my shoulder something appeared to go to my head and I would feel cold as if a river was flowing through my head. When my husband and brother returned Shri Mataji insisted on us having some dinner and then only let us return home. We did not talk about Sahaja Yoga on that occasion, only some years later.'

Sandra Castelli is a businesswoman and interpreter living in Milan.
'In December 1984 I was taking part in the annual tour of India with Shri Mataji and about two hundred Sahaja Yogis. I had been very struck by the enormous respect which the Indian Sahaja Yogis had for Shri Mataji. In Vaitarna, a village some distance from Mumbai, the local people organized

a procession, and Shri Mataji would be taken around the village on an ox-cart, decorated with garlands. The Sahaja Yogis danced around the cart as it advanced through the village streets accompanied by local musicians. I sensed the joy and started to dance and we gradually approached Shri Mataji's ox-cart. Shri Mataji saw me and greeted me.

I started to walk alongside the cart, but at one point I was slightly pushed in the crowd of dancing people. At that moment the cart wheel, wooden with an iron rim, ran over my foot. A nurse tried to stop the bleeding and then a doctor stitched my foot without anaesthetic. Mr. Pradhan, of the local Vaitarna Sahaja Yogis, came see me, lying under a tree.

"Shri Mataji is very sorry for what happened. She sends her vibrations and will work on your foot tomorrow." From this moment, my feet felt a veritable current of cold air. I was taken in a jeep to the bungalow where we were staying. Unknown to me, Shri Mataji was also staying there. Mr. Pradhan worked on my foot with a lemon. He told us that the lemon absorbs negativity, something he had experienced himself after being cured with one from a snake bite. He was already out of danger when the doctor arrived. The next morning Shri Mataji called for me.

"I am here for you," she said. "Come to my room." I followed her, hopping on my good foot. The other had swollen up and I could not put any weight on it. Shri Mataji began to give vibrations to my foot. She put her foot on top of mine, at first horizontally, pressing on the toes, and then pressing first on one side of my foot and then on the other, vertically. Her foot was completely pressed against mine and I not only felt the vibrations on my foot, but I had the impression that my foot had become a band of vibrations.

"Go now and don't think any more about it," she said after some time.

Having entered Shri Mataji's room hopping, I left it walking normally. I could put my weight on my foot without feeling any pain. I walked normally into the centre of the village, where the breakfast was being served.'

In India people accept the deity Shri Ganesha as the eternal child, wise and innocent. Shri Mataji explained how these qualities often protect children.

'... Shri Ganesha, who is the Lord of innocence. He is the ocean of innocence. And though he is such a young, little boy, he can fight the whole world, he can destroy all the negativity. That's the sign of innocence. There have been stories that children who have fallen from a very great height were completely saved, nothing happened to them. Their innocence is such a powerful thing that it doesn't harm anyone who is not to be harmed.'

'They (young children) are not taught anything, they are not conditioned, nothing. But they know how to behave. And they are always looked after by the Divine. I have known children, who have fallen from great heights. Nothing happened to them.'

Here are some stories to illustrate this.

'Our little daughter Janaki fell on her head from a considerable height onto a concrete floor. She fell asleep and did not wake up except for making little whimpering sounds. She had never been like this, and we decided to take her to the hospital, but were able to also show her to Shri Mataji at her home in Italy.

Shri Mataji said that the subtle negativity, which can lodge in a chakra or channel within us, can do such things with children and she gave Janaki a 'bad sight treatment,' as she called it. She asked us if our other children learnt to speak earlier and faster, which was indeed the case. Janaki was very introverted and Shri Mataji worked on her with a candle, moving it around her head.

"Janaki, look at me," Shri Mataji said, and at that instant, Janaki sat up on her own, without remaining on my lap, which she would normally have done in similar situations, and looked at Shri Mataji with absolute big clear eyes. The sun shone in her face and she appeared absolutely still and calm inside – a picture I will never forget. At that moment, I knew that Janaki was completely cured. Shri Mataji gave her a doll. And she was cured.'

Wolfgang Hackl

Editor's note: see Appendix for bad sight treatment.

'I was living in Madras (now called Chennai, in South India) with my wife and daughter in the mid-nineties. My daughter was about a year old and was just crawling. My wife and I were having lunch downstairs, and my daughter had heard us talking from above. That house was not finished, and the mezzanine did not have a railing. To my horror, I saw my daughter fall off the mezzanine on to a marble floor eight feet below. Oh my God, did I scream! It was too much. We rushed her to the hospital, and she had just hurt her nose a little bit.

A year later we saw Shri Mataji in Maharashtra (central India), but we had not mentioned this incident to her.

"See, I saved your daughter and I am protecting her. I was there," Shri Mataji said to me, quite spontaneously.'

Jayant Patankar

In Karun Sanghi's story we again notice the power of Sahaja Yogis to feel vibrations, the cool breeze felt in the palms of the hand and elsewhere. These are our link to the divine information centre and through which we can know about the inner state of a person, even though that person may be far away from us.

'My six-year old daughter fell from a height of twenty feet onto the road, in Calcutta, India. Members of my family took her straight to hospital. I was attending the meditation session at the local Sahaja Yoga centre, where I was phoned to tell me the news. Somehow I answered:

"Don't worry, she is all right." I went to the hospital and a neurosurgeon advised a CT scan of her skull. This revealed a brain hemorrhage and occipital bone fracture. I checked her vibrations and felt no cool breeze, which told me that her condition was serious. However, I was in good spirits, having come from the meditation and, somehow, even the gravity of the situation could not dispel this. I was not worried at all, even though her doctor told me that it was possible she might not survive. I left a photograph of Shri Mataji by her bedside.

That evening when I was returning from the hospital, I heard a question within myself:

"What do you want?" I knew, somehow, that it was from the divine. I replied that I did not want anything except whatever was good for me, which I would gladly accept. The question came many times and each time my answer was the same. Next day I again checked up on my daughter's vibrations and found it was cool. She was improving a lot. On the fourth day she got up from her bed and told me she wanted to be taken home. I asked the doctors for their permission, and they, astonished and reluctant, agreed and the next day she was back at home, without a single bandage. In a few days she was completely all right.'

A similar story from Sudhakar Shukla from India

'It was an evening of 1998 December and our entire family was on the terrace of our first floor house. We were walking on the terrace for about an hour. As it was growing dark, we decided to go down for a cup of tea. My daughter got down by a steel ladder, my son, who was only three years old, started climbing down. He was quite adept in climbing up and down that ladder but suddenly he slipped from the first step and fell down onto the hard marble floor at least 12 feet below. I shouted his name and hurried down the ladder. My wife cried out said, "Mother!" meaning the divine Mother.

As soon as I got down I lifted him in my lap and placed him in front of the table where we have our photos of Shri Mataji. By that time our two neighbours had arrived, having heard my shout. They saw me in front of the photos with my son in my lap and thought I had gone mad!

They suggested to me to take him to a good orthopedic to get a thorough scan done, but I was very calm and composed. I started looking at him for any injuries. To my utter surprise I could not even see a small swelling anywhere on his body. Within minutes he again started playing again as if nothing had happened! I thanked Shri Mataji from the bottom of my heart for this miraculous protection.

The second part of the story is even more interesting. Within half an hour a friend of mine came to our place with his family and kids. I enthusiastically told him about the miraculous incident that had just happened. My wife simply could not believe this, and as a possible explanation, told my friend's wife that my daughter was standing at the last step of the ladder and our son was stopped by her body, and only then fell on the floor. That was why he was not injured.

All the kids were playing on a cane wood swing which was hanging on the veranda, about one foot (thirty centimetres) above the floor, where my son had fallen a short while before. While my wife was giving her explanation my son again fell from this swing, from a height of about one foot, and this time had a big swelling on his forehead.'

Ursula Doring, a flight attendant from San Francisco, USA, relates a story of a lucky escape.

'In the spring of 1983 I mailed a letter to Yogi Mahajan, an experienced

Sahaja Yogi I had met in India. I asked him to come to San Francisco and help spread Sahaja Yoga. I was quite new in Sahaja Yoga at the time and did not yet feel confident to share my knowledge and experience with others.

I went to Delhi to pick him up. He was ready to go, and as we were preparing to depart he mentioned that we should stop off in London on the way to see Shri Mataji. I protested that our tickets had been routed from Delhi to San Francisco through Karachi, Frankfurt, and New York, and that they could not be changed.

One and a half hours after leaving Delhi, we were landing at Karachi after a fast, steep approach and rolled off the end of the runway into some rough ground which tore off the landing gear, severed the hydraulic systems, and made a huge hole in the forward compartment of the 747 near where we were sitting. I remember thinking, "Oh no, we will be stuck in Karachi."

Miraculously, there was no fire, and all the passengers scrambled down the slides to safety and were taken to hotels. The next evening we returned to the airport to retrieve our belongings which had been laid in piles far from the aircraft. Yogi's bag of fresh mangoes which he wanted to give to Shri Mataji was in perfect condition, not one had been squashed, and the fifty or so posters of Shri Mataji, for advertising Sahaja Yoga programmes, that had been placed in an overhead compartment, were unharmed.

The next day Pan Am sent a special plane to pick us up, with no guarantee, however, that there would be room for employees. As it happened we were given First Class seats and were informed the plane would make an extra stop in London. The customer service people were only too happy to rewrite our tickets to include a stop in London - after all, we had just been in a frightening accident.

Before we left New Delhi, Yogi Mahajan requested that I should repeat the mantra of Shri Jagadamba for a while. Shri Jagadamba is the deity associated with the heart chakra on the central channel, the Sushumna Nadi, whose quality is that of courage and confidence. I did so, and after the accident people remarked that I seemed remarkably calm.

We were blessed to meet Shri Mataji in London and only then did I learn that she had been planning a tour of the USA exactly during Yogi's visit. Later, we had lunch with her.

"Just get people to experience the vibrations, and leave the rest to me," she said. Yogi and I went on to San Francisco a few days later to do just that.'

This story is from Deepak Midha, an Indian living in Austria.
'In March 1985 there was a Sahaja Yoga programme at Talnoo, Dharmshala,

Himachal Pradesh, India, just below the mighty Himalayan ranges. The Sahaja Yogis from Delhi left for Dharmshala by bus and arrived in the early hours of the morning. In the evening there was a beautiful musical programme in the presence of Shri Mataji and the next day we did the Devi Puja. The next day, she suggested we should all visit a temple ten kilometres away. We did so, and it was built in a picturesque valley surrounded by high mountains, and inside the temple precincts was a small artificial pond. We decided to dip our feet in the cold water.

I put my foot on the first step and realised it was covered with slippery wet moss, but it was too late. I fell sideways, straight into the water. I climbed out but there was something very wrong with my right wrist, which could not take any pressure and was hurting a lot. The pain increased and I had to use a sling for my arm. I could not sleep at all in the night and was crying in agony.

The next day was Shri Mataji's public programme for the villagers of that area and thousands of people assembled by a nearby lake. I was taken there by car, in a lot of pain. At the end of the programme someone mentioned my accident to Shri Mataji and she immediately called me to the stage. I told her I had slipped and maybe fractured my wrist bone.

"So what?" she said, "We can even cure fractures." She took my wrist in her hand and held it for about ten minutes, at the same time talking to the new people who were queued in front of her. "How is it now?" she said, looking at me. At that moment I was able to take my hand out of the sling, and raise it high in the air.

"Mother, it is nearly gone," I replied.

She was laughing and I could hear applause from the people all around. I thanked her and stepped off the stage. On the drive back to Delhi, that night, I could only feel a little pain in the wrist. When we reached Delhi the next morning the hand was perfectly all right.'

Miodrag Radosavljevic was living in London.

'In 1983, I was going to a Sahaja programme in Geneva, Switzerland. I made my way to our house in Chelsham Road, south London to collect some items we needed there. About fifty yards from there two rough looking guys approached me. They flicked their knives and grabbed my hands and asked for money. I managed to free my hands but they grabbed the little golden locket which I had around my neck. As soon as they did so, for some reason they let it go and ran away.

The locket contained one single hair of Shri Mataji. Many years ago she would give us a strand for protection because she said the vibrations coming from her hair were very powerful.

It was a bit of a shock to be attacked like this, so I called the police and reported it to them. They said I was very lucky, because someone got stabbed the previous night, most probably by those same people. I realised how protected I was and arrived in Geneva the following day safe and sound.'

A Sahaja Yogini from France also tells of her fortunate escape.

'This took place in Tunisia in July 1988, when I was bathing in the sea, about twenty-five metres from the beach, but well within my depth. It was quite rough and I was having fun in the waves with a friend who was an excellent swimmer. We did not realise that little by little the waves were leading us further and further from the other swimmers.

Suddenly, I saw a great wave coming, filling me with fear. I wanted to get back to the beach, but the wave pulled me even further away, towards a deep and jagged rocky depression. A succession of waves, each more violent than its predecessor, burst on me, sucking me in before I even had time to breathe. I could hear my friend calling for help, unable to do anything for me. I was alone and my fight against the elements was vain, however strong my desire to live. I thought I was going to die, but accepted it, stopped struggling and let myself be carried in the movement of the water. The deeper I sank the more

I was completely silent and free of thought. Nothing mattered any more. I was astonished at this detachment from everything that had previously been important for me – my family, my friends, all the people dear to me. Everything was calm in my head, without any trace of fear or agitation. From deep within myself, I called to Shri Mataji and prayed, 'Mother, please, help me, help me.'

I have no words to express the sentiment of peace and serenity which came upon me then. I have never felt anything so intense. Then the miracle happened. I opened my eyes and saw the sea going away from me, as though to form a shield around me. It was like a giant wave, but this time one which wrapped me within it, like a giant bubble of air. I can still see the green-grey colours of the water all around and above me, and I seemed to be wrapped in a soft golden light. I had breathed clean pure, air, even though I was deep under the water.

After a few minutes I found myself once again just a few metres from my friend, desperately alarmed at seeing me disappear so suddenly. He pulled me from the water and I quickly got my breath back.'

Charlotte Turnbull tells of a harrowing escape in South Africa, known for its high incidence of violent crime.

'I live in Johannesburg. Some years ago, in the nineties, I decided to order a pizza for supper. After ordering it I went to another shop to buy a magazine. Upon entering it, unknown to me, some thieves already had everyone on the floor. I walked over to the magazine shelf, near the teller, and heard, "Take the money, take the money." I looked up and saw a gun pointed at the shop owner's stomach, and quickly left the shop. There was a video shop between it and the pizza place and I popped into it, asking them to phone the police. I then went back into the pizza shop and asked the people there to phone the police too.

No one reacted and I couldn't understand why, as I knew there was a panic button underneath the counter. No one moved and their eyes grew bigger and bigger. The gunman had finished robbing the magazine shop, and his accomplices, who were outside, told him about me. Unknown to me, as I walked into the pizza shop, the gunman had the gun at the back of my head – hence no one reacted as they were too shocked. Someone yelled at me, so I swung round to see the gun directly in my face. I stepped back, put my hands in the air and started apologizing to the gunman. He called me a fool, slapped me in the face and raised the gun to shoot me.

While this was happening, the pizza shop owner arrived back from delivering pizzas and walked between me and the gunman to get behind the counter. Only when he was at the other side did he realise something was wrong and shouted at the gunman, who was again demanding money. The shop owner refused, there was a fight and a shot went off.

While this was happening I looked at them and called upon Shri Mataji to look at how South Africans behave. I so wanted her to see through my eyes as to what was happening. The gunman fled as he knew that there was a police station nearby. I ran to the door, and suddenly there were more shots coming from the police station. Later the policeman told me that the gunman turned to shoot me in the doorway, so he fired shots into the air to stop the robber.

The pizza shop owner took the bullet for me - there is no doubt about that. He was shot in the arm, and thankfully we all lived to tell the tale. As I was so focused on the gunman, I did not see the shop owner and his son walk between me and the gunman.

I had another gun incident, in a shopping mall, but this time I ducked and stayed where I was. The hijacker was killed. This time the man ran right past me and could have grabbed me as a hostage but thank God he didn't.

Shri Mataji has given us extremely good techniques to use and I would like to share them with the world. Without her I would not be here today. On one occasion she told the Sahaja Yogis that if ever any of us are in our direst extremity of danger, if we think of her we will be saved. And I was.'

Daniela Picciafuoco of Milan, Italy, tells how her daughter was saved.

'Veronica, my daughter, was saved from the terrible train crash at Paddington, London, in October 1999 where many people were killed. She saw the other train rushing into her coach while she was writing, and luckily she was not sitting normally, but with her legs up, otherwise they would have been completely sheared off. She remembers seeing seats flying around, and thinks she must have fainted, because doesn't recall any noise. She came to her senses very quickly though, before the fire and smoke could reach her, ran towards the exit, and as she did, she saw burnt corpses.

"When I saw the crash coming," she told us, "I suddenly thought of Shri Mataji and my attention went towards the Sahasrara chakra on the top of my head. I only remember silence and thought, "When will it be over?" and somehow got out unhurt.'

The editor tells of a fraught journey.

'I was living in South Africa and went to a Sahaja programme in the USA, via the UK. The first close shave was leaving Johannesburg. The plane roared down the runway but a few metres before the end came to a screaming halt instead of taking off, and the pilot apologised, saying that the left side engines had not powered up and if he had not braked like that we would have crashed. He said we would have to return to the terminal, deplane while they checked everything and possibly wait for another plane. I gave a bandhan and started reading the Hanuman Chalisa, the praise of Shri Hanuman, who fixes problems, especially of travellers. I got half way through the forty verses, and the pilot said, 'It was a mistake, it was just that the instruments did not record that the engines had fired up. Everything is ok now.' So off we went to London without further delay.

I joined a group of Sahaja Yogis from England going to pay their respects to Shri Mataji in the USA, in June 2000. We were just coming into JFK, New York, but instead of feeling the bump as the plane landed, there was a swoop and we went up in the air again, and finally landed some minutes later. The pilot said he had seen a plane stationary just ahead of us on the runway and if we had landed it would have been disastrous. Shri Mataji has said many times that if there are Sahaja Yogis on a plane it will be all right.

After the trip, I was returning to Port Elizabeth, then my home town. The winds were very strong, and we were in for a bumpy landing. We approached the airport, the plane bouncing in the wind, when suddenly there was the most powerful smell of electrical burning. Everyone, even the cabin staff, looked very frightened, the oxygen masks came down and people started to scream.

I felt strangely calm, as if time had stopped, and stared at the panic around me as the smell got worse and worse. Then I came to my senses and gave a bandhan, and in my heart prayed, 'I am living in this town and trying to tell people about Sahaja Yoga, so please, let the plane land safely.' At that precise moment the electrical smell completely disappeared and the plane stopped jumping around in what seemed to be a gale force wind. We landed a little later, and the pilot, in a rather shaky voice, apologised.'

The hole in the plane

When the editor saw this reported on the TV news, her immediate reaction was 'Oh, there had to be Sahaja Yogis on board,' and there were - Robert and Belinda Henshaw, who were returning home to Australia from a Sahaja Yoga programme in Italy in July 2008.

'I will try and put into words the amazing experience I had on the QF 30 (Qantas) flight from Hong Kong in July 2008.

It was virtually a full flight with a lot of children on the plane. We had been flying for approximately an hour and a half, at 29,000 feet. Rob, my husband, woke me up as a delicious smelling fish dish had just arrived. I was about to open it up when we heard a large bang and a strong gust of wind came rushing into the cabin. I heard a man yelling and immediately thought someone had opened the door and people were being sucked out. Rob and I both had our seat belts on so we pulled them tight. I couldn't believe what was happening. I thought this sort of thing only happened in the movies and surely not to me.

Somewhere during this drama I put the situation into bandhan and put my attention at Sahasrara. The plane lurched to the side and then went nose down at quite a speed towards the China Sea. At that point I and I'm sure everyone else on that plane felt that was it. Then Rob was helping me with my oxygen mask and I told him he was meant to put his on first before helping me. I was in a very calm state - no fear or terror, cocooned in the vibrations from Mother's love, because we were returning from a programme with her at Cabella in Italy.

The plane flattened out once we reached 10,000 feet and after a while we had a message that we could take our masks off. Everyone was quiet and the pilot announced that we were going to land in Manila. One of the air hostesses then came around with a slightly panicked tone to her voice telling us to put the lunch trays under the chairs, tables up and seats upright.

I was a bit worried as I felt the crew knew something that we didn't. Were we going to have a crash landing or was the plane going to fall apart before we reached the ground? The plane was rattling around quite a bit and didn't feel very secure. I gave more bandhans and asked Rob to point out the emergency exits, just in case.

We had a very good landing and there was loud applause from the passengers. No one, not even the pilot, knew what had occurred until we got off and saw that huge hole. Everyone felt lucky to be alive! Not one person was hurt in any way. It was a true miracle. May we all have absolute faith that the divine looks after us, protects us and loves us at all times.'

The hole in the plane, just behind the wing

Rob Henshaw's side of the story

'Rarely does any aircraft stay in one piece with a massive hole the size shown in the Qantas QF30 747. Most experts claim that if the airplane were 1000 feet higher, it would have broken up in midair. At any higher altitude an explosive decompression is catastrophic and even at the height we were at it was very difficult, according to the investigating authorities. It was not until we got off the plane that we saw the massive hole and realized we had experienced a major miraculous escape.

I shot various images for news services, although I was just making a record until I spoke with my news chief, who wanted anything I shot. So we were rather busy once on the ground.

Bel mentioned the faith we should all have particularly at these times, and I would add that surrender is one of our greatest strengths, that everything is taken care of and that we need not worry about anything in our lives or families, that a far greater power is working around us at all times and all we need do is surrender to this divine love.'

Editor's note: Rob later mentioned that the sale of the photos to the news agencies paid for their trip.

Chapter 27

Incidents and Accidents with Cars

Some of these stories could be explained as being fortunate coincidences. Maybe they were, but whatever, Sahaja Yogis seem to get more than their fair share of them. Hamid Mehrani-Mylany from Vienna tells this story.

'I was driving in Vienna and absent-mindedly went through a red light into a tunnel. This tunnel was such that when the light went red, traffic from the other direction would come through for some minutes, filling the whole tunnel. When the light went green from my end, all the traffic would be going the other way, and oncoming traffic would wait. Firstly, it was a busy road and there always was traffic coming through, and secondly, once I had entered the tunnel I could not turn round or back out. Also, the oncoming traffic would not be expecting a car to be coming towards it, so it was a very dangerous situation.

As a Sahaja Yogi would, I prayed for help, 'Please stop the traffic in the other direction.' There was a car at the other end of the tunnel, the first to cross the green light. At the further entrance to the tunnel it suddenly broke down, thereby blocking all the other traffic entering the tunnel and preventing any vehicle from driving into me.

I stopped my car to give him a hand, as I was by now out of danger and out of the tunnel. His car, for some reason, started straight away. He thanked me and we both drove off.'

Aniruddha Bhattacharya and his family also had a miraculous escape.

'It was a beautiful day, the first weekend of March, 2000, and we were in the USA. My wife, mother, baby daughter and I had gone to watch a dolphin show. On our way back the car was running smoothly, at around 130 km, on the busiest interstate highway in Connecticut. All in a sudden, I had no control - the brakes, steering, everything completely stopped working.

The next moment our car approached the left side wall of the highway, hit the side railing, started bouncing and finally jumped the side wall to settle down with its wheels on top, at the other side of the highway with extreme risk of getting hit by cars coming from the opposite direction. It looked like a smashed matchbox and the rods, springs, seats and everything else had broken and come out, and heavy smoke covered the car.

At the moment of the accident, just before the blackout, I prayed for help.

We saw people from both sides of the road stopping their cars and running towards ours, which is not common in the USA because of legal restrictions to avoid the unwanted death of victims due to careless handling. They took us out through the broken windows of the burning car much before the police, fire brigade and ambulance appeared. Almost everyone there started crying seeing us all alive; after witnessing the deadly accident they just couldn't believe their eyes.

Where the car had landed on the opposite side of the road, there was a small piece of grass, just on that place and nowhere else, and because our car came to rest on that soft grassy surface cars from opposite direction would not hit us. Also we were amazed to see how in the wreckage all four of us, including our little daughter, had been placed absolutely safely.

Nobody, including the police and fire people could believe that we could all be alive and unharmed, seeing the state of our car. Shri Mataji's photo that I used to keep in the car was on top of the debris. After the accident I felt tremendous vibrations flowing all over my body for a long time.'

Here are two stories which are similar to each other, one in Shri Mataji's presence and the other not. Werner Steindl, a retired librarian from Vienna, told this first one.

'In summer 1985, Shri Mataji went by train from Paris to Den Haag, Holland. The Sahaja Yogis welcomed her at the station and escorted her to a car, which was waiting outside. While Shri Mataji and three other people were seated in her Mercedes, my friend Engelbert stood next to me near the right front wheel of the car. It started to move backwards, turning to the left at the same time. My attention was fully on Shri Mataji and suddenly I saw her face go tense for two seconds, afterwards she relaxed and smiled again. Engelbert started to laugh too at this point. After the car with Shri Mataji had gone, he told me that the Mercedes had driven over his right foot. Although his foot should have been completely crushed, he had only felt a prickle.'

Chris Coles from America was also present.

'The Sahaja Yogis welcomed Shri Mataji and escorted her to a car. She was in the white Mercedes, and Dr Engelbert was standing next to me just beside the right front wheel of the car. As the car reversed and turned out of the parking space it seemed to bounce and there was a loud and unmistakable cracking noise as the car had apparently run over Engelbert's foot. I looked directly at him and for a split second his face froze in shock. The next moment Shri Mataji moved across to the window of the car and laughingly waved her finger at Engelbert. After the car with Shri Mataji had left, he walked away without even a limp.

Later that day we went to the public programme. The main hall where Shri Mataji was speaking was full, so the organisers opened up a second hall. Engelbert was giving an introductory talk in this hall. I was in the corridor outside showing new arrivals where to find a seat. All of a sudden one of the Austrian girls came dashing out of the hall.

'Engelbert is telling the story of the car driving over his foot!' He explained that as an intern at an Emergency Unit, nearly every day he saw patients whose feet had been run over by smaller cars and their feet were completely smashed, but his foot had been run over by a large Mercedes. After Shri Mataji had left, Engelbert could walk with no pain, so he had literally run back to his hotel room, where he had taken his shoe and sock off and there was not even so much as a bruise or sock imprint on his foot.'

A similar near disaster happened to Ambar Chatterjee, the physicist.

'My wife and I arrived in Cabella for a programme in July 2006. We were grateful to Shri Mataji for having brought us to this divine place, where we would be connected amidst the three thousand Sahaja Yogis from the world over who were already here. On Sunday we had a bit of free time, we decided to walk towards the village and ascend to the castle, on the hill, so that we could sit and meditate at the foot of Shri Mataji's abode.

On reaching the main road just above the camp, we saw the possibility of taking a lift with a Sahaja Yogi who was also on the way to the village. She stopped her car, and her daughter began to clear the back seat. I opened the door on the left side to help. My wife was doing the same on the right side. Just then, the yogini took the car forward just a bit, and the rear tyre started to climb over my left foot. I immediately raised my voice, but the yogini spoke only Italian and my English words were not much use. In the linguistic mix up, she took the car forward and parked it right over my foot without realising what she was doing! I remember only that I felt no pain. Shouting aloud seemed to be the only way to communicate. The tyre was parked on my foot for some twenty seconds, then driven forward and reversed once again over the foot before at last the foot was free. The lady got down from the car and was sobbing over the event, lamenting over our communication gap.

There was no doctor at hand in the village on a Sunday, but we did not need one. I felt no pain, although there was some blood visible and marks of the tyre on the foot, and I was wearing soft shoes. We went back and I sat down, received vibrations from some helpful Sahaja Yogis, and after some time I watched the havan from afar, sitting outside the hanger. I looked down again and I saw no trace of blood and I sat and waited for the other part of the programme.

The next day we returned to Caen, France, as normal, carrying our heavy luggage out of the tent, walking and climbing. The foot was as good as ever.'

Jeff Raum, a professional artist, was resident in New York at the time of the story.

'On January 27th 1989 we were driving down a lonely dark road to a Sahaja Yoga seminar, having picked up two Sahaja Yogis from Ohio at the airport. We came to the turn-off to the camp, I was making my left hand turn when suddenly from behind a car came up and tried to pass me on the left. He went zooming by, taking my front bumper with him. We didn't even feel the impact as we watched the car and my bumper continue to fly down the road! It was eleven at night on a deserted street in the middle of nowhere. I stopped the car on the side of the road. I prayed, "What to do?"

At that moment, a state police car slowly drove up and stopped at the stop sign. I walked on over and simply reported the accident. It seemed at the time so natural for that police car to appear. As the officer filled out the report, a car appeared and the occupant announced he had seen the whole thing, followed the car and had taken down the licence plate number. All of this happened in just a few minutes, as if everyone had been waiting in the wings, for their cue.'

This is written by Calin Costian, from the USA.

'My wife and I were once involved in a bad car accident. Our car went off the highway and onto the grassy area between the inbound and outbound lanes. It flipped over and slid on its roof for several long seconds that felt like eternity, at the speed of 70 miles per hour. Then it flipped again and landed on its four wheels. A few cars pulled over and people came to us to ask us if we needed an ambulance. To their stupefaction, my wife and I thanked them but declined, got out of the car and walked away. Our brand new car was totalled, but we didn't have a single scratch. I just had a tiny bump on my head, the kind that hurts only when you press on it.'

This is by Hemangi Pitale from Mumbai, India.

'In 1999, we went to Ganapatipule to help prepare for the December

Sahaja Yoga seminar. The twelve of us started our journey, which takes about ten hours from Mumbai. When we were about fifteen minutes away from Ganapatipule our jeep fell into a deep cutting at the side of the road as we tried to miss a speeding bus. We tumbled into such a position that small stones formed a sort of platform on which our car rested with its two side wheels up in the air, at the edge of the deep valley. One movement and all of us and the car would go straight down over the edge. The villagers saw us and came running but refused to touch us.

"They are all going to die," we heard them say to each other.

One lady with us managed to get out through the driver's window, then opened the door. We lay flat on our stomachs and she pulled us out by our hands. We had a man with us who was quite robust and we had tough time pulling him out. None of us felt disturbed, as we were in a meditative mood and enjoying the beauty within us and outside.

The next morning we went to the temple of Shri Ganesha at Ganapatipule, and thanked all the deities for helping us and being with us. To our amazement when we saw the sky there, on the sea shore, we saw many clouds shaped like Shri Ganesha, with his elephant head and showing its trunk. One of Shri Ganesha's qualities is that he removes obstacles and helps us overcome difficulties.

Afterwards one of the men with us said that the villagers were not ready to help us because they thought there was no hope. On the very same spot where our car tumbled there had been six accidents recently and none of the other people in them had survived. We were the seventh one. They were amazed that any of us were alive. We were all very much alive, and without a single scratch. Not only us, but even our car was intact and without any scratches.

The most interesting thing was that the flowers we offered to Shri Mataji's photo in the car while starting our journey were absolutely fresh the next day, as if they have been offered a few minutes before. In the heat of India flowers fade and die within a few hours. Also while returning we again saw both the ends of a rainbow in the same valley.'

Auriol Purdie remembers an incident from her childhood.

'We had a VW Combi in 1980, when I was very small, about six years old. One time, I stood up on the front bumper and was trying to clean the windows. I had my fingers in the door and someone came along and shut the door on them. When the person opened the door again my fingers were hanging at a very unnatural angle and were obviously broken.

We were going to meet Shri Mataji at Gatwick Airport and one of the Sahaja Yogis held my hand. I was in absolute agony, but my hand was all bandaged up. We met Shri Mataji and she held on to my hand really, really tightly. When she took her hand away it was still a bit sore, but it definitely wasn't broken and it definitely was before that. Before, my fingers were all at a totally unnatural angle, but they weren't after that.'

Shridevi Angurala tells of an escape like a Bollywood movie
'In 1988, my father, Mr Surender Pal Angurala, was coming home and met with a major accident. He crashed into a truck and his scooter went right under it, and it was running. He said the words - Jai Shri Mataji - and somehow came out from underneath, sliding like a movie hero. He drove back home with just some scratches on his body, all safe and sound to tell the tale.'

Shri Mataji has often said that if Sahaja Yogis are in a dire situation, they should think of her, and help will come.
'I live in Malaysia in Kuala Lumpur. In 1993 I had just dropped off my husband at the airport and was returning home alone in the car. Two motorcyclists were a little ahead of me. The first hit the rear of the second motorcycle, causing the first one to fall on its left side. The rider, however, fell to the right side of the motorcycle and into the path of my car. The second motorcyclist was unaffected and sped off.

I could not stop or swerve my vehicle and only managed to cry out, "Shri Ma!" before driving over the first motor cyclist. I brought my car to a halt on the shoulder of the road. My hands and knees were shaking, my heart pumping and I looked into the rear view mirror. I saw him lying in the middle of the left lane, where I had just driven. He slowly got up, brushed some dirt off his trousers, walked to his motor cycle and heaved it up. He checked it, slowly mounted it, started the engine and began to move. It all seemed in slow motion and unreal. My heart was dreading the moment he would pass me by. I was expecting to be verbally abused by him, but as he passed he did not even turn to look at me.

I watched as he rode ahead until he was out of sight. It took me a full five minutes before I could stop my knees from shaking and little more time to just calm down. I recall crying in utter relief and gratitude, for a while.'
Malathi Menon

Not an ideal way to spend Christmas Eve, from Mark Williams, the journalist from Australia.

'Quite a few years ago I was working as a photojournalist with a journalist colleague in the Australian outback. It was Christmas Eve and we were driving towards Birdsville, Australia's most isolated township. It was about 48 degrees Centigrade, the hottest day in 25 odd years, I heard later. We hadn't seen another car o.r any other living thing in two days of driving. Outside it was a harsh almost Martian landscape though with Bach and Mozart playing, the A/C blaring, and with lots of philosophical discussion we were lulled into a cozy comfort zone.

We were on dirt roads and while driving late one morning I noticed at the bottom of a sandy hill an odd looking patch of dust covering the road. Not realising what it was we drove straight through it.

Except we didn't make it through. It was a silty muddy ditch with a dry layer of dust on top. As you can imagine, mud was the last thing you'd expect in the desert heat. Anyway, the 4WD sank all the way down to the door frames. We were stuck. And somewhat ironically, we had just reported on a German couple who got stuck in exactly the same way and died of dehydration.

We tried everything to get it out. We couldn't dig it out of the fine silt and there was nothing to chock the wheels. After about half an hour of trying we were dizzy from the heat and starting to worry.

My colleague was an atheist and much of our discussion was about whether God existed or not. That said, we'd become good friends. We'd tried everything you'd usually do, releasing pressure from tyres, putting our backs under the wheels and so on.

Nothing worked and now it was a real life or death situation. We were 300kms (half a day's drive) from Birdsville with no phone contact. No one knew we were coming. It was a holiday. We had enough water one day only. There was no way we were getting out as the car was all the way up to the door in mud.

Now I had to pray for help. So I sat in the driver's seat, took a bandhan and went into meditation. Strangely, although my heart was racing, it was easy to go silent. My colleague watched on, a little cynical.

I prayed to Lord Hanuman, "Please forgive us Lord, if we've made any mistakes. But please Lord, get us out of here. We surrender this all to you."

I bandhaned it as well. Then I put the car into first gear, revved the engine all the way to redline and popped the clutch. The engine roared and the car leapt straight out of the silty ditch.'

Chapter 28

Grave and Chronic Health Problems

The editor relates a story of Ashwini Koorich, a businessman who lived in Dehra Dun, a town in the foothills of the Himalayas.

'Ashwini had marvellous brothers-in-law. One of them came to Dehra Dun on a holiday and got his self realisation from Ashwini. Then he returned home to Delhi. Shortly before getting self realisation, he had had some x-rays. The doctors said he had a foreign body in his knee and they would have to operate. Luckily, just before they did so they decided to do one final x-ray, and the particle had completely disappeared. The only difference was that he had received self realisation. They were amazed.

Dehra Dun was a newly established Sahaja Yoga group in 1986, and Shri Mataji invited any of the Sahaja Yogis, who wanted to meet her to Pune, in central India. When we reached Mumbai, after an exhausting two-day train journey, Ashwini arranged for us to stay with his Mumbai brother-in-law, a wealthy industrialist. The family had a big flat in the most upmarket part of Mumbai, and in the early morning a taxi would take us to the train station for Pune. As soon as was polite we all, except Ashwini and his brother-in-law, went to bed. Our host had a problem with his spine, which had been bent from childhood, and as a result he had a hump of flesh that protruded at one side of his back. It was quite noticeable and both the lump and his curved spine had been giving him trouble for years.

The next morning we were woken up very early. The taxi didn't come and then Ashwini's brother-in-law said he was taking us, so we all got into his jeep and off we went. After some time we realised he was going a very strange way to the station, over the causeway out of the city on the Pune road. We asked him what was going on. He said he and Ashwini had been up almost all night, and Ashwini had given him self realisation, and also vibrations. By the early hours of the morning, his hump had disappeared and he was standing up straight for the first time in many years.

"I've had a miracle," he said, "and I'm going to drive you up to Pune myself, even though it's quite a long way (a four hour drive) and I should be at my factories today, because I want to personally thank the lady who has made this possible." We reached the flat where Shri Mataji was staying in Pune, and explained that our host, Ashwini's brother-in-law, had insisted coming to thank her personally. She was very touched.'

Anthony Visconti, a chemical engineer in Milan, tells us how the attention of Shri Mataji could relieve the gravest of troubles, but it was up to us to sustain the cure.

'At a public programme in America with Shri Mataji several years ago, after the programme Shri Mataji received all the people who were in the public and she stayed there for several hours, receiving one by one. And during this procession a man who was spastic from birth – and he couldn't walk properly, he couldn't speak, he couldn't do anything properly. He was taken to Shri Mataji and she took some roasted chick peas and passed them over his body and ate them, and said she was taking away his negativity. The man became absolutely normal for at least twenty seconds. He was smiling and enjoying himself but after he left Shri Mataji, after a short while, he went back to the way he was before.

Shri Mataji said he went back to his old identification, his old way of thinking, so that let the negativity come back in. At least he had been able to experience what it meant to be free and find his own potential for that short period of time.'

This account was written in the mid 1990's by a Sahaja Yogi of Chennai, India, many years after he was declared dead.

'In December 1971 I fell sick with serious anaemia, my entire body turned yellow with a hemoglobin count of five – normal being about fifteen. I sank into a coma and was rushed to hospital in Mumbai with a recovery chance of hardly five per cent.

At that time, by divine providence, Shri Mataji Nirmala Devi was in Mumbai and a close relative of ours took my worried children to her. When they told Shri Mataji about me, she assured them that she would put her attention on me and I would be all right in a few days. After two weeks I was discharged from hospital.

Two weeks later I went for a check-up and was found to be perfectly normal and in good health, to the amazement of the doctors. I was put on some strong medicines, but Shri Mataji advised me to discard them all. She warned me that my continued intake of these strong medicines would give me a heart attack. Ignoring her advice and thinking that out of caution I had to take these medicines, I went on for a while till Shri Mataji sent another warning. I then discontinued the medicines, but it was too late.

In 1973 I had a severe heart attack and was rushed to Jaslok Hospital, Mumbai, where I was examined and declared dead, and my pulse having totally failed. Shri Mataji was in London and was contacted over the telephone. Her attention and blessings were given to me from London and I recovered; it was not necessary for her to be physically present. Her collective attention and vibrations travelled like lightning to any distance.'

Brian Bell, a producer and scriptwriter, is a New Zealander now living in Sydney, Australia.

'At the age of six Brian was attacked in the left ankle by osteomyelitis, a disease of the bone marrow. Over the following years, he was regularly in hospital undergoing a number of operations. Most of his youth, he spent on crutches. Through adult life there were continuing flare-ups and crippling seizures.

In 1979, forty years after the first attack, a particularly severe and painful disability was diagnosed as a rare form of tuberculosis, which had settled into what remained of his left ankle. To cure this he was put on a regimen of antibiotics which would last for at least two years.

Shortly after the course of pills started, Brian, on crutches again, received, through the grace of Shri Mataji Nirmala Devi and the agency of the Australian Sahaja Yogis, his self realisation. In a matter of days he was off the crutches. In less than two months, he was walking without even a stick for support. In less than six months the regular check-up proved, to the astonishment of the doctors, that the tubercular infection had completely disappeared.

When Brian first met Shri Mataji, she had him lying on the floor with one of her feet on his ankle and the other on his leg.

"To get the vibrations flowing," Shri Mataji said.

What the doctors had expected to take over two years had taken less than six months and for the first time in nearly four decades, Brian was without pain. He could put his attention on something much more important, his spiritual ascent.'

Sometimes Shri Mataji helped people even if they did not consciously ask for it.

'I received my self realisation in 1992, in Malaysia, at a public programme where Shri Mataji Nirmala Devi was present. When she spoke, she began with, "Truth is what it is….," and her dignity, authority and intrinsic majesty touched me to the core of my being. I felt as though I had finally been brought home after many years of wandering and seeking.

I was born with partial facial paralysis affecting the left side of my face. Also, I had no outer ear on the left side. All through my childhood, I struggled with this. My left cheek sagged since there was no movement on that side, the left side of my lips drooped, and my left eye could never be closed properly.

Two years after I received my self realisation, during a Sahaja Yoga seminar in India, I had the opportunity to present a gift to Shri Mataji, and she gently stroked the left side of her face when I was with her.

Since that day, I began to notice, that bit by bit, movement started on the left side of my face. Now, fourteen years later, my face is more balanced: the left cheek does not droop, my lips are fuller and my left eye closes much better than before. Even my left ear, which used to be closed tight and affected my hearing, is now opening up. This, to me, is a demonstration of the tremendous love of Shri Mataji, who blessed even when you had no words to ask for it, and whose blessings were gentle and gradual, like the soft touch of cleansing rain.'

Latha Nayar

Bogunia Bensaude of Australia relates a biblical style miracle.

'Shri Mataji did a miracle similar to one Christ did, at Nagpur, India, outside the church she attended as a child. The story started in Delhi, about two weeks before Christmas in 1983. Shri Mataji invited any Sahaja Yogis who wanted to join her with her family at Christmas at Nagpur. The family were getting together not only to celebrate Christmas, but also to attend the dedication of a statue to her father, Mr Salve, who had played a prominent part in the emancipation of India and had been the mayor of Nagpur.

On Christmas Day we all went to church, as the Salve family were Christians. Shri Mataji's brother, a bishop, was one of the people giving a sermon. Those of us who were not of the family had been given seats outside the church in the yard around and, as all the doors were open, we could see and hear what was going on. However, it began to rain and we all ran into the church and finished up sitting at Shri Mataji's feet, because she was in the front pew.

After the service all the Salve family went outside into the yard and began talking to each other. We stayed in the church for a few minutes with Shri Mataji, who walked down the aisle and out of the main door. An old man in a wheelchair was in the corner of the atrium at the entrance to the church. As Shri Mataji came out of the main door of the church, she saw him and greeted him.

"Oh, it's little Nirmala. I worked for your father," he said.

He had apparently been in a wheelchair and not walked for years and must have been well over eighty. Mother went over and asked him to get up and walk. She held his hand, then stepped back and said 'Ut!' meaning "Get up!" He got up and walked over to her.'

Mark Daniel tells of his personal voyage

'As a young and precocious teenager it seemed the world was my oyster. I won prizes for my academic success, achieved recognition for my prowess on the sports field and enjoyed home life in the bosom of a large, loving family. But whilst undergoing my A Levels, I suffered the first breakdown of what was to become a recurring nightmare over the next twenty plus years: severe depressive moods, followed by brief periods of calm normality and then the highs of mania.

Salvation came from an unlikely source, in 1996 - a picture on a library wall, a subsequent telephone call and an invitation to a Sahaja Yoga meeting. I had no great initial revelation, no strong sensation, no earth-shattering, mind-blowing experience but an intuitive knowledge that I had come home.

A year later I was in Mumbai, India, attending our clinic which specialises in Sahaja Yoga treatments. This was the breakthrough, the moment of sublime realisation, I could feel the Kundalini energy, which lies within each of us, coming out of the top of my head as a cool breeze - what had been referred to by the great prophets in their scriptures and by many evolved souls was a living reality, and it was happening to me! I could not deny it, even though my background was that of an atheistic Physics undergraduate.

I have returned from the shadows and am very grateful. Above all I am sure this is something we have to share. I am enjoying my retreat from sickness and malaise and am giving something back to the source of this redemption. I have been working as an English teacher in Turkey. As such I, or really we, as another gift, I have been blessed with a beautiful and loving Sahaja Yogini wife and, have been able to give this experience to many of our students and friends, often helping them to overcome the imbalances and imperfections in their lives, and to be fully restored to the harmony and beauty of the universal truth of the spirit, awakening within them. I am now the director of an English Language school in a Turkish university, responsible for three hundred students. I hope to pass on the miracle and blessing of Sahaja Yoga as widely as possible and let all share equally in the profound experience with which we have been blessed.'

Lala Kisbu of Istanbul felt joy.

'When I got my self realisation on 25th of April, 2001, in Istanbul, Turkey, I was having treatment for depression and my psychiatrist told me my sickness was genetic. Fifteen days after getting self realisation I noticed I was feeling joy. Until then I was not sure about the raising of the Kundalini energy inside of me. I went home and called my doctor and told him that I didn't need medication any longer; I had started yoga and I had felt very good. The doctor was very surprised.

"That's impossible," he said. "You may have to take medication all your life. Don't leave the medication suddenly but if you insist on this idea, then take half the dose."

I took the medicine half dose for fifteen days but I was bothered with side effects so I quit it myself. Since then I have not taken any medication of any kind.'

Lale Kisbu

Editor's note: as a general rule, it is advised to use Sahaja Yoga treatments alongside, not instead of, regular medicine, until one is absolutely sure one is alright.

This is Lyudmila Bredyihinav from Novosibirsk, Russia

'Shri Mataji was touring Russia for the first time; the programmes were held in the cities of Togliatti, Saint Petersburg etc. We were going by bus from Togliatti but did not know where the next programme would take place, where Shri Mataji would go. Intuitively we made the decision to go to Moscow to clean Mother's house in Rastorguevo for her coming. As soon as we had finished cleaning, Shri Mataji's car appeared. After some time Shri Mataji invited all of us to the meeting hall.

"How do you live? What problems do you have? What questions do you have?" Shri Mataji kept asking us.

One Sahaja Yogini had broken her leg some time before in the femoral neck. The plaster had been already taken away, everything had knitted together but the leg did not bend at the knee. Shri Mataji put her attention to it when the Sahaja Yogini sat down (she had her leg straight). Shri Mataji asked the Yogini to sit down in front of her and put her hand on the Sahaja Yogini's Vishuddhi chakra. Shri Mataji placed her leg under the Sahaja Yogini's Swadishthan. At the same time Shri Mataji was talking to the other yogis. In 10 - 15 minutes a joyful cry was heard.

"Guys, my leg is bending!" The Yogini leapt onto her legs and started jumping.'

This story tells how Nirmala Verma started Sahaja Yoga, although she had met Shri Mataji socially some years before.

'In 1975 I fell off a rock at the Mahalakshmi Temple, Mumbai. This temple is on the seashore. At that time I saw a lady with thousands of lights around her. When I fell I developed a crack in my spine and in my coccyx bone and was told that this was incurable and I had to live with it. Then in 1978 when we came to Delhi, we read in the newspaper about Shri Mataji's programme. So, I started going to Shri Mataji to learn Sahaja Yoga. One day she told me that the Kundalini resided in the coccyx bone in three and a half coils and the Greeks called it the sacrum bone because it is sacred. I asked her, if I had a crack in my coccyx bone, could my Kundalini still rise.

"I know you have a crack in your coccyx bone," Shri Mataji said, even though nobody had told her.

Later she asked me to sit down and put her feet exactly at the spot on my spine where I had the crack, then asked me to stand up. That was the first time in years that I could stand up without pain. I have felt no pain in my spine since then, thirty years later.'

Shri Mataji said that Jane's life could be saved.

'On the 16th June, 2002, my daughter Kamala and I were driving to Pesaro from Rome to visit grandparents. Suddenly a young man came out of his line of traffic onto my side of the road immediately in front of me and we had a head on collision, both going about 90 km/hr.

Some months later my husband Andrea and I went to see the car, and up until that moment I assumed all the miracles were in the hospital. Seeing the car, there was no doubt at all that at that moment the divine power saved my life. The engine block was right under the windscreen, my seat twisted towards the driver's door, the pedals were up under the radio in front of the gear stick and all the glass was broken. Looking at it, you would be certain the driver would have no chance. While trapped in the car I was very squashed, and knew some things must be broken, but I never lost consciousness. After about 20 minutes a helicopter arrived to cut me out. The man in the helicopter remembered me well because he said it was rare that someone chatted to him on their way to hospital. I was taken to Ancona Hospital, famous for its high standards.

They had to fix many bones and remove the spleen, some intestines, some colon and part of the rectum. Breathing tubes were used for months. Visiting was restricted, and only my husband and one other person were allowed in at a time. They always worked openly, raising the Kundalini and giving vibrations to all the chakras over and over again. They put Shri Mataji's picture on the chakras. As other Sahaja brothers and sisters were doing, with my husband's attention (at his apartment and by the hospital bed) he offered puja for my chakras. Also he did many other Sahaja techniques to help me.

There were many miracles in the hospital. I was in an induced coma for at least six weeks. My kidneys had stopped working for at least two months, and I was receiving regular dialysis. The doctors knew the kidneys were shrivelled and without life and therefore dialysis would always be needed. However, a lot of Yogis put their attention on my kidneys. One evening my husband Andrea went behind the bed to massage the area on the head where the brain controls the kidneys. He asked Shri Mataji to come and help the kidneys and prayed that he could be a completely clear channel for her loving and healing vibrations - and then he experienced a very deep meditation. The next day the kidneys started to work!

"You must understand that this is a miracle," the doctors said.

There was damage to the rectum and some had been removed. There was too much necrotic (dead) tissue in the area which could give a lethal infection to the whole body and the doctors said they had to operate and close it completely. They needed my husband's permission because the operation would be dangerous. He stayed near my bed for a very long time, praying. He put his fingers in that direction and went into a very deep/high meditation. He felt a wind blowing very strongly from the end of his fingers to that area. In this state of complete thoughtlessness the image of a dark tube appeared and he continued to pray to Shri Mataji - then there were flashes like lightning in this tube until it became full of light. Then he 'woke up'. The doctor came to say that after the latest analysis they could not avoid the operation, because it was endangering my life. That night and the next morning, Andrea offered the simplest puja.'

"We don't need to do the operation, it is not needed any more," the doctors said when he arrived at the hospital.

"Why? What has happened?"

"Just before going to the operating theatre, we did the last test and there was no more necrotic tissue. New pink cells have grown in its place."

I was in hospital for five months, and had to learn to walk again. The surgeon was really impressed with my blood analyses, especially the liver. He said the reading for it was better than 'normal'. That is a miracle too, after all the antibiotics!

Many who came to visit in the hospital had incredibly powerful experiences and some said they felt Shri Mataji's presence so strongly. Shri Mataji said that my life could be saved with her picture near me, and with the power of the collective desire. And thus it was.'

Jane Antonioni

Sometimes the doctors do not diagnose correctly, as George Naidu of South Africa explains.

'On May 13, 2004 I was in Johannesburg. My job as an executive often had me travelling the length and breadth of the country, including many international trips. On this particular day, I had a high temperature. The doctor was called and I was diagnosed with a bout of flu. However, I was feeling a catch in the Void (the area around the third subtle centre, in the abdomen, and if there is a catch, or problem it will be felt as a heat or tingling on the outer part of the palm of the hand). I made an appointment with a physician and the tests conducted gave the all systems clear, so the doctor told me to stop worrying.

I felt that there was something wrong and asked to be admitted to hospital. The doctor warned that as this was against his recommendation I would have to pay the medical bills - the medical aid would not pay as the doctor did not admit me. I booked myself in the next day and test results indicated a cancerous tumour, in the area of the lower abdomen, requiring a major operation. Two days later the operation was completed relatively successfully, and the medical aid did pay. I did not want chemo or specific treatment.

Six months later, I went to the Belapur Sahaja Health Centre, Mumbai, India, where intense Sahaj treatment was recommended. This treatment was still practised when I returned to South Africa. There has been no re-occurrence.'

Chapter 29

Dreams and Visions

Many Sahaja Yogis dream of Shri Mataji, and often the dreams give counsel or hope. Others are prophetic. This is Bala Kanayson, who is involved in the type of engineering which requires hard headed precision, accuracy and reliability. On one occasion he told the editor some of what he had designed was at that moment on its way to the planet Jupiter.

'My background was twelve years in a Methodist school, plus at that time I was a newly qualified aerospace engineer just out of college, with all that scepticism. Quite soon after getting my self realisation, in 1977, I was in Shri Mataji's presence at one of the Caxton Hall, London, public programmes, and experienced spiritual ecstasy.

There were relatively few people in the room. At each programme, she would sit down and close her eyes and the Sahaja Yogis would also close their eyes. But I would always watch what was going on, still being rather curious. On this particular day, the 8th of April 1978, I was watching Shri Mataji very closely and she opened her eyes, looked straight at me and then something very amazing happened.

She gazed at me and I felt as though I was being pulled into her eyes. The next thing I knew, I was being whirled into a cosmic flux back through time and experiencing all the things that I had studied in history whizzing past me. I distinctly saw/heard/smelt/felt certain objects like a sabre-tooth tiger, the universe, planets, etc., until it came back to the beginning. There was nothing, just nothing, and, in the middle of this nothingness was Shri Mataji.

It encompassed me, this thick transparent sphere of complete silence. I felt complete love and compassion flowing out of me, and I was in tune with everything. All of nature, all of life, was living and breathing with me. My every gesture made ripples and waves in this completely interlinked creation. This lasted for three days and nights, where I was in a perpetual state of ecstasy. It is impossible to describe.

After I had this experience, I went back home and wrote a letter to Shri Mataji. The next time I went to London, she came up on stage and looked straight at me.

"Bala, that was a beautiful letter you wrote me," she said.

Auriol Purdie remembers one of her dreams when a child.

'Not long before I met Shri Mataji, when I was five years old, in 1979, my parents and I were going through a rough patch and I had a dream that an Indian lady, who I later realised was Shri Mataji, was standing at the prow of a barge looking at me.

"Don't worry, I'll come and get you soon," she said with great love in her eyes, in the dream. She was wearing a sari which had spots on it and I remembered it very clearly. I had another dream where she came to see us at our house in Scotland, on the banks of a loch, in a beige coloured Mercedes.

My parents went to meet Shri Mataji down in London. I didn't go but soon after she came up to our house in Scotland with a lot of the Sahaja Yogis. I was only very small then, but knew she was a great person. When she arrived, her car pulled up and it was a beige Mercedes. She got out and was wearing exactly the same sari as she had been wearing in the dream, so I knew exactly who she was.'

Andrea Cousins, who nowadays has a responsible position in the public sector in America, has two dream stories.

'Shri Mataji came to New York in about 1982 approximately a year after I'd become a yogi. The local Sahaja Yoga leader had explained over the months that Shri Mataji works on several levels, both on the conscious and subconscious. She said that Shri Mataji often worked on us in the dream state. I dreamed of her and the dream was set at a public programme; Shri Mataji turned and pointed her right Vishuddhi (index) finger at me. This chakra is connected with Lord Krishna.

"Open your mouth!" she said in the dream. Her command was so direct that when I awoke, my mouth was wide open.

The day of Shri Mataji's programme arrived and the question of her presence in the dream kept surfacing. Finally, in my heart, I begged Shri Mataji to put the question to rest, "Were you really in my dream telling me to open my mouth?"

Shri Mataji proceeded with her talk but my questions kept surfacing. Then, amazingly, Shri Mataji began telling a story of little Lord Krishna. She spoke of how the mischievous toddler loved to steal the butter, which was supposed to go to the rulers of the land, who were devils, thus weakening their strength. Shri Mataji spoke of how one day Shri Krishna's mother was preparing some food, when the butter disappeared. She asked him where it was and the ever-playful Shri Krishna shook his head.

"Open your mouth," his mother commanded. In his mouth was the sight of the universe. Shri Mataji had given me my answer, not only the answer of my dream, but the answers of the universe. America is the country corresponding to the Vishuddhi chakra as far as the world goes. It is at the level of the throat in the body, and this is the chakra of Shri Krishna.'

How Andrea Cousins gave up smoking.

'When I received self realisation, in the 1980's, I was a two-pack-a-day smoker and had been for fifteen years. This represented a lot of dollars, and what I believed was a great deal of enjoyment. Shri Mataji did not tell people to stop drinking or smoking and I puffed merrily away for two years after getting my self realisation, but in truth, I couldn't or wouldn't quit. Shri Mataji played little tricks with me. Often I would greet her at the airport and be unable to utter a sound when she spoke to me. Time after time, She would look compassionately at me.

"What's wrong with your Vishuddhi chakra?" she would say knowingly. Obviously one couldn't fool her, but admitting to my smoking seemed too embarrassing.

Finally, one night Shri Mataji appeared to me in a dream. The setting was a party filled with a wide variety of seekers. I sat alone at a long wooden table watching the entrance door. "Wait till you see my guru!" I exclaimed to everyone who passed by. "She's incredible, magnificent."

Suddenly the door swung open and there stood Shri Mataji, beautifully dressed, regally posed with … a cigarette. I was mortified! My head filled with conflicting thoughts. What could this mean? How could she appear here like this? Especially now since I'd told everyone how holy, how special and how righteous she was. Shri Mataji entered the room and approached me. Was she telling me it was okay to smoke? Had I agonized all this time for no reason? Our Mother suddenly appeared before me, right index finger pointed squarely at my face.

"You are not to smoke!" she said sternly, and disappeared.

When I woke up, I threw away my cigarettes and have never had another. Nor, by Shri Mataji's grace, have I had a desire to smoke since that night.'

Wendy Barrett of Australia dreamed Shri Mataji embraced her.

'I dreamt Shri Mataji kissed me and embraced me. Then my dream came true when I went to India. I could only stay for one month, instead of two months, the normal length of those early tours. I went to explain to Shri Mataji that I had to leave early and she asked me to come and sit next to her while she ate her lunch, and held my hand. Whilst talking to other people in the room as well, she would turn around and chat to me and ask me whether I'd bought my husband a nice present and how my children were. I had never told her I had children and a husband, nor had anyone else, and I live in Australia. I sat for about twenty minutes.

"Go on, give me a kiss," she turned around and said all of a sudden. She put her arms around me and I responded likewise; she kissed my cheek and I hers. I felt her hair on my cheeks and was in such bliss that I can't remember leaving her, only arriving back in the adjoining room.'

This lady dreamed of Shri Mataji before seeing her photo or meeting her.

'I am from Jaipur, India. Before I started Sahaja Yoga, I used to see a deity like figure in my dreams, but I could not recognise it. One day I suddenly got a pain in my back and was diagnosed as having a big gap between my lower vertebrae. I could barely move and to add to this the problem extended to my knees. After a few days in the hospital, I came home and found it very difficult to walk and even to sit.

One day my sister visited my place and insisted I went with her to the Sahaja Yoga centre. As I reached there I saw the photo of Shri Mataji and realised this was the figure I had seen in my dreams. Whereas before I could not sit for five minutes, I managed to sit there for two hours.

I started walking and went to my sister's house every day and she gave me healing vibrations. I got well in just seven days, and when I went for a rediagnosis, the doctor found the gap in my vertebral column had disappeared.'

Meera Soni

In Sahaja Yoga, we accept that the left side of our subtle system is governed by Shri Mahakali. In Hindu mythology she is described as a dark lady.

'I discovered Sahaja Yoga through someone who wanted me to give French lessons to her son, then I checked it out on the internet and joined the local centre. For nine years I had had a troublesome lump on the chest – on the sternum bone. It was small outside but had grown inside and had almost reached the heart. I was advised to go for immediate surgery, which would be very complicated.

I insisted on going to the Sahaja Treatment Centre before going ahead with the doctors' plan. I was there for a week and then went for the biopsy. The need for an operation was averted and medication was begun. I also continued the Sahaja treatments, as advised by the Sahaja doctors. Later there was a sudden turn of events and I went into renal failure, and was put on dialysis. I continued my prayers to Shri Mataji and felt she was always with me.

One night while I was in the hospital, in my dream, I felt as if I was in a whirlpool, and was being sucked down into the earth. I shouted, "Mother, Mother!" at the top of my voice and a dark lady entered the room and pierced my left side with an iron rod and I was still shouting. Then everything settled down, and I woke up drenched in sweat.

From the next morning the medical reports all changed. Today I'm just fine, and the tumour has gone.'

Vivek Sawhney

Anna Mancini, an actress and producer from New York, tells this story. She comes from a Christian background.

'In mid 1983 I had constant dreams of earthquakes, buildings collapsing and spasms of intense heat being released from my lower back. There was a great emptiness in my life, and I kept desiring something I couldn't explain or understand. One day I was waiting for a bus. A picture flashed into my mind of a woman dressed in a long white gown, with long black hair. She was standing in a wooded area with cabins and there were little stones on the ground. This vision disappeared but then calmness entered my being.

That evening, after dinner, I rested on the couch while my son played with his toys. Suddenly, my hands felt heavy and strong sensations flashed through my palms and fingers. I sat on the floor and my hands opened as if ready to receive something. I heard a powerful sound coming from above my head, a rushing sound, like a wind blowing. The sound came down and pierced the top of my head and filled my whole being. My son also opened his hands and felt this energy. For the next three weeks I felt peace and joy; nothing bothered me. My son was also constantly feeling this.

Three months later, in September 1983, Shri Mataji came to the United States. I went to her public programme and the next month, October, we had a weekend seminar in northern New York State with her. One beautiful evening she spoke to us and then we enjoyed some bhajans, Indian devotional songs. It was quite late and I went outside for a walk. I realised I had been seeking Shri Mataji all my life and she had been the woman in my vision. On my way back to the cabin, I passed the house where she was staying, and saw the cabins and the wooded area that I had seen in my vision months before, and even felt the little stones under my feet. I had finally come home!

Some time later, I wrote Shri Mataji a letter which contained the basic questions all seekers desire to have answered, 'Who is God? Who are we? What are we doing here? Why are we here?' in answer I had a beautiful dream; Shri Mataji appeared, dressed in a white sari and holding the letter in her hand.

"I am aware," she said simply.

I awoke and could only smile because peace and tranquility filled my whole being. A couple of days later, I was sitting on a bench waiting for my son to come out of school, watching the mothers waiting for their children, and started to think about Shri Mataji. All of a sudden my Kundalini rose so quickly and spontaneously. I felt it on the top of my head very strongly, and then saw all the people coming together, as if they were all one.

Mangal Singh Dillon is a businessman from America.

In November 1999 I had cirrhosis of the liver diagnosed. My liver was shrunk, with a spot on it, and my spleen was enlarged. The doctors said I had to have a liver transplant and needed to have the spleen removed. During my two week stay in hospital, Shri Mataji appeared in my dream, sitting by the bedside.

'How come you got disappointed so soon, yet there is a lot of work still to be done?' she said smilingly, in Hindi. The doctors gave me six months to live if I didn't have the liver transplant. Shri Mataji again appeared in my dream.

"Do not let them remove any parts of your body," she said. "Get out of the hospital. If you have your body parts in place, I can work on them. If you do not have the parts in place, there is nothing I can do."

I left the hospital in the USA and in March 2000 came to the International Sahaja Health Centre at Belapur, Navi Mumbai and stayed for six weeks, doing the Sahaja Yoga treatments they advised. After that I went back to the USA and got my blood checked, and the same doctor as before asked me what I had done, because my liver functions were good. The other doctor who was involved with the specialist said that medical science had failed and spirituality had won.

It is now 2007 and I am seventy-two years old.

"What was going on?" asked Merenia Ashwell.

In October 2003, I was in New Zealand and received a phone call saying my niece Hine had been diagnosed with meningacocol, which can be fatal. Upon her arrival at the hospital she was admitted to the Children's Intensive Care Unit and had tubes connected to all parts of her body, and an oxygen mask assisting her breathing. I went there and spent the night with her so her parents could recuperate. I had a photo of Shri Mataji showing her hands, and put it beside Hine.

I was pleased to see her night nurse was a beautiful Indian lady. Even though I was fairly new to Sahaja, I had an immense confidence in Shri Mataji. I prayed with all my might, singing lullabies to Hine to comfort her cries of pain. I dreamed Shri Mataji was standing at the foot of Hine's bed with her hands up, just like the photo, and healing her by giving her vibrations.

The medical staff ran tests and said she had all the symptoms of the disease. However by the third day Hine was trying to pull her tubes out, and was frustrated at being confined to her bed. The specialist came in and explained the meningicocal was in the blood, so she was lucky not to lose any limbs. Another specialist commented on her rapid recovery, saying maybe they had misdiagnosed her condition, because normally with this disease the patient goes up then down for weeks, but Hine just got better and better. The following morning they sent her back to our home town to recover.'

The ability to see the future, auras and other extra sensory perceptions can cause subtle imbalances, but they can occasionally help people to know how Shri Mataji's message can help them. Kogie Pillay is one of them.

'In 2007 our Sahaja Yoga collective from Durban, South Africa, was giving self realisation at a Mind and Body Fair. Next to our stall was a nice lady who had a lot of her paintings on display. I introduced myself and found out that she was not an artist but a psychic. I began to wonder how I should give her self realisation.

Suddenly an idea came to me – I told her to use her psychic powers and place her hand over the photograph of Shri Mataji on the Sahaja Yoga pamphlet and concentrate on the divine – thereafter she was asked, "How do you feel?" At first she became very silent.

"This person has a very warm heart, she is very peaceful, very calming. She has come on this earth to save all the people," she suddenly said, to my amazement.

Instantly after she said that, I felt a gush of cool wind to my heart and the hair on my hands stood on end!'

Chapter 30

The World Stage

Shri Mataji has explained that because Sahaja Yogis have a connection with the divine all-pervading power, if we desire something sensible it often works out. These 'close coincidences' happen time and again, and how many of these close coincidences need to occur before one can draw some sort of cause and effect connection? An early example of this is the story of Grazyna Anslow, from Poland, who left there for London, long before Perestroika and the demise of Communism.

'In 1981 the political situation in Poland was very tense because of the Solidarity uprising, Shri Mataji called me to do the celebration of respect and worship we have at Christmas. She was very concerned about Poland. Shri Mataji asked me to pray for peace in Poland during the celebration and she said that there should be no bloodshed.

The next day I heard that martial law was declared by General Jaruzelski, who was then the head of state. I did not know what to think, as it was such a controversial decision to make. I found out later on that had Jaruzelski not declared martial law, the Russian tanks, already waiting for an order to go in, would have invaded the country and there would have been terrible bloodshed, followed by occupation of Poland by the Russians troops.

Because of the martial law, the bloodshed was avoided.'

Reza Ghaffurian also desired peace, for Iran.

'On the first Friday of May, 1988, and we were preparing to go to Rome for the weekend when we celebrate the opening of the Sahasrara Chakra. On the Monday afternoon a public programme was held with Shri Mataji in attendance. The hall was packed and at the end she asked those who desired to shake her hand or speak with her to come forward. I had a strong desire to go forward to her and thank her for whatever she had done for me, but stepped back to let the newest ones go forward. Before she began to meet anyone, suddenly she looked around and her eyes lit on me.

"Come here," she said. I went to her and she hugged me warmly and held me. I felt it was the love of a real mother and incredible vibrations surrounded us.

"It is your time to ask if you have any desire," she looked at me and said. It came to my mind that I wanted peace for my country Iran, which had been at war with Iraq for ten years with great destruction to our people.

"I want peace for my country," I asked.

"You can have peace," she replied.

This was a spontaneous request, not planned or even thought out beforehand. Less than a month after this had happened, the news suddenly came out that the war, which had been going on for so long, had been stopped between Iran and Iraq.'

Bohdan Shehovych was in Russia when the counter coup threatened to take the country back to the former regime.

'At the time of the coup or 'putsch', in the early 1990's, Shri Mataji was in Moscow when Gorbachev was kidnapped and held prisoner. The people were totally depressed as they felt the old totalitarian ways would return and the freedom promised by Perestroika would be taken away.

All public gatherings were cancelled in Moscow, except for Shri Mataji's introductory programme, where about 4,500 people attended in a stadium. We had been instructed to finish at 10 pm as there was a military curfew starting at that time, but at 10.30 pm Shri Mataji was still smiling and moving ever so slowly. I drove onto the footpath so that she would not have far to go, and in their enthusiasm, the crowd virtually pressed her into the car.

We started south, from the north of Moscow. I was wondering how we would traverse the centre, where rumours suggested that all the streets were closed to traffic. The city lights were out. Suddenly I heard repeated thumping.

"Oh no!" I thought. "What a time to have a flat tyre." I pulled the car over to the kerb, got out, rolled up my sleeves, took out the spare tyre and jacked up the car. Having taken the flat tyre off, I tried to put the spare on but it simply wouldn't go on. Just then a convoy of sixty heavy battle tanks rumbled past us. Their commanders were directing their tanks from open turrets, and each commander had leather headgear covering their ears, but their faces were extremely pale. "These are just boys!" I thought. "Boys fight the world's battles and old men send them to their deaths."

"Are you all right Mother?" I asked.

"Yes yes, I'm studying the tanks," she replied as she scanned each of the sixty tanks which roared past. Later I learnt that these tanks were ordered to help in the putsch, but refused to take part. My attention went back to the car. I realized now how to bolt the wheel on properly, but this kept us in the street for twenty minutes till I had worked it out. Meanwhile Shri Mataji kept her attention on this world problem. I then accelerated the car.

"Turn here," Shri Mataji would say, as we neared a road which appeared blocked, and I would turn. "Now turn there," and I would do so.

We mounted gutters, went through unfenced yards in the dark and miraculously found ourselves on the south side of the blockade. We left danger behind us and proceeded towards Shri Mataji's dacha outside Moscow, and peace.

A few days later Shri Mataji was to fly to Togliatti where about thirty thousand people were to meet her in a stadium. When we got to the airport officials said we couldn't fly because Togliatti was not amongst the several cities stamped on our visas. I went around to various organisations and government departments to get Togliatti added to our visas but everyone seemed scared to make a decision. Finally we got the appropriate stamps, and again drove Shri Mataji to the airport but this time fog prevented us from flying, so we returned to her flat in Moscow. Shri Mataji mentioned she would go to sleep in the bedroom, and the Sahaja Yogis sat in the kitchen for several hours. We were able to receive international calls for the first time since the coup started, and a phone call came from a Sahaja Yogi in England to inform us that the coup was over and had failed. Just then Shri Mataji came out of the bedroom.

"It appears that the coup has failed," we said.

"Yes, yes I've been working on that," Shri Mataji replied in a very simple way. She said the Ritambara Praghya had worked it out, in that she had to stay in Moscow, so the coup would fail. Each time Shri Mataji had said something simple, like, "Yes, yes I am studying the tanks," or "I have been working on that," it seemed to point towards the end of the coup.'

This story shows the close coincidence, timewise, between a Sahaja Yoga havan and events which helped improve a political situation.

'My name is Victor Vertunni and I came to live at Shri Mataji's castle at Cabella, Italy, in the early 1990's. We were blessed to be in her presence when she started to put her attention on Italy and its problems. She was reading the book by David Yallop, In God's Name: An Investigation into the Murder of Pope John Paul I, at the time. Also there was something emerging called Tangentopoli, a big corruption scandal.

One of the flaws in the Italian constitution is that it did not provide for the financing of political parties, so they had to find ways of getting round this. One way was kickbacks on public contracts, and the proceeds were divided between five parties who held the balance of power in this country. One person to be exposed when this all came out was the Prime Minister, Andreotti, of the Christian Democrats and linked with the Vatican which sustained this party. Money was recycled through the Vatican Bank - Mafia money - and so on. One evening we were sitting with Shri Mataji in her sitting room.

"Can you imagine that these people are sinning, but they are sinning in God's name!" she said.

This was all starting to come out, but no significant convictions were made - everybody knew about them but no one could do anything because it implicated so many people.

Shri Mataji asked us to do a very powerful havan which would enable the param chaitanya to work on this particular problem. As many Italian Sahaja Yogis as could be mustered came and it was only a matter of days before a major event happened, which appeared in the newspapers. Shortly after, a prominent Italian won his first case against a man called Mario Chiesa, a small man in a big chain of corruption, and soon big names came up and a whole avalanche of prosecutions were made. It was a revolution in Italy and broke the link between political parties, finance, Freemasonry and the Vatican.'

The editor tells of a time when South Africa was on the verge of a violent conflict.

'In South Africa in 1989 the dark days of apartheid were drawing slowly to a close but violence could and did erupt at any moment. When I arrived in Cape Town to start Sahaja Yoga there, I hadn't much clue of the political situation, having been in India for some years. Some people came and got realisation, and we decided to have our first havan. When it came to asking the power of the fire to absorb negativities, we offered the problems of the ruling Nationalist Party, the negative tendencies of key members of the government and the damaging apartheid policies. We did the havan on the beach some way up the coast and when we returned to the flat where I was staying some hours later, one of the new South African Sahaja Yogis turned on the TV. There was a man saying, in a very distraught way, that he was resigning.

"It works. This havan really works," said one man, astonished. "That's the Prime Minister, Botha. He has unexpectedly announced his resignation, out of the blue, leaving the way clear for FW De Klerk to take over." FW released Nelson Mandela and paved the way for the peaceful transformation process.

Was it coincidence? Was it the result of our havan? Or that we were in tune with the all-pervading power of divine love? The timing was perfect though.'

Editor's note: Botha resigned very suddenly, for no apparent reason, on the 14th August 1989.

Israel is not so easy, but for seven weeks there was peace.

'It was the beginning of June 2001 at the Adi Shakti Puja in Cabella, Italy. That weekend there was a suicide attack in a discoteque in Tel Aviv, Israel, and things were looking very grim. Shri Mataji said she was very concerned about Israel, about all the wars in the world and how serious things were everywhere there was conflict. I went up with flowers on behalf of Israel after the puja, and felt really bad and weak at the knees, I could barely stand.

"How are you?" Shri Mataji said, as if she was aware that I was not ok.

"Please save Israel," I said, even though I don't know where from.

"What?" she said.

"Please save Israel," I repeated.

"Write it down," she smiled and said. I thought she meant to make a bandhan.

"Write it down?" I repeated, to make sure.

"Write down what you want me to do," she looked at me and said.

I stepped off the stage, quite perplexed, not really knowing what she meant. Next to me were some ladies who suggested I write a letter to Shri Mataji expressing my prayers and wishes, so I wrote there and then, actually sitting in the hangar, within five or ten minutes. I wrote from my heart, asking her to save the children of both the Palestinians and the Israelis before they should be got hold of by this hatred. As soon as I finished writing, I felt a strong cool breeze tumbling from the stage where Shri Mataji was sitting; it washed over the writing paper and my hand.

Following this incident, there was an unexpected and unprecedented cease fire, which lasted seven weeks.'

Michal Gal

Djamel Metouri tells his story of that fateful day in New York, 9/11/2001. A

number of people who had received their self realisation were actually in the buildings when the planes struck, but all got out alive.

'My bank, which has its headquarters in Paris, sent me to New York in August 2001, five weeks prior to the Twin Towers attack. My flat was located a few minutes away from them and every day I used to walk to Fulton Street underground station, virtually at the bottom of the two huge towers.

Very soon after I arrived in New York, I started feeling a very bad pressure moving between the centre and left heart chakra, like a clutch. The vibrations were very weird for the whole of August, oscillating between rushes of coolness through the central channel and pouring tremendously out of the Sahasrara, followed then by serious pains in the chest as I had never experienced before.

At first I thought it was my own problem, until I acknowledged this disturbance had started in New York, so I put my attention on Manhattan, especially on the stock exchange and the Twin Towers, where the world business rhythm was actively challenging the spirit. Yet, for several weeks, I had mixed feelings as to whether the sickness was coming from me or from my surroundings. But one thing was sure: I was suffering badly. The last days before the suicide-bombing attack, I felt a kind of a silence before the storm.

I woke up that morning with something inside telling me, "Hurry up! Go to work early!" I felt I had to get ready quickly since I had arrived a bit late the day before. So, to my great surprise, I found myself running in the street to catch the train. I usually left my flat at 8.40 am every day, but on this particularly day I dashed out at 8.30, ten minutes earlier than usual. I ran to the subway, with the towers above me, grabbed a newspaper and took what was probably the last train before the tragedy struck.

I travelled to work safe and sound, completely unaware that I had been spared from the sight of a horrible battlefield, and great danger of falling glass, debris and so on, from above.'

Editor's note: the first plane hit the World Trade Centre at 8.46am, the second at 9.03am.

Here Sahaja Yogis from countries that often oppose each other joined together.

'During the Shri Krishna Puja of 2006, on the August 13th, a prayer was offered by the world collective for the war between Israel and Lebanon to end. A joint gift was offered, from Lebanon, Israel and Iran, which charged the whole room with emotion. Oleg, one of the presenters, wrote to the yogis later, 'It was so great a moment when we came up to the stage, Emad from Lebanon, Akbar from Iran and me, Oleg, from Israel, offering the gift from Hala in Lebanon and flowers from Israel and prayer from all of us.'

The conflict started on 12th July 2006, and continued until a United Nations - brokered ceasefire went into effect on 14th August 2006, the day after the gifts were offered to Shri Mataji.'

James Murdock

'In 1982, Shri Sanjeeva Reddy, the then President of India, was returning to India via London, after open heart surgery in a reputed hospital in the USA. As he was very weak and in great physical pain, accentuated by the long journey from New York to London, he made a request to Shri Mataji to come and help him during his short stopover in London. Shri Mataji graciously attended on him and through her divine vibrations cured him of his pain and restlessness. He had a restful time and good sleep. From then onwards, Shri Mataji was a welcome guest at Rashtrapati Bhawan (the President's residence) whenever she was in Delhi.

I must mention a very prophetic and important speech made by Shri Mataji in 1976 before a gathering of eminent doctors at the All India Institute of Medical Sciences in Delhi. She said that the indiscriminate sexual promiscuity which was spreading its tentacles across many countries would result in some deadly disease for which there will be no cure. At that time no one had even heard about HIV or AIDS. In a few years, the deadly scourge of AIDS had appeared on the health scene of the world.'

S. Venugopalan

Chapter 31

A Little More about Shri Mataji

If people asked Shri Mataji at public programmes, 'Who are you?' sometimes she would insist she was 'Just a housewife and mother'. On other occasions she said, 'It is all done – we are not doing anything.' Done by whom or what? The param chaitanya, the all-pervading power of divine love.

Shri Mataji had the most extraordinarily auspicious and powerful horoscope. A well-known Austrian astrologer looked at it, from the Western point of view, and stated the subject of that particular horoscope would become more and more famous as the years and centuries pass. A horoscope drawn up by a highly respected Indian astrologer, on the Indian system, was even more complimentary and in awe of what it purported. Even someone who has no knowledge of astrology can see from the large number of lines, or connected aspects, that it is extremely unusual looking.

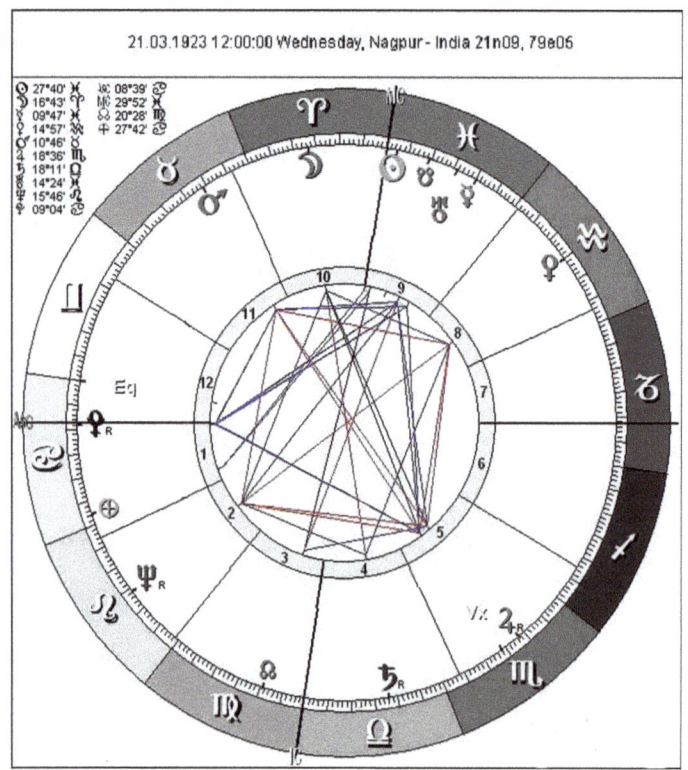

The following stories may give some insight.

'In May 1983 Shri Mataji had just completed a lecture tour of Australia and stopped over at Kuala Lumpur, en route to India, to give some public programmes. At Singapore Airport, a friend of mine and I had the privilege of being able to join her for the onward flight to Mumbai. We were waiting in the queue of people to go through the metal detector prior to boarding the aircraft. As Shri Mataji started to walk through, all the lights started to flash and the buzzers to sound. Shri Mataji was called to one side by a security attendant. After we had gone through without a murmur from the alarms, we followed to where she was detained.

Shri Mataji was wearing a typical traditional Indian sari and blouse. The security attendant was using his hand scanner to check for any metal objects and, to his surprise, it continued to sound while scanning Shri Mataji, even on her bare arms. He checked his device on himself by scanning his arm and it only buzzed when going over his watch. A little confused, he once again scanned Shri Mataji, especially her bare arms and the device continued to buzz.

According to the metal detector, this Indian lady, wearing only a silk sari with a short sleeved blouse, was clad in a suit of armour. In the confusion and in disbelief in what was happening before his eyes and with a queue of passengers building up and walking through the detector without supervision, he waved to Shri Mataji to carry on. She chuckled and walked on into the boarding lounge. All this happened in a matter of ten to fifteen seconds. We both saw it and were totally bemused.'

Albert Lewis

'I was with Shri Mataji in Vancouver, going from the airport to where she was staying overnight. As we arrived there was a huge thunderstorm and Shri Mataji said it was Shri Vishnumaya, the sister of Shri Krishna, two of whose powers are lightning and electricity. We arrived in the house and Shri Mataji sat down and some of the yogis came to greet her respectfully. As they did so a lightning stroke came through the room to between her feet and the people. The vibrations were absolutely amazing.'

Antony Visconti

A story of superhuman strength: Ruth Eleanore, Duilio Cartocci and Giovanni Albanesi tell this story.

Ruth: On that same weekend that the miracle happened with the endless cement at Brompton Square in London, some people were supposed to come and visit the house. Many of the men were moving furniture. Shri Mataji asked some strong young Italians to move her bed of solid wood and they were trying to push it, but could not move it a centimetre.

Duilio: Three of us had to move a very heavy wooden bed. We were at the foot of the bed on our knees and we pushed and pushed, but the bed didn't move.

Ruth: I was in the room, packing Shri Mataji's suitcase. She approached the bed and just pushed it with her knee and the bed moved.

Duilio: At that moment I turned my head and saw Shri Mataji touching the foot of the bed with her knee. In the same moment, the bed flew against the wall in the right position and we fell on the ground.

Ruth: The Italian yogis said, 'Ah,' in big shock and surprise.

Giovanni: On that same day, there was a big wardrobe for clothes. The men needed to move this cupboard and no one could move it. When Shri Mataji just touched it with her finger, it moved easily.

Here is a similar story.

'One time, before leaving Cabella for India, Shri Mataji called me and a few others to do some packing. We were in one of the bedrooms filling up suitcases. Shri Mataji asked us to close a certain suitcase, but it was over full, and the things were spilling out everywhere. We could not close it.

"Stand on the suitcase," she said to me. I am almost a hundred kilos, but we still could not close it.

"Bring the suitcase over to me, close to me," she smiled and said. She just put her right foot on the case, and after that we could close the case without any effort at all.

On another occasion I brought a briefcase to Shri Mataji. It had a lock which was numbers, but none of us knew the correct number. Shri Mataji asked her grandson to try to open the briefcase. So he tried every number he could think of - triple zero, one, two, three and so on. After about five minutes he gave up because he couldn't do it. Shri Mataji was smiling.

"Bring it to me," she said, and looking and smiling, moved her fingers on the lock, and did not even look at it. After a few seconds there was a 'click!' and both of the locks were open. She wasn't even looking at the numbers, and nobody had any idea what the numbers were.'

Raju of Cabella

The flame would shudder.

'When Shri Mataji was giving vibrations, or curing someone by giving vibrations, sometimes she would look at their back. Then suddenly she would look up, and there would always be a candle put in front of her. The moment she would look at the candle, the flame would shudder. Then she would look at another flame, because there would always be two or three candles. As she looked at a particular flame, that candle would shudder as she would be driving the negativity out and into that particular flame. It was fantastic to watch.'

John Watkinson

Meenakshi Murdoch, who lives in London, describes how she felt the chakras in Shri Mataji's body.

'After Shri Mataji had given realisation at the public programmes, we all would stand in a queue and go to her. I still remember the Kundalini rising or throbbing at each chakra in the new people as she used to clear it out. If there was a problem in a chakra, then you could sometimes see the Kundalini throbbing or pulsating at that place for a short time.

When Shri Mataji asked you to put your hand on her head, on the Agnya chakra or whatever chakra, you could feel the rotation of the chakra spinning so fast.'

This is from Kay McHugh of Australia.

'I was on the train from Pune to Mumbai, India opposite Shri Mataji, on the window seat. With us were an Australian man and an Indian man. She had the Australian stand up, she was sitting down and he was pushing down on the top of her head, her Sahasrara chakra, with his hands, and she was doing this to try to open his Sahasrara chakra. He was over six foot and pushing down as hard as he could.

"Harder!" she kept saying, for him to push on her head, "Harder!"

She was laughing because he couldn't push any harder. He was sweating, he was pushing so hard, and she was sitting there, laughing and talking and turning her head. He was pushing as hard as he could and Shri Mataji was not affected at all and was talking so charmingly to the people on the train.

On another occasion, we went to a hospital where there was a Sahaja Yogi's mother-in-law, who had gone to a fake, or as we say false, guru. She'd gone blind and Shri Mataji went to the hospital out of compassion.

"Don't come in," she said to me.

She went into the hospital and after some time came out again. I was amazed because she sat in front of me in the front seat of the car and, because Shri Mataji had worked on this woman's blindness, her back Agnya chakra, the back of her head, had sucked in all the negativity and it was pulsating out about an inch and a half. You could see it. I sat there with my mouth open and watching the back of her Agnya chakra go in and out and in and out. That was a pretty amazing experience, to see the bones move and pulsate.

Editor's note: the sixth, or Agnya chakra, at the level of the forehead, corresponds to the powers of Christ: forgiveness and resurrection. Every chakra is associated with an aspect of the divine, and the spiritual evolution of mankind is reflected within the Kundalini.'

A similar story from Marilyn Leate

'In about 1979, we went to Shri Mataji's flat after the public programmes in London and were given cups of coffee. She continued to work on people, help them in every way and cure them. One time she asked me to put my hand on her left Swadishthan chakra, on her back at the level of the hip, and put my other hand out. I felt an incredible force going through me.

"Powerful, isn't it?" she said, looking at me.'

Miodrag Radosavljevic again

'There was a miracle, which I experienced when we had a seminar in the English countryside. It was a long time ago, 1979, and Shri Mataji came. It was a very dark day with no sun, heavy clouds. It was very, very dull and heavy. Shri Mataji was talking to us and saying that she expresses the powers of the divine, like the sun and the sunlight. At that moment the beam of sunlight came out of nowhere and shone on her head and went away. To prove it, she said that the beam of sunlight should come again on her head. That happened two or three times. Out of nowhere the sun came. I witnessed this together with about fifty other Sahaja Yogis who were present at that time.'

This type of story, here told by Felicity Payment, has been repeated many times.

'We were standing with Shri Mataji in the nave of a beautiful 13th century abbey in Sherbourne, Dorset, England. We had just had a weekend seminar at our house, Mill Farm in Dorset, England and Shri Mataji was visiting the area. She looked way up at the limestone ceiling full of vaulted buttresses.

"How do you think they made those arches?" she said, gesturing with her hand, as if wondering to herself. I was clutching a guidebook.

"Maybe it will tell us in here," I said, but before I could find anything, Shri

Mataji launched into a complete architectural explanation, as if she knew the answer all along.

Later a specialist in his field said that he had had a conversation with Shri Mataji about aerodynamics and she had talked with him about very technical aerodynamic concepts. She knew everything about everything.'

This Sahaja Yogi, Hari Jairam, who was living in the UK at the time, is a telecommunications engineer.

'Some years ago, in my work I had to develop a new type of radio antenna. I was at first unable to make much headway. One morning as I sat in meditation, I asked in my heart, 'Shri Mataji, are you the telecommunications expert of the universe?' I started to feel cool vibrations. Then an idea came to me of electromagnetic waves spreading through the universe like the vibrations which we experience in Sahaja Yoga, and being helped in their radiation through the use of certain auspicious shapes and forms. In Sahaja Yoga we find that certain shapes, for instance the bandhan or horseshoe shape, attract and channel vibrations, hence they are said to be auspicious, and pleasing to the divine.

Later that day, I began to design my new antenna taking these forms as a base. The antenna we built to this design worked extremely well and the company went on to win enormous orders worth many millions of pounds. When they asked me for information about the theoretical basis of the new design, I just told them that I had consulted a higher authority.'

Shri Mataji has a profound awareness of Jesus Christ.

'For a number of years Shri Mataji did a Sahaja Yoga introductory programme at Versiliana, in northern Italy, at an open air café or tea garden. One time she had lunch there with two Sahaja Yogis and a journalist, the organiser of the programme, Romano Battaglia. She was explaining Sahaja Yoga to him.

"Jesus Christ transformed the water into wine," he said at a certain point.

According to the bible that we have today, Christ went to a marriage at Cana, and when the host ran out of wine he changed water into wine, and it was said to be the best, much better than the earlier wine which had run out.

"This, I can also do," Shri Mataji answered.

She put two fingers in a glass of water and then gave it to him to drink. Mr Battaglia said that this was normal water, but was also like wine. Shri Mataji also said that Christ did not make the water into wine. She explained that this must have been a mistranslation, because to make an alcoholic beverage it would be necessary to let it ferment, which is a process similar to rotting and this would have taken time. She told the journalist to drink the contents of the glass, because it would be good for him.'

Sandra Castelli

Shri Mataji referred to this in one of her lectures.

'... marriage is necessary and, as you know, Christ went to attend a wedding. Why did he pay so much attention to a wedding? Because that sanctifies your relationships with each other. ... relationship between husband and wife has to be sanctified. ... That's why he went, to sanctify the marriage institution.

But it is absolutely wrong and nonsense that he created alcohol. What he did was to change the water into the taste of grape juice. Alcohol is called as grape juice in Hebrew language. I mean it is not called, but wine means alcohol as well as grape juice. But it cannot be, because instantly you cannot create alcohol. Alcohol takes time; it has to rot and rot and rot, then it becomes alcohol. But if Christ has made it in such a Sahaja manner, spontaneously, how can it be alcohol, that is intoxicating? ... He never sanctified alcohol. He changed the grape juice into wine taste.

The other day I happened to meet a person and he said, "Mother please give me realisation." I said "Alright, get me some water." They brought some water, I put my fingers into it and then he tasted it and said, "Mother it tastes like wine." I said, "That's it, that's what Christ had done." So there is no sanctity of alcohol. How can you expect Christ to do something like that by which your awareness absolutely goes?'

Shri Mataji Nirmala Devi, Cabella, Italy, 2000

Chapter 32

The Mother who 'Just Knew'

For all of us in Sahaja Yoga, Shri Mataji was and still is our loving, caring mother. Below is a photo of her with her great grandson when he was a baby, some years back. Here are some stories which show how much she knew and cared.

Gail Pottinger had one of those food cravings so many of us get when expecting a child.

'When we were living in Bramham Gardens, London in the early 1980's, and I was pregnant with my first child, I had an incredible desire to eat dates. I didn't tell anyone, though. One evening, my husband Graham came up from Shri Mataji's apartment, which was downstairs.

"Shri Mataji sent you these," he said, and she had sent me a huge box full of stuffed dates, which was quite amazing as obviously I hadn't told her.'

Rosie Lyons of Australia tells how Shri Mataji just knew.
'My desire to have a baby was really strong. I was in a room with a pregnant woman.

"This couch should be moved," Shri Mataji said, then looked at us and continued, "pregnant ladies can't move furniture. Go and find someone else."
I looked around, wondering who was pregnant. I was the only one there. I found out I was pregnant the next day from a test.

Alison Rovina was sure that Shri Mataji felt her fear.

When I was working in Shri Mataji's house at Brompton Square on renovations in the early 1980's, somebody had put me to papering a ceiling over a staircase. They left me there on a little plank over the well. I was too shy to say that I was terrified of heights. All of a sudden the plank wobbled and I felt a sudden fright in my heart, but didn't say anything out loud.

Shri Mataji was right at the other side of the house, and could neither see nor hear me, and in the over thirty years I knew her, I never saw her run, before or since. But she ran into the room where I was standing on the plank and told me to get down immediately'.

Elizabeth Ravenscroft came across the world to give Shri Mataji a flower.

'In 1993 I had just arrived in Bristol, England, from South Africa, to stay with a friend. We had a phone call from London saying Shri Mataji was going to be at Heathrow Airport at five o'clock that day. So we drove to London, about a three hour drive. We arrived quite late and didn't have time to get flowers, but someone very kindly gave us some. They didn't look very fresh and I decided that because they weren't so beautiful, I wouldn't make a great effort to go to Shri Mataji with them.

She arrived and the crowd surged forward. I stayed put. Shri Mataji walked around, and as she was going back towards the car, I began to feel heartsore because I had travelled so far to come and see her and, although my flowers weren't beautiful, I still wanted to give them. As she bent down to get into the car to leave, in my heart I cried out, 'Please Shri Mataji, take my flowers. I've come six thousand miles to see you,' although naturally I didn't say anything out loud.

Before she actually sat down, she began to rise again and must have been about fifteen metres away. She turned around and looked at me through the sea of faces, and the many people in front of me just parted like waves. Shri Mataji walked right up to me.

"I think I have to take these flowers," she said.

My tears just flowed with joy.'

This is Frances Henke again, who observed these events with the sharp eye of a journalist.

'I have been collecting 'miracle' or anyway 'most unusual' handbag stories that my husband and I witnessed. It started in India one year when we were on the tour and the Indian government put up the price of train tickets. Some of the Indian Sahaja Yogis could not afford the new price and Shri Mataji reached into her handbag and started pulling out seemingly endless piles of cash to give them for the tickets, which seemed unlikely to have been there in the first place.

Later, deep in rural Maharashtra, a child was fidgety and she suggested reading it a story. Did anyone have a children's story book? No one did, so she reached into her handbag and pulled out a book, bigger than the bag.

On another India tour a woman came to one of Shri Mataji's programmes and she fainted. Shri Mataji asked if anyone had a thermometer to see if she had a fever. No one did, so she opened her handbag and took out a thermometer.'

This is Carolyn Vance from the United States.

'When I was very new to Sahaja Yoga, Shri Mataji suggested I should try to get back together again with my husband, because she said, "He has the vibrations of a seeker." How did she know I was divorced and in great agony about this? I had never discussed it with her or anyone else in our Sahaja circle. I was utterly flabbergasted and yet overwhelmingly happy to have the opportunity to try and redeem myself.

Another time, I was still a new yogi and was beginning to realise more fully the horror of the problems in America. Shri Mataji had come to New York and I was riding in the back seat of her car.

"Don't feel so responsible for America. You weren't here for all your lives, you know," she said to me after a long silence.

I immediately relaxed and felt the joy - she knew exactly what our worries or obstacles were and removed them instantly. She was the kindest of the kindest, her grace was the most gracious and her love and compassion made it impossible for anyone to feel anything but joy when one was in her physical presence.'

We all make mistakes, often unknowingly, but Shri Mataji puts us at our ease, as was the case for Liallyn Fitzpatrick of Australia.

'On one occasion I did something which I felt was wrong involving my young son, and which I was concerned might have offended Shri Mataji. As it happened, She took a taxi to the public programme that evening and invited a few of us to come along in the back seat. My son and I were squeezed in and I was sitting on the edge of the seat, right up against the front seat with my son in my arms.

I was silently praying for her forgiveness and Shri Mataji opened her purse – I was sitting just behind her left shoulder – and drew out a small bottle of perfume. I knew beyond a doubt that it was the very same bottle of perfume I had sent her the year before with a message of love and gratitude for my self realisation and for the opportunity of seeing her in New York. She sprayed some of this perfume on her wrists and put the perfume back in her handbag. At that moment I closed my eyes and the weight of the world was lifted from me. I suddenly felt very light and very much loved. We hadn't exchanged even a glance.'

Maria Galabova's story shows the extent of Shri Mataji's concern, and there are many similar stories.

'Shri Mataji Nirmala Devi visited Bulgaria in September 1993. We had decided to organise a small exhibition of traditional handmade Bulgarian lace and embroidery. I had to bring a big pack of these to Sofia where Shri Mataji was going to come. The day before my departure I sprained my ankle badly and the pain was severe and persistent, so when the coordinator of the projects connected with Shri Mataji's visit called me that day I explained, full of despair, that I could neither bring the handicrafts nor go myself. She calmed me and said that she would ask the collective to give me a bandhan. A miracle happened - half an hour later the pain in my left ankle was gone.

The following day I, alongside with many other yogis went to Sofia and welcomed Shri Mataji at the airport. That same evening I had the immense blessing to go close to her and while doing so, I saw that her left ankle was swollen and bruised at that exact same place where mine had been before the bandhan. I could freely move around, using my ankle normally, where it had been badly sprained the day before. On remembering how painful it was I felt extremely miserable that I had burdened Shri Mataji with my pain.

However, some time passed and the worries that were plaguing me got their answer. I read one of Mother's talks where she said that she had taken an oath to cure us and to take the pain away and that we shouldn't feel guilty.'

This is a similar story, from India.

'In 1983, when we were at Satara, Maharashtra, staying in the guesthouse, one of the Sahaja Yogis had become quite sunburned. He was very ill and someone told Shri Mataji. During those tours she would travel alongside us, and would be with us pretty much every single day.

Shri Mataji was sitting at the foot of a tree, and in India a lot of the trees have seats built of concrete almost like a step around the bottom of the trunk.

She was sitting on one of these at the guesthouse and we were all sitting round her. She called this boy out and he came and sat next to her. She worked on him for quite a long time and he was sent off to go to sleep. When he woke up, he was feeling infinitely better and the next morning someone who had been close to Shri Mataji said that she had had a very bad night; her skin was dark and black and looked as if it was covered in sunburn.

Apparently what had happened was that Shri Mataji had taken the sunburn from this person into her own body and had worked it out through herself.'

Auriol Purdie

And another

'At Ganapatipule, on the coast some way south of Mumbai, at our Christmas gathering in December 1985, some Sahaja Yogi boys were enjoying themselves on the seashore and not realising the intensity of the midday sun, had got badly burnt. They were brought to Shri Mataji's bungalow and she graciously worked on them, laughing and joking with them.

"Ah! You look like Greek gods with your suntans now!" she told them, and lovingly massaged their backs with oil and talc, patiently removing each blister. When her work was done the boys thanked her profusely and they floated out of her room on cloud nine. When they had gone, Shri Mataji asked me to massage some talc on her back. She pulled aside her sari showing me many heat blisters that had erupted all around her Nabhi chakra, the area of the abdomen. Her body was pure love. She had absorbed their pain in such a matter-of-fact way, yet not letting them feel in any way hurt or guilty.'

Danya Martoglio

Nanda Tagliabue didn't want to trouble Shri Mataji.

'I was living at Shri Mataji's house at Cabella and was really ill. For fifteen days I couldn't even get up at all, but I didn't want to trouble Shri Mataji. After fifteen days, I didn't know what to do because I had a little boy of a year old. I went to the doctor and he gave me a lot of medicines and I was about to take them. That very morning, Shri Mataji called to see me. I could hardly get up the stairs.

I was in the big room, the salone. She had me put one hand towards her and one out of the window. I was there for about twenty minutes the fever had gone and I walked downstairs. I took all the medicine and threw it in the bin. I didn't even know she had been healing me, because she was writing something at the same time.'

Shri Mataji's motherly quality showed itself even with fiery sages like Gagan Giri Maharaj, who lived on a hilltop in Maharashtra, India. This is from a transcript of one of her lectures.

'There was a story about a person who was supposed to be a great guru, and I went to see him. I had to climb quite a lot because he lived in a small, little cave. When I reached there, he was very angry within and going on like this, like this (Shri Mataji shakes her head from side to side). It was raining so I was completely drenched! I went and sat in his little cave. Then he came back and he asked me a question:

"Mother, it was raining. Normally I can stop the rain, but you wouldn't allow me to stop the rain. Why?" I could have told him, "Because of your ego," but I didn't.

"You see, you are a sanyasi (recluse) and you have got a sari for me," I told him in a very sweet manner, "if I had not got drenched, I could not have taken your sari from a sanyasi." He completely melted! He had tears in his eyes and fell at my feet.

So the technique of Sahaja Yoga is like this. It's not anger. It's not repulsion. It's not hatred. But the technique is such by which you suggest your love. This is how one has to understand the difference between a Sahaja Yogi guru and other gurus. No question of beating your disciple, no question of spoiling, no question of shouting at them. Love is the most powerful thing! Of course it doesn't work on some people, I agree – forget them. But (it) works in most of the people because God has made us out of His love, and we have a capacity to yield to that love and to enjoy that love.

For a Sahaja Yogi, what he has to do is to understand the powers of love. The powers of love, if you can understand them, will grow within you. Try to understand that this param chaitanya is nothing but the power of God's love – or you can say 'Mother's love! This power works so beautifully, in such a secret manner, that you call it as 'miracle', because you can't see how it has worked.'

Shri Mataji Nirmala Devi, July 2001, Cabella, Italy

Shri Mataji could understand many languages.

'Shri Mataji came to stay with us at Givrins in Switzerland, and spoke to all the yogis there. At one point someone gave her a letter and she asked for her reading glasses. No one could find them so she opened the letter and read it without them. She answered each question in the letter, and afterwards we found out that the letter was written in French, even though she did not know French.

A few years later we were at Cabella in Shri Mataji's room. The news came on the TV and Shri Mataji wanted someone from Austria, where we usually speak German, to translate it, but there was no one in the room who could speak Italian well enough to translate the news. So Shri Mataji started to tell us everything that the man on the television was saying, even though he was speaking Italian.

She said that the ladies also have to know what is going on in the world so she translated it from Italian, even though officially she did not speak Italian.'

Laxshmi Ward

'At Diwali Puja in Istanbul in 1994, Shri Mataji's talk was being translated into Russian and Turkish, with one Sahaja Yogi translating into Russian and another into Turkish. At one point Shri Mataji said something and then paused and when the Russian Sahaja Yogi translated it, Shri Mataji corrected her.

"No that was not what I said, what I said was…" So the Russian Sahaja Yogi translated it again. Shri Mataji again corrected her, "No that was not what I said, what I said was …" The Russian Sahaja Yogini was a touch surprised

"Do you understand Russian, Shri Mataji?" she said.

"No, but I understood from your abstract thought that you had the wrong concept," Shri Mataji replied.'

Anonymous Sahaja Yogi

The pink bangles

It was my first India Tour, in the 1990's, where some of the Western Sahaja Yogis would accompany Shri Mataji around India when she went on tours giving self realisation. A friend had told me before going to be careful what I desired because in India, on the India Tour, all your desires are answered. Near the start of the tour, I would often 'speak' to Shri Mataji in my heart, sometimes a deep and profound thank you for something.

Everyone was buying the glass Indian bangles that tinkle and jangle on the wrists. My hands, being quite large, I couldn't find bangles that would fit. I found myself having one of my 'chats' with Shri Mataji, it going through my mind how nice it would be to have some pretty pink bangles that would actually go over my right wrist to cool down my rather Western right side.

Time passed and one evening we went to a programme in the presence of Shri Mataji. When we all got back to the camp, tired and contented, I noticed tissue paper on top of my suitcase. I opened it to glean what it was and inside was a set of large pink bangles. Thinking that someone must have put them down there I asked around to give them to whoever they belonged to. No one seemed to know anything about them.

It took a while before I remembered that I had in fact made this fleeting, almost humorous, request for them and these bangles must be for me. I wore them on my right wrist for as long as I could.

Philippa Newman

Chapter 33

The Last Word

Calin Costian, originally from Romania, has some sobering words to offer.

One day I was walking on the Purdue University Campus, Indiana, USA, in between my classes and noticed a strange weather pattern. It would rain for ten to fifteen minutes, then it would stop for half an hour and the sun would come out, then again rain vigorously for a short time, then again stop, and so on for several hours. I didn't think much of it until our next public program, when the same lady told me what had happened to her on that very day, while moving some furniture to her son's place. It was a rainy day to begin with, and she was a bit worried that the furniture will get wet. However, when she pulled up the truck to her door to start loading, the rain stopped. She was able to load everything she needed without a drop of rain, and then as soon as she got behind the wheel the rain started to pour. When she reached her son's place and got ready to unload, the rain stopped again, just long enough to allow her to unload everything. When she got back in the truck, the rain started again. All this kept happening until she finished moving all the furniture, which took her the whole afternoon.

"Ah, it was you!" I exclaimed with a smile.

This lady had also had great success with using the bandhan of request: she was able to help a relative of hers to give up smoking in three months. What surprised me more than these events is the fact that this lady, despite all the proofs she had received since starting to practice Sahaja Yoga, didn't recognize what this was. She eventually stopped practicing it in favour of some other disciplines which promised a lot of fantastic things, used big words and in the end gave her nothing except confusion and maybe a drained bank account. This made me think of the parable used by Christ who said that in some future, special times to come, salvation and true knowledge will fall on the earth like seeds, but some will fall on a rock, some will be eaten by birds, some will sprout but then soon die, and some will grow into beautiful, strong trees and produce fragrant flowers and fruits.

Our emancipation as human beings and the fulfillment of our destiny depend on our desire, and also on our intelligence to recognize the truth once we see it. The all-pervading divine power could cure people of smoking, move the clouds and control the rain, but there was one thing it could not do:

change this lady's mind, or force her to evolve spiritually by embracing the path she had found.

Why? Because this is one of the fundamental rules of the cosmic game that has been playing since the beginning of creation. Human beings are given free will, and this is something the Divine will never trespass. The Divine could instantly change a stone into a flawless angel, but the contribution of the stone to this process would be nil. In these modern times of confusion it is easy to go down the wrong trail and difficult to choose the path of ascent. However, if we succeed and embrace the correct path, the rewards of our spiritual evolution are tremendous, because these are the blossom times, when we can bloom into flowers and fulfill a destiny that maybe we didn't even know was awaiting us.

There are many miracle stories I could recount, of my own as well as of many other Sahaja Yogis, but above all these stories is our own experience which no one can take away from us, which helps us steer through times of confusion and reminds us of what is real.'

The Sahasrara Chakra is the final development of the subtle nervous system within man, enabling him to rise in every sense above the world of mental activity and emotional concepts. The collective consciousness which arises when the Kundalini energy rises through the Sahasrara chakra allows for the direct perception of reality on the central nervous system. We can know ourselves as pure spirit: pure joy, pure attention, pure truth.

Vibratory awareness allows our perception to transcend the senses and go to the essence of all creation. Once the Sahasrara chakra is opened, all the others can be purified and enriched. Often at the same time, and sometimes a little later, a great expansion of the heart takes place, and a sense of deep, radiating joy is experienced as the Heart chakra, which is the seat of the spirit within each of us, opens.

Thus we come to the end of an infinitesimal sample of the events which have occurred to many of us when we have had our self realisation, are involved in Sahaja Yoga and have received countless blessings from Shri Mataji, both directly and indirectly. She once said that all her powers, her love and her wisdom had to be given to us. She had a tremendous vision as to how humanity could be, if we all allowed ourselves to be one with the power of the divine which is awakened in us when we get self realisation.

This book shows how Shri Mataji did astonishing miracles, and benevolently, compassionately and untiringly gave of her love and healing blessings, enabling us to also be part of many miraculous events. We can enjoy and spread the same magic, from Kazakhstan to Chile, from South Africa to Canada.

To quote Shri Mataji in her great book Meta Modern Era:
'I knew my mission very well of collective awakening, but I was born in such a blind world. … I am being used as the desire of God Almighty to emit these forceful holy vibrations to give realisation to thousands and thousands of people very happily. In my life, to my amazement, the time has come – the blossom time, where there are so many flowers on this earth who are seekers of truth, and they can easily become the fruits.'

Maybe these unusual things happen because we are allowing a different form of free will to guide us, so we are moving into a different realm of possibilities, with different physics and laws governing it. Here another quote from Shri Mataji, again in Meta Modern Era.
'You have seen, experienced, in your lifetime how miracles are taking place, how things are working out.
This is how the en masse evolution of human beings will take place. These are the signs of advent of the Golden Age of Truth.
Let us forget whatever hardships we have suffered in our search, in the past. It does not matter if some could not find it before this. You have to open your mind and understand that, though the discovery is unprecedented, it does not make any seeker or predecessor small. If some experiments are made, it does not matter if ultimately we have found out the way. It is a collective achievement.
Perhaps in the chaos of Kali Yuga (the 'Dark Age') it was to happen, and many of us who have been earnestly searching in many lives are reborn to have their promises fulfilled by the Divine.'
Her Holiness Shri Mataji Nirmala Devi

This is an extract from a poem written by Shri Mataji, when she first encountered the lost American and English hippies of the seventies.

Now rest in the petals of the lotus flower
In the lap of your gracious Mother
I will adorn your life with beautiful blossoms
And fill your moments with joyful fragrance

I will anoint your head with Divine Love
For I cannot bear your torture anymore
Let me engulf you in the ocean of joy
So you lose your being in the Greater One
Who is smiling in your calyx of Self
Secretly hidden to tease you all the while
Be aware and you will find Him
Vibrating your every fibre with blissful joy
Covering the whole Universe with light.

So, we come back to the premise at the beginning of the book, that this is an account of close coincidences, unusual occurrences and miraculous events that could possibly happen to anyone who reads it with an open mind. If you have already received your self realisation, put out your hands and ask if this statement is true, and your awakened Kundalini should tell you.

Appendix 1

Instructions for Awakening the Kundalini

By far the best way to awaken the Kundalini is to watch or listen to Shri Mataji herself demonstrating and leading a self realisation programme. Nearly everyone who reads this book will have access to the internet, so the editor's advice is to go to one of these links and follow the instructions: www.sahajayoga.org/experienceitnow or www.youtube.com/watch?v=FaRHIWgp1-k

If for some reason this is not possible, we can try something a bit different.

One way to awaken the Kundalini and experience the cool breeze of the spirit is to hold one's hands out, palms raised and ask for it to awaken. In the following photo of Shri Mataji is demonstrating how to do it.

Sit in a quiet, undisturbed place and give yourself a bit of time. Put your hands out with the palms upwards as Shri Mataji was doing in the photo above. Look at this photo as you do so.

Now put your left hand out towards the photo, and your right hand on your heart, the seat of the spirit within us. Ask, 'Please, Shri Mataji, awaken my Kundalini,' or 'Please awaken the Holy Spirit within me.'

At this point you will find it easier if you close your eyes, so read on and then you will know what to do before closing them.

Put your left hand out and your right hand across your forehead, and with the eyes closed, say 'I forgive everyone,' and really mean it! Below is a picture to help see where the hand should go.

Next, with your eyes still closed, put your right hand at the back of the head and say, 'I forgive myself, and please, forgive me if I have made any mistakes, knowingly or unknowingly.'

Now put your left hand out and your right hand on top of your head and say, 'Please give me my self realisation.'

After you have done this, open your eyes again, put your right hand above your head and the left one out towards the photo. See if you feel coolness above your head, as the people are doing in the next photo, below. Reverse your hands so the right one is towards the photo and the left one is above your head. Finally put both hands in front of you, and maybe you will feel some coolness on the palms of your hands. At this point, open your eyes again.

If you do feel some coolness, then your Kundalini - the subtle, motherly energy within all of us - has risen from its dormant state at the base of the spine to the top of the head. This means the Holy Spirit has awakened within you and you have your self realisation. You may also feel peaceful, joyful, and your thoughts may settle down so you feel an inner stillness. If you feel heat, or a combination of heat and coolness, this just means some impurities are coming out.

Once the Kundalini has been awakened, we can reawaken it and we can also protect this awakened energy. Put both hands in front of your body and twirl the right hand round the left one, simultaneously raising them up until they get to the top of the head. Then make a gesture like tying a piece of string. The first time, do this once, then put your hands back in front of the base of the spine and do it again. The second time, make two knots when your hands are above your head, and finally the third time make three knots. That is the reawakening part and the two drawings will help make it clearer.

Then there is the protection part. This is called a bandhan. Put your left hand out with the palm upwards, and with the right hand make an arch over your body. Then bring your right hand back to your left hand and do this seven times each way. The drawings should help explain how to do it.

It is necessary to establish and strengthen the experience of the cool breeze and thoughtless awareness which we begin to enjoy when the Kundalini is awakened. The easiest way to do this is to do a simple meditation for a few minutes each day. If we do this we start to experience more benefits.

Sahaja Yoga meditation is very simple. The 'classic' way of doing it is to put a photo of Shri Mataji up in front of us, because as has been seen in some of the earlier stories, this photo radiates tremendous healing vibrations and is very relaxing to look at. If possible light a candle or lamp and place it in front of the photo. Having done this, one can just sit comfortably, either cross legged on the floor or in a chair, put the hands out with the palms up, either look at the photo or close the eyes, put the attention on top of the head and allow the thoughts to float away. It is that simple. Give it a try.

The Bandhan of Request

To do the second bandhan, write something on your left hand or the name of someone you want to help, with your right index finger. Then circle just above the left hand, with your right one. Otherwise think of a problem, or just do it without thinking anything specific. The idea is not to desire any particular outcome, but rather to feel, 'Let whatever is the best solution work out'.

If we feel a cool breeze on our hand when we do this, it is the all-pervading power affirming our request, because when our Kundalini is awakened we are in touch with that

The Relationship between the Chakras and the Parts of the Hand

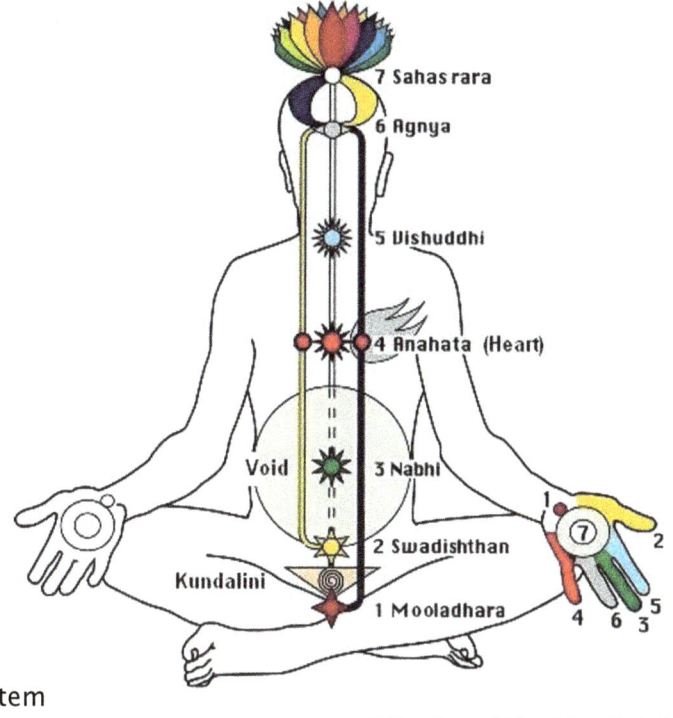

The Subtle System

At this moment, we start to feel a cool breeze, generally on the palms of the hands and the top of the head. Also, if there are any problems in the chakras, they are registered as a pricking or tingling, or heat, on the appropriate parts of the hand. The fingers and different parts of the hand correspond to the different chakras, see the diagram below, and we can learn how to direct the cool breeze, or vibrations, to the area of the body which needs help, as indicated by the sensation we feel on our hands. If we put our attention on another person rather than ourselves, we can feel if there is something wrong with them, and can help them.

The Liver Diet
Apart from the normal Sahaja meditation and basic clearing treatments, the basic, simplified liver diet is a diet: high carbohydrate, very low or no fat, with no red meat, alcohol, coffee, strong tea or refined foods, apart from white sugar, which is good, and white rice. Plenty of fresh fruit and vegetables are recommended, and also plain yoghurt. One also puts an ice pack on the liver fairly often, to cool it down.

To Clear the Agnya Chakra
Because the qualities of the Agnya chakra are those of Jesus Christ, forgiveness and resurrection, if any reader has a similar problem, one can also try saying the words, 'I forgive, I forgive,' a few times. Otherwise one can look at the photo of Shri Mataji through a lighted candle and say the 'Our Father who art in heaven' prayer

To Help with Eye Problems, and Using Fire and Light for Healing
Many people who have eye problems have been helped by Shri Mataji's photo, and photos of her hands are especially effective. Here is a photo which has helped a lot of people. Try lighting a candle and putting in front of the photo. Sit down and if possible put a second candle behind the head. Just look at the photo and let the thoughts float away. You will probably feel peaceful and relaxed.

Another treatment for the eyes is to meditate with the back of the head where the rays of the morning sun fall on it, just as it is rising, for a few minutes. This is another form of light. The subtle element of the Agnya chakra is light, and this chakra is placed in the head and governing the eyes, so it responds well to the rising sun. This treatment can be done on the flat roof of an apartment block, a garden or even the seashore – wherever. Try it out and you will find it is very restful and helpful.

The use of flame often clears left side problems, which can come from past conditioning. One common treatment is the three candle treatment. One lighted candle is placed in front of the photo of Shri Mataji, one at the left side of the person and the third is held, either by the person him or herself, or by someone else. This candle is rotated clockwise from the front, or anti-clockwise from behind, of the chakras of the left side.

Some Treatments to Help Overcome the Desire to Smoke Cigarettes
If the Vishuddhi chakra, at the level of the throat, is in good order and the vibrations are flowing strongly we often find we have no further desire to smoke. To clear and purify this chakra, which is damaged by smoking, one simple treatment is to put the left hand towards Shri Mataji's photo and the right hand on the base of the throat while we sit in meditation, for a short time. We can also put our index fingers in our ears, look up, and say 'Allah hu

Akbar' sixteen times. This Muslim prayer, which means 'God is great, God is all pervading', also helps to clear this subtle centre. A third treatment is to inhale the smoke rising from parched ajwan, or amjo seeds, available at any Indian food shop. Put some seeds on a dry frying pan, or chapatti pan, on a hot stove, or on a piece of glowing charcoal, and when the seeds begin to smoke, lean over it and sniff it up for a short time.

To Put Vibrations in Food

To put vibrations into food is very simple, and Sahaja Yogis usually do this before they eat, or give food to anyone else. Once one has had realisation one can feel the vibrations of food, or anything else, by putting one's attention on it and registering the coolness or 'catches' (tingles or heat which indicate problems, on specific fingers which correspond to certain chakras). Then one can usually clear the catches so the food radiates coolness – even if it is a hot dish. One puts the left hand out, if possible towards a photo of Shri Mataji, and circles in the air over the food with the right hand, until coolness is felt on the hands.

Instructions for Doing the Matka Treatment

The matka treatment allows lemons and fresh green chillies to absorb the negativity which is causing the dog's illness. It is known as a matka after the porous clay pot these items are put into in India. If one is in a country where these little pots are not available, a simpler way of doing this treatment is acceptable one should put seven lemons and seven green chillies in front of Shri Mataji's photograph for some time.. Then put the left hand to the photo, and with the right hand circle clockwise in the air above the lemons and chillies at least seven times, ideally until a cool breeze is felt coming from them. Put the lemons and chillies in a plastic bag and place this under the bed, or in a bedside cabinet. In the night, open the bag and in the daytime close it and put it out of sight. After seven nights put the lemons and chillies in running water, or if that is not possible, under the earth.

Suggestions for Farmers and Gardeners

We have a farm near Grosseto, in Tuscany, Italy. Shri Mataji told me a few things about farming, and especially how to vibrate the crops. For the crops that are irrigated, she said to put one of her photos into the well, which I did. I had a badge with Shri Mataji's photo on it, which had been made waterproof with a silicon treatment, and we put that in.

For crops which are not irrigated – such as wheat or sunflower – Shri Mataji said that to get the vibrations into the seeds, you have to take a small quantity out of the whole amount of the seeds and put them in front of her picture. Then you must put it back with the whole quantity of seed and mix it and this will vibrate all the seed, which you have to put in the ground. If you can't vibrate the ground with vibrated water through irrigation, this is an alternative solution. So even if the farm is big, like ours is, if you vibrate only a small quantity of seed and mix it up, this is enough. Shri Mataji also said we shouldn't use hybrid seeds, but only the F1, the first hybridization. It is not good to use seeds which are further hybridized.

Alessandra Pallini

The Bad Sight Treatment

The bad sight treatment, to stop attacks of subtle negativity, is as follows. Take a pinch of black mustard seeds, a pinch of salt, and a dried red chilli. Put them on a piece of cloth or even a tissue, and vibrate them by making a bandhan over them – left hand to the photo and with the right hand circle clockwise over these items until coolness is felt. Then wrap them in the cloth or tissue, hold it in the right hand and make a bandhan around the body of whoever is to be protected, seven times each way. Raise the Kundalini of the person and give them another bandhan to protect them – and then burn the package of mustard seeds, salt and chilli.

Appendix 2

Contributors

1. Ajay Arora
2. Alan Wherry
3. Albert Lewis
4. Alessandra Pallini
5. Alex Henshaw
6. Alice Abergal
7. Ambar Chatterjee
8. Ambiga Ramiah
9. Andrea Cousins
10. Anna Chicos
11. Anna Mancini
12. Annette Haines
13. Antoinette Wells
14. Antonio Masella (Dr)
15. Aniruddha Bhattacharya
16. Antony Visconti
17. Auriol Purdie
18. A.V. Izmailovich
19. Avdut Pai
20. Bala Kanayson
21. Belinda Henshaw
22. Bertrand de Techtermann
23. Bhakti Iro
24. Bill Hansel
25. Bogdan Shehovych
26. Bogunia Bensaude
27. Bokwe Mafuna
28. Brian Bell
29. Brijbala Samii
30. Brigitte Saugstad
31. C. Ranganayakamma
32. Calin Costian
33. Catherine Hallé
34. Cheryl Bradshaw
35. Chris Coles
36. Chris Kyriacou
37. Chris Marlow
38. Christina Rosi
39. Christina Sweet
40. Christine Haage
41. Christophe Sous
42. Claire Nesdale
43. Daniela Picciafuoco
44. Danya Martoglio
45. Deepali Bandakar
46. Deepak Midha
47. Derek Ferguson
48. Devibehn Kalam
49. Didier Goven
50. Djamel Metouri
51. Douglas Fry
52. Duilio Cartocci
53. Edward Saugstad
54. Edith Petermann
55. Elizabeth Ravenscroft
56. Elizabeth Schulz
57. Felicity Payment
58. Frances Henke
59. Françoise Kazakov
60. Gaelle Sattarshetty
61. Gail Pottinger
62. Gauri Mehrani-Mylany
63. Geoff Godfrey
64. George Naidu
65. Giovanni Albanesi
66. Gillian Woltron

67. Gisela Matzer
68. Graciela Vázquez-Díaz
69. Grazyna Anslow
70. Greg Turek
71. Gudrun Ortner
72. Guillemette Metouri
73. Günter Woltron
74. Hamid Mehrani-Mylany
75. Hanna Rentola
76. Heidi Stornier
77. Heidi Zogorski
78. Helga Adams
79. Hemangi Pitale
80. Hermann Haage
81. Ingrid B
82. Jadunandan Prasad
83. James Murdock
84. Jane Antonioni
85. Jayant Patankar
86. Jeff Raum
87. Jenny Brown
88. Jeremy Lamaison
89. Jim Thomas
90. Joanne Langdon
91. Joanne Moore
92. John Watkinson
93. Kapil Goyal
94. Karun Sanghi
95. Kavitha Mohan
96. Kay McHugh
97. Kay O'Connell
98. Kevin Anslow
99. Kogie Pillay
100. Kristine Kirby
101. K.T. Tan
102. Lale Kisbu
103. Latha Nayar
104. Laxshmi from Vienna
105. Laxshmi Ward
106. Lena Koli
107. Lev Doronski
108. Liallyn Fitzpatrick
109. Lily Rai
110. Linda Williams
111. Liselotte Wiehart
112. Lucia Coutinho
113. Lydia P
114. Lyn Roles
115. Lyudmila Bredyihina
116. Madhavi Dejust
117. Madhavi Fordham
118. Malathi Menon
119. Mangal Singh Dillon
120. Mara-Madhuri Corazzari
121. Maria Galabova
122. Marie-Laure Cernay
123. Marilyn Leate
124. Mark Daniel
125. Mark Mays
126. Mark Williams
127. Martin Purcell
128. Mary Heaton
129. Maryanne Berman
130. Matthew Fogarty
131. Meenakshi Murdoch
132. Meera Soni
133. Meera Szegvary
134. Merenia Ashwell
135. Michal Gal
136. Miodrag Radosavljevic
137. Mirriam Oweke
138. Mitesh Gandhi
139. Murarti Lal Lodha
140. Nanda Tagliabue
141. Naveen Navlani
142. Nea Alanen

143. Nirmala Verma
144. Pamela Lewis
145. Patti Prole
146. Patrick Anslow
147. Patrick Redican
148. Paulette Oddo
149. P. D. Chavhan
150. Pradeep Singh Rawat
151. Philippa Newmann
152. Prakash Sreshthaputra
153. Purna Vertunni
154. Rabi Ghosh
155. Raju of Cabella
156. Raju Koli
157. Rama Iurili
158. Ramesh Manocha
159. Ray Harris
160. Rekha Das
161. Reza Ghaffurian
162. Richard Payment
163. Robert Henshaw
164. Robert Ruigrok
165. Rosaria Tagliacia
166. Rosemary Maitland Hume
167. Rosie Lyons
168. Roxana Sindici
169. Ruth Eleanore
170. Ruth Mattison
171. Said Ait-Chaalal
172. Sandeep Gadkary
173. Sandra Castelli
174. Savita Arora
175. Sergiy Fadyeyev
176. Sergei Utenkov
177. Shannon Shapovalov
178. Sharmala Hader
179. Sheena Sivaprasad
180. Shridevi Angurala

181. Shyam Etchepareborda
182. Sno Bonneau
183. Stavros Neofytou
184. Sudhakar Shukla
185. Sue Sutcliffe
186. Suman Mathur
187. Suresh Thacker
188. S. Venugopalan
189. Theresa Biara
190. Toni Panayiotou
191. Trupta de Graaf
192. Ursula Doring
193. Vera Pinheiro
194. Victor Vertunni
195. Vivek Sawhney
196. V.K. Kapur
197. Wendy Barrett
198. Werner Steindl
199. Wolfgang Hackl
200. Zuhra Dundjerski

www.ingramcontent.com/pod-product-compliance
Lightning Source LLC
Chambersburg PA
CBHW071309110426
42743CB00042B/1234